Programming in C++

An Applied Approach

Habib T. Kashani

Langara College

Prentice Hall

Upper Saddle River, New Jersey   *Columbus, Ohio*

Library of Congress Cataloging-in-Publication Data

Kashani, Habib T.
    Programming in C++: an applied approach/Habib T. Kashani.
        p. cm.
    Includes bibliographical references and index.
    ISBN 0-13-228818-4
    1. C++ (Computer program language)   I. Title.
QA76.73.C153K37   1998
    005.13'3--dc21

97-17979
CIP

Cover photo: Digital Art, Westlight
Editor: Charles E. Stewart, Jr.
Production Editor: Stephen C. Robb
Design Coordinator: Karrie M. Converse
Cover Designer: Rod Harris
Production Manager: Patricia A. Tonneman
Illustrations: Custom Editorial Productions, Inc.
Production Supervision: Custom Editorial Productions, Inc.
Marketing Manager: Debbie Yarnell

This book was set in Times Roman by Custom Editorial Productions, Inc., and was printed and bound by Quebecor Printing/Book Press. The cover was printed by Phoenix Color Corp.

© 1998 by Prentice-Hall, Inc.
Simon & Schuster/A Viacom Company
Upper Saddle River, New Jersey 07458

Printed in the United States of America

10 9 8 7 6 5 4 3 2 1

ISBN: 0-13-228818-4

Prentice-Hall International (UK) Limited, *London*
Prentice-Hall of Australia Pty. Limited, *Sydney*
Prentice-Hall Canada, Inc., *Toronto*
Prentice-Hall Hispanoamericana, S. A., *Mexico*
Prentice-Hall of India Private Limited, *New Delhi*
Prentice-Hall of Japan, Inc., *Tokyo*
Simon & Schuster Asia Pte. Ltd., *Singapore*
Editora Prentice-Hall do Brasil, Ltda., *Rio de Janeiro*

To my wife, Nahid, and my children, Mathew, Suzanne, and Cyrus.

Preface

Programming in C++ is intended to meet the needs of both the student and the professional programmer. This book may be used in a second programming course, after an introductory course in computers and programming, for students with computer science majors and students with other majors. It may also be used as a supplement to an introductory computer science or software engineering text, if the topics take students into abstract data types and object-oriented programming. In addition, this text is recommended for students of computer information systems (CIS), business, technology, and continuing education programs. Finally, professional programmers who want to learn how to write programs in C++ and those who are looking for a resource reference will find this text useful.

PEDAGOGICAL APPROACH

This book's thorough treatment of C++ includes a comprehensive view of the features of the language as they apply to both structured programming and object-oriented programming. The book's focus is the fusion of concepts and applications; its purpose is to demonstrate how to apply theory to practical problems. To that end, concepts move from simple to complex so that each one is a foundation for the next level. Each concept is discussed in a clear and concise manner to make the learning process enjoyable, fast, and effective.

The discussion of each concept includes a variety of examples, which demonstrate how to apply the concepts and reinforce the principles of good programming. Each major topic is followed by a list of self-check questions and exercises, for which answers are supplied at the end of the book. Moreover, since the best way to learn how to write good programs is to see well-written ones, several sample programs, with internal documentation and necessary comment lines, are included at the end of each chapter. The sample programs are deliberately placed at the end to provide full discussion of the material without interruption, making the discussions more cohesive and understandable. Although the programs presented here have been tested using the Borland C++ compiler, they were designed to work without modification on almost any C++ compiler.

Finally, the style tips at the end of each chapter tell students how to write programs that are easy to read and maintain. They include schemes for using meaningful identifiers and specifying their case and symbol set (e.g., DaysOfWeek or days_of_week or Days_Of_Week) as well as methods for documenting the program, its interfaces, and classes. The intent behind this initiative is to develop and establish a consistent style in writing code. Good programming style also makes the programmer a more productive team member in a joint development project.

ORGANIZATION OF THE BOOK

Programming in C++: An Applied Approach is organized into six chapters, each of which covers a group of logically related topics. The chapters cover almost all facilities of the language in an orderly manner and explain the mechanical underpinnings of C++ supported by application examples for each topic. This innovative approach assures easy progression for the novice and offers a clear reference for the professional.

- Chapter 1 provides the fundamental programming concepts of C++. To ensure thorough understanding, readers should study the material in the sequence in which it is presented. The chapter also covers in detail the standard *I/O* facilities of the language.
- Chapter 2 focuses on more advanced topics, including language constructs, arrays and strings, pointers and references, and storage management.
- Chapter 3 discusses functions and describes in considerable detail how they interact with each other, the way in which they are invoked, and the values that are returned, as well as storage classes, scope rules, and lifetime of variables.
- Chapter 4 covers the features that help readers develop more advanced applications. Topics include enumerated data types, the type definition construct (*typedef*), different types of C++ functions, library functions, the preprocessor, and command line arguments.
- Chapter 5 addresses the structures and techniques for file processing. Structures and unions, bitfields, classes as unique C++ features, and an in-depth discussion of files are the topics of this chapter. Because there is some variability in readers' comprehension of these topics, the chapter is aimed at presenting them with the means to understand thoroughly, to design readily, and to implement easily the structures and files.
- Chapter 6 introduces the notion of an Abstract Data Type (ADT) and its practical use in object-oriented programming. The chapter gives students a clear understanding of the advantages of object-oriented programming before they invest time and effort to learn how to do it. To that end, it presents many ADTs of different levels of complexity. Finally, the chapter takes the reader through the design and implementation of each ADT in the following steps:

    Specifications

    Representation

    Implementation

    Application

Since the most important advance offered by C++ is its support for object-oriented programming, the level of detail in this chapter is considerably higher in order to address adequately the prominent features of the language, including:

- Classes
- Constructors and Destructors
- Inheritance
- The Keyword *friend*
- Virtual Functions and Dynamic Binding
- Polymorphism
- Pure Functions and Abstract Classes
- Static Members
- Operator Overloading
- Type Conversion
- Generic Classes Using Templates and Void Data Types
- Embedded Objects

ACKNOWLEDGMENTS

I would like to thank the following students at Langara College for their comments and suggestions: Balash Akbari, Kristian Erickson, Raymond Chan, Yan Teplitsky, and Graham TerMarsch.

In addition, I express sincere appreciation to the following colleagues who provided valuable input for the manuscript: Judy Boxler, Michael Kuttner, Pierre Massicotte, and Fred Parvaz.

I also thank executive editor Charles E. Stewart for his encouragement, support, and patience, and the other good people at Prentice Hall, Steve Robb, Kate Linsner, and JoEllen Gohr.

Finally, I gratefully acknowledge the contribution of these reviewers for their comments, criticism, and helpful suggestions: Michael Bush, Carl C. Hommer, Jr., Usha Jindal, and Philip Regalbuto.

Habib Kashani
Langara College

Brief Contents

Contents

1   Fundamental Concepts

1.1   PREVIEW

In this chapter you will learn:

- A Historical Overview of Programming
- The Origin of the C++ Language
- Program Structure
- The Elements of C++: Functions, Identifiers, Keywords, Literals, and Operators
- Expressions
- Data Types
- Variable Declaration and Scopes
- Standard Input-Output Operations

1.2   A HISTORICAL OVERVIEW OF PROGRAMMING

Over the past forty years programming languages have gone through an evolutionary change. The journey started with assembly language. The first assemblers made programming a relative pleasure by providing mnemonic names for operation codes (such as *mul* for multiplication operations and *add* for addition operations) and by allowing programmers to refer to memory locations by symbolic names.

Advances in computer technology, including those in both hardware and software on the one hand and experience in programming and software development on the other, led to the appearance of high-level languages in the 1960s. The focus of programming has shifted from compact code to structured programming using procedures and functions. Many new programming languages have emerged in a short period of time to support this concept of using data types, control statements, functions, procedures, and modules. Programs became structured and procedural abstraction became pivotal to software design and the programming paradigm. For the past twenty-five years, structured programming has worked very well for environments in which programs tended to be relatively stable and the code did not change significantly. Almost all of the business and scientific applications of this period have operated under these criteria.

Recent achievements in microprocessor architecture and data communication technology have created unprecedented computing power and opportunities for the software industry. In the last decade alone, applications for computers have increased dramatically and literally thousands of software packages have been developed for every purpose imaginable. New areas for software applicability arise each week, and applications are required to be more functional. The continuing demand for ambitious applications with many capabilities have led to programs that are voluminous and complex.

The volume and complexity of applications demand a new approach to software design and engineering. The software for today's applications must be

- Reliable
- Reusable
- Easy to develop
- Easy to maintain

Code reliability plays a critical role in software design. Reliable code is correct and robust: Correct code does exactly what the specifications state and robust software handles exceptional cases in a reasonable way without sudden program termination.

Ability to reuse code increases the programmer's productivity and facilitates development, allowing him or her to use as much as possible of the existing functionality in writing new applications. Ease of maintenance implies that an application ought to be flexible, extendable, and readable. Maintenance has always played an important role in software development. This role in today's applications is even more critical in light of continuing changes in hardware and software requirements. A maintainable application allows easy modification, refinement, and improvement.

1.3   THE ORIGIN OF THE C++ LANGUAGE

C++ is a general-purpose programming language based on the C programming language. In 1972, the language C was designed for programming under the UNIX operating system. The language was named C because it was based on an earlier version called B. Both B and C represent different versions designed after the earlier systems programming language BCPL (Basic Compound Programming Language). The primary difference was that B, the first letter of BCPL, was an essentially typeless language, while C, the second letter of BCPL, had an extensive collection of standard types. In 1973 UNIX itself was extended, and more than 90 percent of it was rewritten from assemby language in C. The current versions of the C language are mostly based on the ANSI Standard C. For more information, obtain a copy of a publication titled "American National Standard Information Interchange—Programming Language C" (1990) from the American National Standards Institutes in New York.

The C programming language has attracted considerable attention internationally because of its popularity in the software industry. The reasons for this popularity are its power, flexibility, efficiency, compactness, and portability. However, the need for greater modularity within programs and support for the development of large and complex systems with maximum efficiency led to the evolutionary development of C++. Developed by Dr. Bjarne Stroustrup at the Computer Science Research Center at AT&T Bell Laboratories in Murray Hill, New Jersey, and this language became available in 1985. The cryptic name C++ implies that it is an enhanced version or superset of its predecessor C.

C++ is not a completely new language. It can be thought of more as an evolutionary advancement of C. Both languages share the fundamental concepts for using statements, data types, operators, function definition, and separate compilation. The primary aim in extending C++ has been to enhance it as a suitable language for data abstraction and object-oriented programming. Data abstraction, in contrast to procedural abstraction, is a new approach to programming and software development. To this end, C++ has provided a stable platform for implementing these concepts and developing high-quality tools for complex environments. (The topics of data abstraction and object-oriented programming will be discussed later in Chapter 6.)

Dr. Stroustrup implemented the language as a C++-to-C translator called CFRONT. CFRONT translated the C++ code into C code so that it could be compiled and linked in the traditional way. Today, there are CFRONT ports as well as full compilers available for the C++ language. In contrast to CFRONT ports, full compilers such as Borland C++ generate object code directly rather than going through a conversion process.

1.4   PROGRAM STRUCTURE

A typical C++ program consists of two parts: the **global part** and **the main function part.** The global part contains necessary declarations, definitions, and files needed by the entire program. The main function, referred to as *main( ),* is the most important part as the program execution starts with this function. We begin by examining a simple program that displays a one-line greeting on the terminal screen.

The first step is to create a file that contains the program. The file can be named something like *hello.c, hello.cpp, hello.cp,* or *hello.cxx,* depending on the conventions required by the compiler used. For example, the Turbo C++ compiler requires *filename.cpp.*

```
// File name: hello.cpp
// This program displays a greeting to the user.

#include <iostream.h>    // for input and output operations

void main ()             // main program part
{
cout << "Hello, Reader!";
}
```

A terminal session with this program looks like this:

```
Hello, Reader!
```

The first two lines comprise comment lines in C++. Comments are helpful remarks that appear in the program listing but have no effect on the way the program runs. Their purpose is to make programs more readable. The comment after the // symbols extends to the end of the line. C++ also provides another commenting style, one in which the line starts with /* (slash and asterisk) and ends with */ (asterisk and slash).

The third and fifth lines are blank for clarity. Line 4 includes the **Stream I/O header file** which, among several other things, contains the definitions needed to allow the program to read input and write output. A typical C++ program normally starts with this unique feature, which is known as a **preprocessor statement.** It is an instruction to the compiler to retrieve the necessary code from the Stream I/O header file into the source code on the line requested. The **cout** (standard output stream) object of this file is used for output. Header files normally have a .*h* extension. In some implementations, the extension may be .*hpp* or .*hxx*. We will explore these entities in greater depth later in this chapter.

The sixth, seventh, and ninth lines include the usual *begin* and *end* of the **main** function of the program. Note that a C++ program consists of one or more functions as the basic building blocks. The function *main( )* is the major function that points to the place in the program where execution starts. Moreover, each function name is followed by a pair of parentheses to indicate that the name refers to a function and not another construct.

The body of the function—a group of statements that specify the actions to be performed—is enclosed between two **curly braces** as shown on the seventh and ninth lines. The purpose of the *cout* statement on line 8 is to print out the desired message. Notice that this statement is indented within the braces. Proper indentation of statements is a style matter. Although it makes no difference to the compiler for the translation of the program from human-oriented form (source code) to machine-readable format (object code), it helps us read the program more easily. Programming style will be discussed throughout this book. In addition, there is a style guide summary at the end of each chapter.

> **Note:** C++ is case sensitive. Unless otherwise specified, all keywords of the language are to be written in lower-case letters. User-defined names can be either in lower- or upper-case letters.

We will now look at another short program to show how computations are performed in C++. The following program takes the length and width of a field and computes the number of meters of fence wire required to enclose the field.

```
//   File name: fence.cpp
//   This program computes how many meters of fence is
//   required for a rectangular field.

#include <iostream.h> // Allows the program to read input and
                       // write output.
void main()            // the main function of the program
{            // The opening brace indicates the beginning of the program.

//   Declaration part: shows the constants and variables used in
//   the program.

const int two = 2; // A constant declaration: two is of type int

int length, width, perimeter; // integer variables
```

```
cout << "Please type the length and width ";
cout << "of the field each separated with a space: ";

        //  Input part
  cin >> length
     >> width;

        // Processing part
perimeter = (length + width) * two;

// Output part
cout  << "\nThe field requires "
      << perimeter
      <<" meters of fence wire.";
}              // The closing brace shows the end of the program.
```

A terminal session with this program is shown below. The underlined numbers are the values entered by the user.

```
Please type length and width of the field, each separated by a space: 100 50
The field requires 300 meters of fence wire.
```

In the example above, the program's name is *fence.cpp* as written on line 1. Lines 2 and 3 explain the purpose of the program. Blank lines are included for readability. Line 5 includes the Stream I/O header file to support input and output operations. Lines 7 to 26 define the function *main( )* of the program. It contains a sequence of statements that are enclosed in the curly braces. There are four distinct parts within the braces: **declaration part, input part, processing part,** and **output part.** The declaration part specifies precisely the constants and variables of the program as well as the kind of information each one will contain. In our example, the first declaration is the constant declaration:

```
const int two = 2; //A constant declaration: two is of type int
```

The keyword *const* indicates to the compiler that the data *two* is a constant and declared to be a value of 2. The value of data *two* cannot change during the life of the program. In addition, *two* is declared to be of type *int*. The abbreviated word *int,* for integer, is one of the keywords in C++. The keyword int must always be typed in lower-case letters. A semicolon separates this declaration from the next declaration. The second declaration is the variable declaration:

```
int length, width, perimeter;  // integer variables
```

A variable is a named location in the computer memory where a data value is stored. This location is referenced by a variable name such as *length, width,* and *perimeter* in our example. The content of the location is the value of the variable. The value of the variable may vary during the execution of a program. A variable in the computer memory looks like Figure 1.1:

Figure 1.1   Example of a Variable in Memory

length

```
┌─────────────┐
│    100      │
│             │
└─────────────┘
```

The type *int* on line 15 tells the compiler that the variables to follow are of the type *integer*. Variable names are separated by commas, and there is a semicolon after the last variable name.

The action of *cout* << on the seventeenth and eighteenth lines display the following message: "Please type length and width of the field, each separated by a space:".

The *cin* >> (the standard input stream) on the twenty-first line reads the values entered by the user and assigns them to the variables *length* and *width*.

The statement on the twenty-third line means that the perimeter of the field will be computed and stored in the variable *perimeter*.

As a result of the final statement, the following will be displayed:

```
The field requires 300 meters of fence wire.
```

The characters '\n' on the twenty-fifth line, normally used with the **cout statement,** is called the **newline character** and causes the following output to start at the beginning of the next line. It operates similar to a typewriter's carriage return, which advances the input to the beginning of the next line. The newline character can be represented as either "\n" or '\n'. C++ also offers another option, allowing the user to enter the keyword *endl* (End of line) to end the current line or start a new line.

The enclosing brace on the last line indicates the end of the program.

Self-Check Questions 1

1. Describe the general format of a C++ program.
2. What is the purpose of a comment line?
3. Describe the correspondence between a variable and its value.
4. What is the purpose of a semicolon(;) in a C++ program?
5. Write a program to print your complete home address on several lines. Write appropriate comments for each line of code.
6. Write a program to input three four-digit positive numbers and to output the sum of the values.

1.5   THE ELEMENTS OF C++

Functions

A function names a set of instructions or operations, the result of which is a single value. The returned value may be a typed datum, an address, or nothing at all. If the function does not intend to return a value, it will be preceded by the keyword *void*. Void functions are comparable to procedures in other languages. Like mathematical functions, each C++ function has a name followed by a pair of parentheses to show its arguments (if any). In other words, a name followed by a pair of parentheses normally indicates that the name refers to a function. Each function has the following form:

```
Type FunctionName (argument list)
{
    Variable Declaration
    Operational statements
    Return statement
}
```

For example, the following function displays the sum of two integer values. It behaves similarly to a procedure in Pascal.

```
void DisplaySum(int x, int y)   // This function does not
                                // return a value.
{
    cout << '\n'            // \n is an escape sequence character
         << x + y;          // and signifies a new line.
}
```

On the other hand, the following function computes the sum of two integer values and returns the result.

```
int Sum(int x, int y)    // This function returns an integer
                         // value (a typed datum).
{
    return x + y;
}
```

The design of both C and C++ is based on using functions. Functions are the fundamental building blocks of C++ programs. Each function is a self-contained unit designed to accomplish a well-defined task. Functions are also autonomous and cannot be nested within each other. Moreover, a C++ function definition cannot occur within a block. A block is a collection of statements enclosed within a pair of braces.

In addition, every C++ program consists of a collection of both user-defined functions and those provided within the language **library,** a collection of pre-defined functions, operators, and other entities. The execution of a C++ program starts with the first executable statement in the *main()* function. Any of the statements in the *main()* can be a call to another function. A called function may also call other functions, and so on. The only function that cannot be called is the *main() function* because the *main()* signifies the beginning of the program.

As with other languages, when a function is called, control is temporarily turned over to the first executable statement in the function. Once the called function finishes the execution, it returns control back over to the calling function.

> **Note:** Functions communicate with one another through passing arguments and returning values. A C++ function may have no arguments or it may include arguments, depending on the program's design requirements.

C++ also requires function prototyping, which is a function heading or a function definition without a body. Consider the following example:

```
int SumOf( int, int );     // function prototype
void main()
{
    int x = 5, y = 10;
    cout << "\n"
         << SumOf(x, y);   // call to function SumOf
}

int SumOf( int a, int b )   // function definition
```

```
{
    return a + b;
}
```

A function prototype allows the compiler to check the return type, the type of arguments, and the number of arguments. It also tells the compiler what type of code to generate when a function is called. A function prototype also leads the programmer to more suitable code generation because all prototypes must appear at the beginning of the file. If the programmer has many function prototypes, one might argue that the design needs a bit more work. Note that if a function is fully defined before the main function, it does not require a prototype.

Self-Check Questions 2

1. What is a function?
2. What is meant by *function arguments?*
3. Write a function that will receive a time in a four-digit format, also known as military format, such as *1125, 1835, 0815,* and *2310,* to compute and return the number of seconds passed since midnight. For example, if the time is *1125,* the number of seconds passed since midnight will be $11 \times 60 \times 60 + 25 \times 60$, which is 41,100 seconds.

Identifiers

An identifier is a sequence of letters and digits of an arbitrary length. The first character must be a letter; however, the underscore (_) counts as a letter. Upper-case and lower-case letters are considered to be different. All characters are significant. Note that while the standard C++ does not set a maximum length for an identifier, some compilers do.

Keywords

The identifiers in Figure 1.2 are reserved for use as keywords and may not be used otherwise.

> **Note:** Identifiers containing a double underscore (__) are reserved for C++ implementations and standard libraries. Identifiers starting with a single underscore (_) are reserved for C implementations. Ordinary users should avoid both.

Figure 1.2 Keywords

int	short	long	unsigned	char
register	float	double	if	else
switch	case	default	break	while
do	for	const	enum	static
void	return	private	public	virtual
protected	friend	union	typedef	volatile
throw	template	new	inline	goto
extern	delete	auto	catch	signed
operator	typeid	struct	class	sizeof
this	asm	try		

Literals or Constants

Literals or constants are:

> integer-constants
> character-constants
> floating-constants
> string-constants

Examples:

> 12 (a decimal value) = 014 (octal) = 0×C (Hexadecimal)

'x' or 'a' are examples of character constants.
"abc" is a string constant.

> **Note:** Single quotes around specific characters specify a character as constant. Double quotes around two or more characters specify a string as constant.

Self-Check Questions 3

1. Which of the following are illegal C++ identifiers?

   A. _Accounts   B. Accounts_Receivable   C. Sales-Table

   D. 4DigitNumber   E. Dot.Two   F. Const

   G. INT   H. integer   I. MAIN

2. Distinguish between 1234 and "1234".

> **Note:** C++ has been designed as a strongly typed language to treat each entity appropriately and distinctively. For example, character constants in C are of type *integer,* while in C++ they are of type *character.* In contrast, C may be called a loosely typed language.

Operators

There are several classes of operators in C++. They are classified according to the number of operands they take and the type of values they return. Table 1.1 summarizes the commonly used operators of C++.

Table 1.1   Common Operators

Arithmetic Operators	+ - * / % ++ – –
Relational Operators	> >= < <= == !=
Logical Operators	&& || !
Bitwise Operators	& | ^ << >> ~
Assignment Operators	= += -= *= /= %= <<= >>= &= ^+, etc.
Conditional Expression Operator	?:
Comma Operator	,

The extensive range of operators in C++ makes the language very powerful. Not only do these operators provide facilities similar to those of other structured programming languages, but they also allow bit manipulation at the lowest level. Since there are many operators in this language, there are situations in which the same symbols may be used for more than one operation. This is called **operator overloading.** For example, the operators >> and << have been overloaded to perform both I/O operations and shifting memory bits. Operator overloading also plays an important role in object-oriented programming because one can overload operators that can be applied to user-defined objects. (We will cover this topic again in Chapter 6.)

Notice that in C++ if an operand is not of the correct type the operation may still be performed but the result may be different from what is expected. This may seem unusual for programmers who are familiar with other strongly typed languages such as Pascal and Modula-2, in which the compiler or run-time environment captures incorrect types. This system obligation has been removed from C++ in order to provide run-time efficiency. Therefore, C++ programmers must be careful to enter operands of the correct type. Having learned the general characteristics of C++ operators, we are now going to look at all of them and then discuss each class separately.

Precedence of All C++ Operators

The arithmetic operators in Table 1.2 are arranged from highest to lowest precedence. The arithmetic operators of C++ are binary operators; that is, they operate on two values. The operators (+) and (-) may also be used as **unary operators;** that is, they may be used with

Table 1.2 Arithmetic Operators

Type	Associativity*	Operators
Postfix	—	[] () . -> ++ —
Unary prefix	left	++ — sizeof ~ ! - + & *
Type cast	—	(cast)
Multiplicative	left	* / %
Additive	left	+ -
Shift	left	<< >>
Inequality	left	> >= < <=
Equality	left	== !=
Bitwise and	left	&
Bitwise or	left		
Bitwise xor	left	^
Logical and	left	&&
Logical or	left	||
Conditional	right	?:
Assignment	right	= += -= *= /= %= <<= >>= etc.
Comma	left	,

*Associativity refers to the order of operations (i.e., left to right or right to left) among several operators of the same procedures.

a single operand to indicate its sign. When using two consecutive operators such as **m + -n,** it is better to place the operand in parentheses with a unary operator, as in **m + (-n)**. The arithmetic operators are listed below:

- + (addition)
- - (subtraction)
- * (multiplication)
- / (division)
- % (modulus: yields remainder after integer division)

There is only one operator for both integer and floating-point division. The type of the operands determines the result of operation. In integer division, the result is truncated. For example,

```
int m = 5, n = 2;
int q;
q = m / 2;          // yields 2
```

In floating-point division, the result is always a floating-point value. If the operands are of mixed types, the result will be promoted or demoted depending upon the situation of the operands in the expression and the conversion rules of the language. Examine the code segment below to see the effect of mixed data types in division operations.

```
int     m = 9,  n;
float f = 2.7,  q;
n = m  /  f;        // yields 3: demoted to integer
q = m / f; // yields 3.33: promoted to float
```

The remainder operator, also known as the **modulus operator,** requires two positive integers and the result is always positive. Negative integers lead to unpredictable results. For example:

9 % 2	will yield 1
5 % 2.5	undefined
5 % -2	undefined

An arithmetic expression may contain one or more sets of parentheses. In such expressions, you must deal with parentheses first. Start with the innermost set of parentheses and evaluate the subexpressions according to the following rules.

1. First, do all multiplication and/or division operators, including modulus operators. All three have the same priority. Then do all additions and subtractions. These operators also have the same precedence as each other.
2. If there are several operators of the same precedence, they have left associativity, so perform the operation from left to right.

Let us now apply the rules to the following arithmetic expression. Remember that in any language the readability of a program is very important, and this is particularly true for C++. Therefore, you should leave a space on both sides of each binary operator.

$$m * 12 - (m * n \% 13 + m / n) * k / 10$$

Assume $m = 12$, $n = 5$, and $k = 20$. Now apply these values to the examples in Table 1.3.

Table 1.3 Associativity Example

Subexpression Evaluate	Result	Expression After Each Step of Evaluation
m * n	60	m * 12 + (60 % 13 + m / n) * k / 10
60 % 13	8	m * 12 + (8 + m / n) * k / 10
m / n	2	m * 12 + (8 + 2) * k / 10
8 + 2	10	m * 12 + 10 * k / 10
m * 12	144	144 + 10 * k / 10
10 * k	200	144 + 200 / 10
200 / 10	20	144 + 20
144 + 20	164	164

Relational Operators

Relational or Boolean operators are also binary operators and compare two values. The result of a relational operator in C++ is either 1 *(true)* or 0 *(false)*. This is also known as a Boolean value, according to whether the result is true or false. Following is a list of relational operators:

- < (less than)
- <= (less than or equal)
- = = (equal)
- != (not equal)
- c> (greater than)
- >= (greater than or equal)

Table 1.4 contains some examples of relational expressions.

Logical Operators

Logical operators of C++ are:

- && (logical AND)
- || (logical OR)
- ! (logical negation or NOT)

Logical operators **&&** and || are binary operators, whereas operator **!** is unary. They take any numerical argument, including *char,* and yield either 1 or 0 to indicate true or false according to the truth table (Table 1.5). Logical operators also combine relational expressions to form complex relational tests.

Table 1.4 Relational Expressions

Expression	Boolean Value
4 == 5	0
4 > 3	1
4 != 5	1
4 <= 3	0

Table 1.5 Truth Table

P	Q	P && Q	P || Q	!P
Nonzero	Nonzero	1	1	0
Nonzero	Zero	0	1	0
Zero	Nonzero	0	1	1
Zero	Zero	0	0	1

The logical negation operator (!) has higher precedence than &&, which in turn has higher precedence than ||. In addition, both && and || have lower priority than the relational and equality operators. Therefore, expressions can be evaluated without parentheses, although parentheses enhance a program's clarity. Furthermore, arithmetic operators have priority over both logical and relational operators. The following list summarizes the operators according to their precedence:

- Parentheses
- Logical Operator (!)
- Arithmetic Operators
- Relational Operators (inequality and equality)
- Logical Operators && and ||, in that order

Use Table 1.6 to evaluate the following logical expressions and show how the rules apply. Given:

```
a = 2;
b = 5;
c = 'a';
d = 'h';
```

In C++, the evaluation of logical expressions is **short-circuited.** That is, C++ evaluates only enough of the subexpressions, from left to right, to determine the value of the entire expression. Examine the following piece of code. (Note that the code contains a conditional statement. Conditional statements will be discussed in the next chapter.) Given:

```
a = 5;
b = 10;
if ( a < 0 && b > 0 )// conditional statement
      cout << "ok!";
```

Table 1.6 Examples of Operator Precedence

Expression	Equivalent Expression	Result
a > b && b > 0	(a > b) && (b > 0)	0
a + b < b * 2 && d >= 'a'	(a + b) < (b * 2) && (d >= 'a')	1
a + b > b * 2 && d >= 'a'	(a + b) > (b * 2) && (d >= 'a')	0
!(a - b > 0) || b == 0)	!((a - b > 0) || (b == 0))	1

Since the first subexpression is false, the second subexpression will not be evaluated. The first part alone can determine the result of the whole expression. This is a useful property for testing certain conditions and avoiding run-time errors. Consider the following:

```
if ( m != 0 && n / m > 2 )// conditional statement
        cout << n / m;
```

If m == 0 then the division by zero, as a fatal run-time problem, will be avoided. This property also helps you arrange the subexpressions in a suitable order.

Assignment Operators

The main C++ assignment operator is the equals (=) sign. It associates the result of the expression on its right side with the variable on the left side. There are two varieties of assignment operators: a simple assignment operator, such as x = m + n, and a compound assignment operator, which is a combination of the equals sign and other operators. C++ programmers commonly use compound assignment operators because they are shorthand notations and in some cases can produce more efficient code. The examples in Table 1.7 show the application of compound assignment operators.

> **Note:** If the operands of both sides of the assignment statement are of mixed types, the operand on the right side of the assignment will be promoted or demoted depending upon the type of the operand on the left side.

For example, in the following assignment statement, the type of *sum* will be promoted to float.

```
int sum = 100;
float half = sum / 2; // an example of promotion
```

Increment and Decrement Operators

Mathematicians have never liked notations such as x = x + 1 or x = x - 1, though one should never read the assignment operator as an equals sign. In C++, however, there is an alternative notation that satisfies everybody. You may write both notations as x++ and x- -, respectively. These operators are called **auto increment** and **auto decrement** operators. Both take one

Table 1.7 Examples for Using Compound Assignment Operators

Operator	Example	Equivalent
+=	m += n	m = m + n
-=	m -= n	m = m - n
*=	m *= n	m = m * n
/=	m /= n	m = m / n
%=	m %= n	m = m % n

operand. The first example, x++, could be rewritten as ++x. Both have the same results. In the first case the auto increment is in the prefix notation and in the second case the operator is in the postfix position. Notice that either case has the same result as long as they are not a part of an expression, or used independently. When they are used within expressions, postfix and prefix positions of the operators do have differences. Consider the following example:

```
n = 10;
m = 20;
p = ++m + n;
```

The last statement involves three operators:

- Assignment Operator
- Addition Operator
- Auto Increment Operator

Among the C++ operators, the auto increment and auto decrement operators have the highest priority and the assignment operator has the lowest priority. Therefore, the value of *m* will be incremented, updated, and stored first. Then the sum of the values of *n* and new value of *m* will be assigned to variable *p*. The equivalent of this statement in other languages such as Pascal is two statements. We can also rewrite it into two separate statements in C++, as follows:

```
m++;  // means m = m + 1
p = m + n;
```

The next statement also has three operators:

- Assignment Operator (p)
- Addition Operator (+n)
- Auto Increment Operator (m++)

```
n = 10;
m = 20;
p = m++ + n;
```

The process of operation is similar to the first one. The auto increment operation is performed as the highest priority. However, since the auto increment is in postfix form, the original value, not the incremented value, of *m* is yielded to the expression for evaluation purpose. When the evaluation of the expression is completed, the updated value of *m* is stored for future reference. We may also rewrite the statement p = m++ + n into two separate statements:

```
p = m + n;
m++;
```

The Sizeof Operator

This operator returns the number of bytes in its operand. The operand may be a variable, a constant, or a structured data type. The syntax of **sizeof** is as follows:

sizeof (*type*)
sizeof *variable* or sizeof (*variable*)

If the variable is a structured data type such as an array, the value returned represents the size of memory, in bytes, used for the array.

Exercise

Run the following program and see the results on your system.

```
#include <iostream.h>
void main ( )
{
    char ch;
    int a;
    long b;
    float f;
    cout << "\nThe size of the character data type is: "
         << sizeof(char)
         << " byte";
    cout << "\nThe size of the integer data type is: "
         << sizeof(int)
         << " bytes";
    cout << "\nThe size of the long integer data type is: "
         << sizeof(long)
         << " bytes";
    cout << "\nThe size of float data type is machine"
         << "independent"
         << " and is: "
         << sizeof(float)
         << " bytes";
}
```

The *int* data type is typically the word size of the machine, either 16 or 32 bits, on which the compiler is used. However, most of the C++ compilers for PCs use a 16-bit *int*, which is equivalent to 2 bytes. The size of *long int* on the same compilers is 4 bytes. The *char* data is typically 8 bits or 1 byte. The *float* data type is stored in scientific notation and uses 32 bits or 4 bytes. The storage requirements for both *float* and *double* data types have been defined by the IEEE (Institute of Electric and Electronic Engineers) notations as 32 and 64 bits respectively. (We will see the data types of C++ later.)

The Comma Operator

The **comma** operator combines a number of related expressions into a single expression, making programs more compact. It guarantees left-to-right operations on a list of expressions. The value of the rightmost expression is returned as the expression's value. The comma operator has the lowest precedence of any C++ operators. For example, in the following code segment, the value of *p* is 32.

```
int m = 10, n = 20;
int p;
p = (++m, ++n, m + n);
```

Self-Check Questions 4

1. Suppose that first, second, third, fourth, and result are numeric-type variables that have been assigned the following values.

Variable	Type	Value
first	integer	250
second	integer	- 2500
third	integer	1025
fourth	float	10.25
result	integer	

Determine the value of the result on each line.

result = (first + second / first * 5) / 2 + third;

result++;

result += first + (int) fourth;

result = first > second && fourth > 0.0;

result = second < 0 || third < 0;

result = ++second - third;

2. What is wrong with the following operations?

result = first % second + fourth / 0.5;

result = fourth % first * 2 - third;

The Bitwise Operators

C++ has a powerful set of operators to access computer hardware and manipulate the bits of memory locations. There are many situations in which there is a need to decode and read a particular device status, to test a desired bit of a device interface, and so on. The bitwise operators operate on integral values bit-by-bit; that is, they may not be used on float, double, and other non-numeric data. The bitwise operators are

- & (Bitwise AND)
- | (Bitwise OR)
- ^ (Exclusive OR)
- ~ (One's Complement: NOT)
- >> (Shift Right)
- << (Shift Left)

The bitwise operators AND, OR, and NOT work in a fashion similar to the logical operators, except they operate individually on each pair of corresponding bits of their operands. This means that 1 & 0 yield 0, 1 | 0 yields 1, and ~1 produces 0. Consider the following example. Given:

```
x = 11001011
y = 11110000
z = x & y;          // Yields 11000000
k = x | y ;         // Yields 11111011
m = ~x;             // Yields 00110100
```

Table 1.8 Truth Table

P	Q	P ^ Q
1	1	0
1	0	1
0	1	1
0	0	0

Table 1.9 Examples for Using Bitwise Operators

Operator	Example	Equivalent
+=	m += n	m = m + n
>>=	m >>= n	m = m >> n
<<=	m <<= n	m = m << n
&=	m &= n	m = m & n
|=	m |= n	m = m | n
^=	m ^= n	m = m ^ n

The exclusive OR behaves like the human OR. The human OR can be defined as the disjunction of two propositions, the result of which is true if, and only if, one of the propositions is true. Let's now look at the truth table of the exclusive OR (xor) operator (Table 1.8).

A combination of an equals sign and bitwise operators, similar to arithmetic operators, may be used, as shown in Table 1.9.

Self-Check Questions 5

1. Examine the following code segment and explain what it does.

```
int num = 65;
num = num ^ num; // exclusive OR
cout << num;
```

2. Rewrite the code segment in the first question, using another bitwise operation, to produce the same result.

The one's complement operator (~) is a unary operator that changes all 0s with 1s and all 1s with 0s. For example, if x = 0000 0001 0101 1001, then the new value of x after the operation

```
n = ~x;
```

will be

```
1111 1110 1010 0110
```

Note that the difference between each bit of the new value and its corresponding bit in the original value is 1. This means that each new bit is one's complement of its old bit. One's complement is used for representing and storing negative numbers. The shift operators (>>, <<) are unary operators to shift the bits of an operand. The shift-left

Figure 1.3 Shift Operations
Example

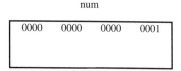
num

| 0000 | 0000 | 0000 | 0001 |

operator (<<) shifts the bits of its operand to the left and moves zero bits into the vacated positions. For example, given a = 00000111, examine the result of the following shift statement.

```
a = a << 3;
```

The statement yields $a = 00111000$. What happened to the value of a? The value of a was multiplied by 8, which is 2^3. Thus, each left-shift operation multiplies a number by 2. What if we shift the bits back to their original state as follows?

```
a = a >> 3;          // (equivalent to a >>= 3;)
```

The statement yields $a = 00000111$, which means the number was divided by 8 this time.

In another example (Figure 1.3), assume that an integer takes 16 bits of memory on your system as shown. Examine the following piece of code and explain what happens. Write a short program and run it to see the result.

```
int num = 1;
num <<= 15;
cout << num;          // (1000 0000 0000 0000)
```

The value of num will be -32768, which is equal to -2^{15}. What about one more left shift? You will lose the value of num and you will get zero. By shifting the original bits of num fifteen times to the left, the sign of the number was changed from positive to negative. This phenomena is called **overflow.**

Let's now do another exercise and look at the result.

```
int num = -32768;        // --> (1000 0000 0000 0000)
num >>= 15;              // --> (1111 1111 1111 1111)
cout << num;
```

Notice that if the leftmost bit of the number is 1, then the shift right operations move ones, rather than zeros, into the vacant positions. This process is called **sign extension.**

Self-Check Questions 6

1. What does the following piece of code do?

```
int n = 10;
int m = 6;
m = ~m;              // Reverse bits.
m++;                 // Increment m by 1.
n += m;              // n = n + m
cout << n;
```

2. Show how the data will appear on the screen if they are written out in accordance with the following statements.

```
int n = 26;
int m = 8;
n = n >> 2; // Shift the bits of n to the right two times
cout << n << '\n'; // Display n.
n = n << 2; // Shift the bits of n to the left two times.
cout << n << '\n';
m = n & 1;  // bitwise AND
cout << m;  // Display n.
```

3. Why was the value of n changed from 26 to 24 after the shift right and shift left operations?

Overloaded Operators

In C++, the operators may be overloaded; that is, the same operator can perform different operations. For example, the operator >> can be used to cause a right shift of binary bits, or it can be used with *cin* to extract data from the standard input stream. The compiler recognizes the role of an overloaded operator by examining the operand or operands in the context of the use of the operator. All operators except the following ones can be overloaded. (We will cover this topic in detail in Chapter 6.)

.	Class Member Operator
.*	Pointer-to-Member Operator
::	Scope Resolution Operator
?:	Conditional Expression Operator

Expressions

An **expression** is a sequence of operators and operands that defines the computation of a value. An expression is reduced to a single value by applying the operators on the operands. Major issues with expressions are the order of precedence of operators and the type of data used. Higher precedence means that an operator is applied before those of lower precedence. In addition to the precedence rules in evaluating C++ expressions, consider the associativity rules when precedence of operators are the same. That is, while the majority of the C++ operators associate from left to right, a number of them—including the unary operators, the assignment operators, and the conditional expression operator ?:— associate from right to left. Left associativity means that the expression *m* operator *n* operator *k* is equivalent to (*m* operator *n*) operator *k*, and right associativity in the same expression is equivalent to *m* operator (*n* operator *k*).

Exercise

Given the values of *a*, *b*, and *c*, try to compute the following expressions and find the answers to *x*, *y*, and *z*. Then write a short program to check your work.

```
int a = 3, b = -4, c = 1;
int x, y, z;
double d;
```

```
d = sqrt (b * b - 4 * a * c);          // The function sqrt() is
                                       // in math.h library file.

x = (-b + d) / ( 2 * a );
y = (-b - d) / ( 2 * a );
z = (-b - d) / 2 * a;
```

You should have found 1 for *x*, 0 for *y*, and 9 for *z*. The difference between the values of *y* and *z* is due to the precedence of operations; the first expression has parentheses around the denominator and the second one does not.

Notice that when variables and constants of different types are mixed in a mathematical expression such as in $x = (-b + d) / (2 * a)$ they are converted to a common type either automatically or through a process called **casting.** The rules of automatic, or default, type conversion are reasonably natural, except when dealing with conversions involving *chars* and *unsigned int.* This is done operation by operation, in the right side of expression, as described in the following automatic type conversion rules:

1. All *chars* and *shorts* are converted to *ints.*
2. If one operand is a *double,* the other is converted to a *double.*
3. If one operand is an *unsigned long,* the other is converted to an *unsigned long.*
4. If one operand is a *long int* and the other operand is an *unsigned int,* then both are converted to an *unsigned long.*
5. If one operand is an *unsigned int,* the other is converted to an *unsigned int.*
6. Otherwise, both operands are *ints.*

Moreover, when the type of the variable or constant on the right side of the assignment operator is different from the type of the variable on the left side, the type of the data on the right side will be demoted or promoted depending upon the type of the data on the left side of the expression. For example:

```
float first = 2.5;
int     next;
next = first;     // First is demoted to int.
first = next;     // Next is promoted to float.
```

Notice that the type of the left side variable of the expression forces the process of demotion or promotion.

Conversion and Casts

In C++ you can force a type conversion in the language by using a construct called a **cast.** A cast is specified by the type to cast to, followed by the expression to be cast, as shown below.

```
(type)expression
```

For example, the following cast explicitly demotes a float value to an integer value.

```
float pi = 3.14;
cout << (int)pi;  //prints out integer 3 as the value of pi
```

In the second example, the expression **average(first + second) / 2** uses a cast to ensure that it evaluates to type *float* to prevent possible truncation of the remainder.

```
int first = 17, second = 24;
float average;
average = (float)( first + second) / 2;
cout << average; // will display 20.5
```

Self-Check Questions 7

1. What are the types and values of the expressions on the fifth through eighth lines?

```
int first = 12;
long int second = 1234566L; // The suffix L indicates
float  offset = 3.5;        // a long integer.
char   ch = 'B';
second = second + 25;
second = second + offset;
ch = ch + first;
second = second + (int) offset + first;
```

Statements

As a unit of execution, a **statement** is an instruction to the hardware. It controls the execution flow of a program. A statement may consist of keywords, expressions, and other statements. Therefore, we can classify two types of statements in C++. These are single statements and compound statements. A single statement ends with a semicolon (;), while a compound statement is delimited with braces ({ }). For example, $x = y + m * n - 2$; is a single statement, and the following block of code represents a compound statement:

```
{
    x = y -3 * n;
    y = y + 2;
    m = m - 2;
}
```

> **Note:** Each single statement within a compound statement ends with a semicolon (;). In C++ the semicolon is considered a statement terminator; therefore, each individual C++ statement needs a semicolon at the end.

C++ defines a rich and powerful set of twelve statements (Figure 1.4). Although C++ allows *goto* statements, the wide selection of the language's control constructs leaves virtually no situation that requires a *goto* statement. Let us examine some of the statements that we need in this module.

Figure 1.4 *Statements*

assignment	if	for	while	do	return
goto	switch	exit	function call	input	output

The Assignment Statement

An *assignment* statement causes the end result of the expression on the right side of the assignment operator to be associated with a variable on the left side. For example, given:

```
n = 4,  m = 5,  and d = 10,
```

the value of *x* in the *assignment* statement $x = m * n + 4 - d$ is 14.

The If Statement

An *if* statement is a control statement that requires a condition. The condition is an expression that produces a value of either *true* or *false*. Examine the following code fragment using an *if* statement. (We will discuss conditional statements in Chapter 2.) Note that true or false are not part of the language.

```
int FirstNumber, NextNumber, Max;

FirstNumber = 10; // assignment statement
NextNumber = 12;  // assignment statement

if ( FirstNumber> NextNumber ) // a standard if…else statement
   Max = FirstNumber;
else
   Max = NextNumber;
```

Note that in C++ we can rewrite the above *if* statement in a different notation using the conditional operator (?:), as follows:

```
Max = (FirstNumber > NextNumber) ? FirstNumber : NextNumber;
```

The While Statement

A *while* statement causes certain steps of the program to be executed more than once. It has the following syntax or basic form:

```
while (expression)
   statement (this may be a single or compound statement)
```

Example:

The following code segment computes the sum of integers from 1 to 10. The *while* statement executes as long as the value of *n* > 0; it terminates when *n* reaches 0.

```
n = 10;
sum = 0;
while ( n > 0 )
{
   sum += n;
   --n;
}
```

Self-Check Questions 8

1. Write a code segment using a simple *if* statement to determine the maximum value in a set of three integer quantities.
2. Write a *while* statement to determine the sum of digits in a positive integer.

Comments

As was discussed in this chapter, a comment line is not executable and is used for internal documentation. In C++, a comment line starts with a special symbol (*//*) and extends to the end of the line. C++ also recognizes the comment line of the C language, which begins with the symbols /* and ends with the characters */. In contrast to a C++ comment line, a C comment line may extend over multiple lines, but it may not be nested. This book uses both types of comment lines.

1.6   DATA TYPES

The term **data types** refers to the capacity for a language to support the representation of different data values (integers, floating point numbers, and individual characters) and a set of valid operations for those values. Data types allow the programmer to define meaningful computations on real-world objects.

Data types in C++ are classified as simple or scalar and structured (arrays, structures, unions, and classes). Simple data types are also referred to as primitive types, that is, the types that are part of the language. We cover only primitive types here.

Integral Types

short	2 bytes	-32,768 to 32,767
unsigned short	2 bytes	0 to 65,535
int	2 bytes	-32,768 to 32,767
long	4 bytes	-2,147,483,648 to +2,147,483,647
unsigned long	4 bytes	0 to 4,294,967,295

In C++, you may declare an integer as *register type* to impose interim storage of data in a register rather than in the main memory. Therefore *register type* is not a new type; it relates to the way that data is stored. *Register type* is normally used when a variable is planned to be used intensively such as a control variable in a *for-loop* statement. During the execution of the loop, the *register* variable may be kept inside the CPU, hence reducing the memory cycle time of the program. You may declare a *register* variable as follows:

```
register int number; // to be stored in a register
```

You may use decimal, hexadecimal, or octal notation for integer type constants. To use hexadecimal notation, place the prefix *0x* before the number. To use octal notation, place *0* in front of the number. To indicate a *long* data type, type a suffix *L* after an integer literal.

Example:

1234	decimal 1234
-8976	decimal -8976
014	14 octal = 12 decimal
0x1A	1A hex = 26 decimal
125L	125 long decimal
624006UL	624006 unsigned long

> **Note:**   C++ interprets 125*L* as a *long* integer literal and allocates memory for *long* integer and the same is true with 624006*UL* which is an *unsigned long* integer. Both suffixes are necessary to specify the desired types.

Character Types

The character type (type *char*) represents individual characters or small integers up to 127. The type *char* is classified as:

```
char                     1 byte -128 to 127
unsigned char            1 byte 0. to 255
```

> **Note:**   Since C++ links characters closely with their ASCII values, you may perform arithmetic on characters.

Example:
```
char ch = 'a';
char ch = ch + 5;
```

Real Types

C++ provides a family of types for floating point numbers to represent numbers with decimal points. There are three floating point types in C++:

float	single precision (32-bit format): at least six decimal digits
double	double precision (64-bit format): at least ten decimal digits
long double	extended precision (96- or 128-bit format): at least fourteen decimal digits

1.7   VARIABLE DECLARATION AND SCOPES

A variable is a location in the computer's memory where a data value is stored. This location is referenced by the variable name, and its contents are the value of the variable. All variables must be defined before use. A declaration has a type and a list of variables of that type following it:

```
int   that, next;
int   n=0xFFF;          // hexadecimal notation
char c;
char name[20];          // an array of characters
```

Variables can be declared in any order:

```
int     both;
char    last;
int     num;
float   radius;
```

Variables can be initialized when they are declared:

```
int    first  = 1;
char   ch     = '\n'
char   *say   = "Pleasure to help you!";
```

The **scope** of a variable declaration is from its declaration point to the end of the block containing the declaration. A block is specified as a code segment between two C++ *begin* and *end* ({...}) delimiters. If the block starts immediately at the beginning of the function, it will have function scope; that is, its impact will be visible throughout the related function. The following program shows such a declaration.

```
void main ()
{
        int     n;
        float   f;
        .

        .

}
```

On the other hand, if a declaration happens to be within a desired block, it is called a **block declaration.** A block declaration is only visible within its defined delimiters, not beyond that:

```
void main ()
{
   int n = 4;
   .

   .

   {                // a new block
   int m = 10;
   .

   .

   }                // end of block
   cout << n;    // displays 4
   cout << m;    // m is undefined outside the block.
}
```

Variables may also be declared before the *main ()* but in the same source file. These sorts of declarations are called **global declarations** and they are visible within all the functions contained in the file. In order to access these variables, use the **scope resolution** operator (::) as shown in the following example:

```
int m = 10;
void main ()
{
        int m = 15;
        cout << m;      // Displays 15 because it
                        // refers to m as a local variable.
        cout << ::m;    // Displays 10 because it
                        // refers to the global variable m.
    .
    .
    .
}
```

Self-Check Questions 9

1. What does a declaration of variables do?
2. What is meant by *scope* of a variable?
3. What is a block variable?
4. How may we change the data type of an expression?

1.8   STANDARD INPUT-OUTPUT OPERATIONS

The term **standard input-output** normally refers to two logical devices, named **standard input** and **standard output.** These names are assigned to the keyboard and screen, respectively. The C++ **iostream library** provides the necessary stream objects for standard input and output (standard I/O) operations. This library predefines a set of operations for handling input and output of the built-in data types. It transfers the input and output data in the form of a sequence of bytes, regardless of their types. Note that the term *stream* means a sequence of bytes and refers to the way that C++ interprets the data. The iostream of C++ provides three objects to handle standard I/O:

- cin: an object linked to standard input (keyboard)
- cout: an object linked to standard output (screen)
- cerr: an object linked to standard error (screen)

All three objects use the (>>) and (<<) operators, which show the direction of input and output flow. The (>>) is called the **extraction operator** and the (<<) is called the **insertion operator.** Notice the arrow shape of the operators. The *insertion* and *extraction* operators have been defined to accept arguments of built-in data types, including string arrays, as well as class argument types.

Now we will write a program to demonstrate the use of the extraction and insertion operators. This program will compute the area of a triangle.

```
#include <iostream.h>
void main()
{
   const int two = 2;
   int base, height, area;

   cout <<"\nThis program computes the area of a "
        << "triangle.";
```

```
    cout << "\nType the base and height: "
         <<"separated by at least one space: ";

    cin  >> base >> height; // The extraction operators
                            // can be concatenated.
    area = base * height / two;

    cout << "\nThe area is: " << area; // The insertion
             // operators can also be concatenated.
}
```

Another code fragment demonstrates the use of the extraction and insertion operators with strings:

```
const int size = 32;
unsigned char name [size];// an array of string type to
                          // hold more than one character
cout << "\nPlease enter your first name:";
cin  >> name;
cout << "\nWhat a beautiful name is "
        << name;
```

Exercise

Write a program to test the above code fragment. Test the program with your first name and with your full name. What difference do you observe? When you type your full name, observe that only your first name was read in and the rest is ignored. The program in the next paragraph shows this behavior of the *cin* statement clearly.

Note that the *cin* statement, using the *extraction* operator >>, reads in values only and places them into variables. It ignores any white space (blanks, tabs, newlines) in the input stream. In other words, it uses white space to delimit input fields, unless there is an explicit *cin* statement used for formatted input. To understand this better, examine the following sample program. The program prompts the user to enter a sentence. It then displays the sentence word by word on a separate line.

```
#include <iostream.h>
const int length = 80;        // a global constant
void main()
{
    char word[length];
    int  WordCount = 0;       // to count the words of a text
    cout << "\nPlease type a sentence and press enter: ";
    while (cin >> word) // reads the text word by word
    {
      cout << "\n" << word;
      ++WordCount;
    }
      cout << "\nThe number of words read in is: "
          << WordCount;
}
```

Table 1.10 Format Flags

Flag	Meaning
skipws	skips white space characters (spaces, tabs, and new lines): used with input statements
left	left justify
right	right justify
internal	pads after sign or base
dec	turn on decimal number base
oct	turn on octal numeric base
hex	turn on hexadecimal numeric base
showbase	display numeric base
showpoint	display decimal point and trailing zeros if needed
uppercase	use upper case for hex characters
showpos	shows '+' for positive numbers
scientific	use scientific format
fixed	use decimal notation
unitbuf	flush all streams after each output operation
stdio	provide compatibility with the C I/O library

Formatting I/O

C++ **I/O libraries** provide the needed support to manage input and output operations. The C++ stream contains functions that specify the width, precision of floating-point numbers and the shape of the output, as shown here:

```
int x = 25;
cout.width(4);
cout << x << '\n';      // Displays 25.
float f = 5.789;
cout.width(4);          // field width
cout.precision(2);      // digits after decimal points
cout << f << '\n';      // Displays 5.79.
int n = 20;
cout.fill('*');         // Fills unused places with asterisks.
cout.width(5);          // Assigns a field of 5 characters.
cout << n << '\n';      // Displays ***20.
```

In addition to its basic functions, the C++ stream provides special features called **format flags** to control the input and output data. The definitions of format flags are listed in Table 1.10. They are used with the **setf (long)** and **unsetf (long)** functions. These primitive functions are available to programmers to achieve the desired format on the input and output of the programs.

You may include **escape sequence** characters in the output. Escape sequence characters are a group of unprintable characters used for special functions such as **newline, tab, backspace,** and **carriage return.** All of these characters are started with the backslash character (\), called the **escape character.** Common escape sequence characters are

```
cout <<'\r';        // return
cout <<'\n';        // new line, similar to endl
cout <<'\t';        // tab
cout <<'\f';        // form feed
cout <<'\b';        // backspace
cout <<'\a';        // audible alert
cout <<'\'';        // single quotes
cout <<'\"';        // double quotes
cout <<'\?';        // question mark
cout <<'\\';        // back slash
```

There are also a few other flags for formatting the output. They are used with the setf(long, long) function. The setf(long, long) does two operations: first, it resets the format field to 0; then it sets the format bit of its first argument. This function also returns a long integer, which represents the previous state of the format field. This is useful because you can save it for future restoration by passing it to the *setf(long, long)* function. For example, the following piece of code sets the format field to decimal base, then alters this state and resets it to hexadecimal base, and finally resets the format to its original state, which was hexadecimal. Examine the following program and comment on each line.

```
#include <iostream.h>
void main ( )
{
    int x = 100;
    cout.setf(ios::showbase );     // shows in hexadecimal format
    cout.setf(ios::basefield );    // for whole numbers
    cout << x << endl;             // Displays 0x64(hexadecimal)
    x = 20;
            // to print out with left justified format
    cout.setf( ios::dec | ios::showbase | ios::left );
    cout.fill( '*' );
    cout.width( 6 );
    cout << x << '\n';             // Displays 20****.
    x = 100;
    cout.setf( ios::oct, ios::basefield ); // octal format
    cout << x << endl;    // Displays 0144 (octal format)
    cout.setf(ios::dec);  // Back to decimal format.
    cout << x << endl;  // Displays 100.
}
```

> **Note:**   The **ios::basefield** is a format bit field that represents the integral base of hexadecimal, octal, and decimal systems. In contrast, the **ios::floatfield,** another format bit field, represents the floating point notations of fixed (conventional) and scientific numbers.

Example:
```
cout.setf(ios::fixed, ios::floatfield );   // floating-point output
cout.setf(ios::showpoint );
cout << 3.0;                                        // Will display 3.0.
```

(Using the | for the bitwise OR operation sets appropriate flags on and leaves the others intact.)

Self-Check Questions 10

1. What is meant by standard I/O?
2. What is the purpose of the *cin* statement?
3. What is the purpose of *cout* statement?
4. What do escape sequence characters do? How are they used in C++?
5. What is the purpose of the format flags?

The C++ Manipulators

Another approach to format output is to use **C++ manipulators.** The standard manipulators with their meanings are shown in Table 1.11. They are straightforward and powerful.

Example:

```
int n = 20;
float m = 1.125;
cout   << setw(4)
       << n <<endl
       << setw(5)
       << setprecision(2)
       << m  << endl;
cout   << setiosflags( ios::oct | ios::showbase )
       << value;
```

Input Operations Revisited

As we discussed before, C++ uses the *cin* object as an aid for standard input. For numeric types, *cin* skips leading white space characters and then reads in the value. In the following example, if you type number *2* followed by blanks and then *123x, cin* will skip over the blanks and input will point to the value of 123x.

Table 1.11   Manipulators

Manipulator	Meaning
dec	turn on decimal base input and output
hex	turn on hexadecimal input and output
oct	turn on octal base input and output
ws	extract white space characters
endl	insert new line character and flush stream
ends	insert null at the end of string
flush	flush the output stream
setbase(int)	set conversion base (0, 8, 10, or 16) (0 means default or decimal)
resetiosflags(long)	clear all format flags or bits
setiosflags(long)	set the format flags
setfill(int)	set the fill character
setprecision(int)	set the floating-point precision
setw(int)	set the field width

```
int n;
cin >> n;
```

Be careful when using *cin* for reading in a single character or a string. The default for *cin* is to skip over leading white space characters and then extract the single character or string. Also, the input of a string by *cin* will stop when a white space character is encountered in the middle, unless you turn the **skipws** (skip white space) flag off. For example, to force the input of leading blanks by turning off the skipws flag:

```
char a_character;
cin >> resetiosflags(ios::skipws)
    >> a_character; // read white spaces, i.e., space, tab, newline
cin.width(20);
cin >> full_name;  // The blanks between names are also read in.
```

The *cin* object also provides the following facilities for input operation.

- **get()** function, which reads in a character or a string.
- **peek()** function, which returns the next character (or **EOF**), but it does not extract it.
- **putback()** function, which pushes the character just read back into the iostream.
- **ignore()** function, which discards the iostream up to a certain specified size or a specific character, whichever comes first.

Example:

Assume that input stream is "abcdef." Examine the effect of the following piece of code.

```
char character, next, another;
cin.get(character);       // Will read in 'a' from "abcdef".
next = cin.peek();        // Will see 'b' but will not extract.
another = cin.get();      // Will read in 'b'.
cin.putback(another);     // 'b' will be returned to iostream.
cin.ignore (3, '\n');     // Ignore 4 characters (0 1 2 3) from
                          // the beginning or up to the end of
                          // line character, whichever comes
                          // first; the iostream will be reduced
                          // to "ef".
cin.get(character);
cout.put(character);
cin.get(character);
cout.put(character);      // The last two statements display "ef".
cin.ignore(5, '\n');      // Removes the leftover iostream.
```

- **cin.get()** function, which lets the program read either a character or a string from the keyboard.

See the following examples and watch the syntax.

Example:
```
while (( ch = cin.get()) != EOF)
...
(EOF is signalled by pressing CTRL/Z keys in DOS)
```

Notice that the **cin.get()** function allows you to correct the input with a backspace before pressing the ENTER key. For example:

```
cin.get(name, 20);
```

- **getline()** function, which extracts a specified number of characters and places them in the addressed array. It stops at a new line and adds a null character to the end of the addressed array to make it a legal C++ string. As a result, the function call will extract one character less than what is specified by the array size. When you call this function, you can count the actual number of characters read in by invoking the **gcount()** function.

Example:

```
const int size = 512;              // bytes
...
char  buffer[size];                //maximum size of a line of text
short int  line_count = 0;
int   char_count = 0;

while (cin.getline(buffer, size))  //Reads in from the keyboard
{                                  //until CTRL/Z keys are pressed.
   line_count++;

   char_count = cin.gcount();           //Gets the number of characters read in.
   cout << char_count
        <<'\t'
        << line_count;
   cout.write(buffer, char_count);
}
```

- **read()** function, which extracts a block of data specified by count into the array. This function has two arguments as shown in the example.

  Example:

  ```
  cin.read(buffer, count);
  ```

Output Operations Revisited

As we discussed before, C++ uses the *cout* object as an aid for standard output. This object, similar to *cin* object, provides extra facilities, such as the *cout.put()* and *cout.write()* functions for output operations too. Let us examine them.

- **put()** function, which displays a character on the output device.

  Example:

  ```
  ch = cin.get();    //Reads a character.
  while (ch !='\n')
  {
        cout.put(ch);      //Writes a character.
        ch = cin.get();
  }
  cout.put('\n');
  cout.put('\n');
  cout.put('\n');    // Watch the syntax.
  ```

- **write()** function, which writes out a string array (its first argument) with a specified length indicated by its second argument.

  Example:
  ```
  char buffer[1024];

      ...

  cout.write(buffer, 1024);
  ```

Self-Check Questions 11

1. Explain the purpose of the following C++ input stream functions.

   cin.get()

   cin.getline()

   cin.read()

   cin.peek()

2. What does the input stream function *gcount()* return?

Other I/O Facilities

The I/O facilities of the C language are also available to C++. The functions and macros of these facilities are available from the header file *stdio.h*. This header file must be included before being used. You should notice that there are two useful macros in the *stdio.h* file for handling character I/O. They are:

- **getchar( )**, which reads a character from the console *(stdin)*. It recognizes the '\n', not '\r', escape sequence as the end of line character. The escape sequence character '\n' is generated after you press the ENTER key by converting it to a carriage-return and line-feed sequence.
- **putchar( )**, which displays a character on the screen *(stdout)*. For example,
  ```
  char ch;
  ch = getchar();
  if (ch != '\n')
  putchar (ch);
  ```

  Notice that both *getchar()* and *putchar()* provide input and output facilities for general I/O devices such as the printer and communications ports.

The **conio.h** header file contains the following functions for character I/O operations. Its two main functions are:

- **getche()** function, which allows the program to read characters directly from the key-board, bypassing the buffered input streams of C. The *conio.h* also provides another function for fast screen input called the **getch()** function. *getch()* performs in a fashion similar to the *getche()* function; however, it does not cause echo on the screen. It is useful when you want to write a password, for example, and you do not want anybody to see what you type. Both the *getche()* and *getch()* functions recognize '\r', not '\n', as the line terminator.
- **putch()** function, which performs fast screen output.

The *conio.h* file also declares several functions that enable you to control your screen operations.

- **clrscr ( )** function, which clears the screen and places the cursor at the top left of the screen.
- **clreol ( )** function, which clears to the end of the current line.
- **gotoxy (int, int)** function, which moves the cursor to a desired location.
- **wherey ( )** and **wherex ( )** functions, which return the row and column numbers. Examine the following program:

```
#include <conio.h>
void main ()
{
    clrscr();
    gotoxy(10, 20);


    // cprintf is an output function from conio.h
    cprintf( "Write at row 20 column 10" );
    gotoxy(wherex() + 5, wherey() + 5);//advance to row 25 column 10
    putch('*');
}
```

SUMMARY

- C++ is a powerful object-oriented language to write large programs. Its characteristics have made it attractive for advanced applications such as databases, visual-based systems, communications, and user interfaces.
- A fundamental design philosophy of C++, similar to C, is based on using functions as autonomous units of a program. In this language, all procedures are considered functions.
- Execution of a C++ program begins with the first executable statement in the *main ( )* function. Functions can call each other from anywhere but they cannot be nested within each other.
- All C++ functions except the *main ( )* function must be prototyped.
- The basic elements of C++ , similar to other structured programming languages, are:

    Functions

    Identifiers

    Keywords

    Literals

    Operators

    Expressions

    Statements

    Comment lines
- C++ offers a rich set of operators. They are powerful and easy to use.

- The primitive data types in C++ are as follows:

  char, signed char, unsigned char

  short, signed short, unsigned short

  int, signed int, unsigned int

  long, signed long, unsigned long

  float

  double

  long double

- The I/O stream of C++ provides the necessary facilities for input and output operations. It is implemented as a collection of class definitions and standard objects. You also have the choice of using the file I/O functions of C to gain more power and flexibility.

STYLE TIPS

C++ programs may easily become unreadable unless you follow the rigorous style tips as listed here. Remember that unreadable programs are difficult to debug, too.

- Case is important in a C++ program. Do not use upper-case text unless you want to follow the language conventions such as using an upper-case *L* to specify a *long* integer.
- All programs should begin with comments including a short description of the program and possibly the conditions under which it will run. Also, the name of the program, i.e., *sample.cpp,* the date the program was created, and the name of the author are useful documentation comments.
- Line up the opening and closing braces.
- Choose the program name as well as variable names carefully. Meaningful names enhance program clarity.
- Separate variable declarations from the rest of the program with one or two blank lines. C++ allows you both function declaration and block declaration. Try to place all declaration statements at the beginning.
- C++ allows you to initialize program variables during their declaration. Do not mix initialized and non-initialized variables. Place them on separate lines.
- Indent statements three or four spaces.

SAMPLE PROGRAMS

> **Note:** Knowledge of how to write an algorithm is crucial to program development. Never rush to the computer to enter code when you have no design ready to be implemented. A language is a means of communication, and a program is the way that we articulate a solution to a digital computer.

Having finished the first chapter, you now have a chance to look at four different sample programs that will give you an understanding of program organization, language elements, and simple input and output operations. The programs illustrate concepts, proper style, and the use of some of features of the language that might be new to users of this book.

The first program shows how to declare variables, use a simple arithmetic expression, handle a compatibility issue, and use I/O operations. The program simply obtains two integer values to compute and display their average.

```
//    Purpose:     To obtain two integer values, compute and
//                 display their average.
//    File name:   average.cpp
//    Author:      Arthur Unknown
//    Date:        25 July, 1998

#include <iostream.h>
void main ()
{
       // Data declaration;
       const int two = 2;
       int   first, second;
       float average;
       cout << "\nPlease enter two integer values separated by "
            << "a space: ";
       cin  >> first
            >> second;
                        // explicit type conversion through casting
       average = (first + second) / (float)two;
       cout << "\nThe average of "
            << first
            << " and "
            << second
            << " is: ";

       cout.setf(ios::fixed|ios::showpoint); // Shows decimal point
       cout.width(6);                        // field width of 6 spaces
       cout.precision(2);                    // with two decimal places.
       cout << average;
}
```

The second program gives us a chance to use bitwise operations. A good example of such an operation is the ability to see how an integer is stored on your system; that is, how many bits have been allocated for it in main memory. One way to solve this problem is to take advantage of the sign concept in integer locations. The sign of an integer is determined by the value of the leftmost bit of its memory location. If the leftmost bit is zero, the integer is considered positive; otherwise, it is negative.

Let us declare an integer variable and initialize it to 1. This means that the integer location inside the main memory will have a binary digit 1 on the rightmost end of the location and a number of leading zeros. We now shift the digit 1 to the left one step at a time until it reaches the leftmost end of the location. A 1 digit on the leftmost location of an integer means that the number is a negative number. In other words, we changed the sign of the number from positive to negative. We now stop shifting and count how many times we have shifted our digit 1 in order to move it from the rightmost to the leftmost position. The total number of shifts indicates the number of bits allocated to integer locations on your system.

```
//      Purpose:        To determine the size of an integer in bits
//      File name:      intbits.cpp
//      Author:         Arthur Unknown
//      Date:           25 July, 1998

#include <iostream.h>

void main()
{
        // data declaration

        int number = 1, count = 1;

        // Iterate as long as the number is positive.
        while (number > 0)
        {
           number <<= 1;
           ++count;
        }

        cout << "\nThe size of the word in this machine is "
             << count
             << " bits";
}
```

The third program is another example using bitwise operations. The program shows how to display the bits of a memory location that contain an integral value. Remember that a bit is the smallest unit of information in computing. Bits may be tested in different ways, but they are not printable. One way to print the value of a bit, to see whether or not it is on, is to shift it to the rightmost position of its location and perform a bitwise operation between its location and another integral location that has been initialized to one and then display the result. For example, to determine the value of the fourth bit of a number, i.e., 27, do the following operations:

```
const int one = 1; //A mask value for and operation
int number = 27;    // the binary of value of 27 is:
                    // 0000 0000 0001 1011
int offset = 4;     // for the 4th bit starting from 0
                    //   from the rightmost
number = number >> offset ;
                    //   will change the number to:
                    //   0000 0000 0000 0001.
number = number & one;     //   The result is :
                    //      0000 0000 0000 0001.
cout << number;
            // Displays 1, the value of the desired bit.
```

Note that if the value of bit were zero, the result of the operation would be zero.

Let us look at the program. Examine the program first by tracing its statements to help you understand these concepts better.

```cpp
//  Purpose:        To display the individual bits of a
//                  positive value (e.g., 1234)
//  File name:      allbits.cpp
//  Author:         Arthur Unknown
//  Date:           25 July, 1998

#include <iostream.h>

void main()
{
    // Data declaration
    unsigned int hold;
    short shift_val;
    const short byte = 8;                 // A byte contains 8 bits.
    unsigned short number = 1234;         // an arbitrary value
    short count = 0;

    hold = number;
    shift_val = sizeof(short)* byte;      // the sizeof operator yields
                                          // the number of bytes

    while (count < shift_val)
    {
       hold >>= (shift_val-1);            // Shift the value to the right.
       cout.width(3);
       cout << hold;
       count++;
       hold = number;                     // Reset the original value.
       hold <<= count;                    // Discard the bit just printed.
    }
}
```

The fourth program is a practical introduction to ASCII values as well as a smooth approach to learning the C++ libraries. (We will cover these libraries at a later time.) The two new libraries used in the program are *ctype.h* and *limits.h*. The former *ctype.h* is used for character processing and has a rich set of functions for this purpose. The *limits.h* file contains a collection of macros that define the maximum and minimum sizes of different data types. The program also uses the *for* statement of C++.

The following program displays all printable characters and their related ASCII code values.

```cpp
//Purpose:   To display all of the printable characters and
//           their related ASCII code values.
//File name: ascii.cpp
//Author:    Arthur Unknown
//Date:      25 July, 1998

#include <iostream.h>
#include <ctype.h>
```

```
#include <limits.h>

void main()
{
        // Data declaration
        int number = 0;

        // CHAR_MAX is defined in limits.h
        while ( number < CHAR_MAX )
        {
                if (isprint(number)) // if n is printable
                        cout << number << '\t'
                                << char(number) << "\n"; // character represented by n
                n++;
        }
}
```

PROGRAMMING ASSIGNMENTS

1. Given the length and width of a rectangle, write a program to compute and display its area and perimeter as shown below:

Length	Width	Area	Perimeter
100	50	5000	300

2. Write a program to encode your first name by replacing each letter with its ASCII value. Separate each pair of numbers with a single space. For example, if your name is John, the answer will be 74 111 104 110. (Hint: You do not need to know the ASCII values; you can display them through casting.)

3. The area of a triangle can be calculated according to Heron's formula:

$$\text{area} = \sqrt{s\,(s - a)\,(s - b)\,(s - c)}$$

where a, b, and c are the sides of the triangle and the semi-perimeter.

$$s = \frac{a + b + c}{2}$$

Write a program that obtains the sides of a triangle and then computes and displays its area. A sample run of the program could look like this:

> This program computes the area of a triangle. Please enter the sides of a triangle as three positive whole numbers.
>
> Given a: 5
>
> Given b: 4
>
> Given c: 3
>
> The area of the triangle is 6.

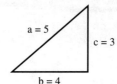

> **Note:**   Use the C++ library function *sqrt( )* to calculate the square root by including the header file *math.h*. For now, ignore the necessary data validation. Errors may occur such as zero values and situations where the two smaller sides are not greater than the largest side.

4. Write a program to display the following tongue twister: Sally's selfish selling shellfish.

   a.   On one line, enter each pair of words separated by a tab space.

   b.   Enter each word on its own line using a single output statement.

   c.   Enter each word on its own line using the format as shown:

   Sally's
         selfish
               selling
                     shellfish

5. Write a program that reads a positive integer and displays it in reversed order. For example, if the number is 2345, the answer will be 5432. (Hint: Use simple division and modulus operations. The *while* statement discussed briefly in this chapter may be used in this exercise.)

2 Control Statements, Arrays, Pointers, and References

2.1 PREVIEW

In this chapter you will learn:

- Control Statements
- Arrays
- Pointers
- References
- Storage Management

2.2 CONTROL STATEMENTS

The control statements of C++, as in other languages, specify the order of execution of program statements. The statements of a program may execute one after another, similar to what we have done so far. Some of the statements may be needed to execute in a desired order, rather than in a sequence, depending on certain conditions present when the program is executed. Moreover, a set of program statements may be required to repeat until certain conditions are met. Therefore, a program might have three types of control structures:

- Sequencing Statements
- Selection Statements
- Repetition Statements

The **sequencing statements** are straightforward and were covered adequately in Chapter 1. Here we will address the other two statements, **selection** and **repetition,** in the C++ context.

Selection Statements

A selection statement controls the execution of one or more embedded statements based on certain conditions. It is a decision-making process. You choose a course of action. For example, you purchase a car, if your financial condition is right. Similarly, C++ takes a condition, as an expression, evaluates it to *true* or *false,* and based on the result, chooses a set of statements for execution. In C++, the logical values *true* and *false* are represented by 1 and 0 respectively. For example, given $x = 2$ and $y = 3$, the following selection or conditional statement will display the value of *y*, which is 3.

```
if  ( x > 5 )
       cout << x;
else
       cout << y;
```

Note that if there is no relational operator in the conditional expression to evaluate the expression for *true* (1) or *false* (0), then the statement after *if* for a *true* condition will execute only if the expression has a nonzero value. For example, given $n = 110$, examine the following statement.

```
if ( n ) // if n has a nonzero value
       cout <<  "\nThe line is hot!; be careful";
else
       cout <<  "\nThere is something wrong!";
```

One-way Statements

Selection statements are classified as one-, two-, and multi-way selection, depending on the design of the program's algorithm. The format for a one-way statement is as follows:

```
if ( condition )
{
   statement;
}
```

Notice that *if* is a keyword and it, along with the parentheses around the condition, are required in a selection statement. The condition is the result of an expression that is to be evaluated to a logical value of either 1 or 0. Selection statements body that have more than one statement to execute are called **compound statements.** A compound statement is included within the braces and defines a code block. Consider the following syntax example:

```
if ( condition )
{
   statement;
   statement;
   ...
   ...
   statement;
}
```

For example, the following selection statement swaps data in two integer variables. Can you rewrite it using the comma operator?

Table 2.1   Tax Schedule Example

Net Income	Surcharge
less than $15000	0
$15001 - $30000	100
$30001 - $45000	150
more than $45000	200

Example:
```
if ( first > second )
{
   first = first - second;
   second = first + second;
   first = second - first;
}
```

Two-way Statements

The format for a two-way statement is

```
if ( condition )
      statement;
else
      statement;
```

Example:
```
if ( number < 0 )
      sign = -1;
else if ( number > 0 )
      sign = 1;
else
      sign = 0;
```

   Now write a short program to show the use of selection statements. The program will calculate the tax surcharge on the basis of the schedule in Table 2.1. The surcharge will be added to the taxable amount.

Example:
```
#include <iostream.h>
void main ()
{
    const unsigned short FirstRate  = 0,
                         SecondRate = 100,
                         ThirdRate  = 150,
                         HighRate   = 200;
    double NetIncome;

    cout << "\nPlease enter the net income amount: ";
    cin >> NetIncome;
```

```
    if ( NetIncome > 45000.0 )
        cout << "\nThe surcharge is: "
            << HighRate;
    else if ( NetIncome > 30000.0 )
        cout << "\nThe surcharge is: "
            << ThirdRate;
    else if ( NetIncome > 15000.0 )
        cout << "\nThe surcharge is: "
            << SecondRate;
    else
        cout << "\nThere is no surcharge ";
}
```

Be aware that each single statement ends with a semicolon (;). Also, C++ selection statements, unlike other structured languages, do not require the keyword *then* after the conditional expression.

The conditional operator (?:), used in selection statements, is a **ternary operator** (meaning it requires three operands) that uses two characters, the question mark and the colon. It is used as a shorthand for simple two-way conditional statements. The format of an expression using the conditional operator is shown below:

```
(expression1) ? (expression2) : (expression3);
```

Note that the parentheses are not required but are used to improve readability. Now we will write two selection statements, one using an *if* statement and another by using the conditional operator.

```
if ( FirstValue > SecondValue )
    larger = FirstValue;
else
    larger = SecondValue;
```

Or:

```
larger = FirstValue > SecondValue ? FirstValue : SecondValue;
```

The conditional operator is evaluated from left to right. That is, first *expression1* (FirstValue > SecondValue) is evaluated for truth. If it evaluates to true, then the value of *expression2* (FirstValue) is used as the answer in the assignment statement; otherwise, the value of *expression3* (SecondValue) will be yielded. The question mark in the statement plays the role of the *if* and the colon behaves like *else* in a normal two-way statement.

One may argue the need for the conditional operator. It is certainly an easy way to handle simple two-way statements that are very common in programming. For practice, try the following code segment.

```
number = (number > 0) ? number : -number;
```

Note the selection using ?: is at expression level instead of the statement level.

Multi-way Statements

In addition to two-way selection, there are many situations that require one selection from a variety of possible options. Each of these options might be a single or compound statement (code block). These situations can be handled in different ways depending on the size and complexity of the problem. Multi-way statements can be written in three different formats:

- Using paired *if-else* statements
- Using nested *if* statements
- Using the C++ switch statement

To see how each format works, consider the following examples. In order to make the code readable and avoid confusion, line up each pair of *if* and *else* terms and use indents.

A Paired If-Else Statement.   The format for this statement is

```
if (StudentGrade > 89)
     LetterGrade = 'A';
else if (StudentGrade > 79)
     LetterGrade = 'B';
else if (StudentGrade > 69)
     LetterGrade = 'C';
else
     LetterGrade = 'D';
```

A **paired *if-else* statement** may be rewritten as a **nested *if* statement.** A nested *if* statement is a combination of several consecutive *ifs* and consecutive *elses*. The flow of logic continues from one *if* to the next as long as the expression of the previous *if* statement evaluates to true. If an expression evaluates to false, the *else* alternative will be chosen. The following code segment is the nested *if* statement version of the previous code. Note that both formats do the same job addressing situations in which more than two conditions are to be tested and appropriate decisions to be made based on the outcome of each condition.

A Nested If Statement.

```
const int high_end   = 90,
          middle     = 80,
          low_end    = 70;

if ( StudentGrade < high_end )
    if ( StudentGrade < middle )
        if ( StudentGrade < low_end )
            LetterGrade = 'D';
        else
            LetterGrade = 'C';
    else
            LetterGrade = 'B';
else
            LetterGrade = 'A';
```

Although both formats do the same job and solve the problems effectively, the first one (paired *if-else* statements) is more readable. If you decide to use a nested *if* statement for a particular reason, use indentation and line up the related *ifs* and *elses* of the statement.

The Switch Statement.   An alternative method for multi-way selection is the **C++ switch statement.** A *switch* statement is useful when the value of an expression determines which statement (single or compound) is to be executed. The switch statement has the following format:

```
switch (expression)
{
       case constant 1:
              statement 1;
              break;
       case constant 2:
              statement 2;
              break;
       ...
       ...
       case constant n:
              statement n;
              break;
       default:
              statement x;
              break;
}
```

The *switch* expression is evaluated and compared to each case constant from first to last. If a case constant is matched by the value of the expression, program execution continues at that place. If no matching case is found, the **default** case is executed. The case constant can be any simple ordinal data type, including *integer, char,* and *enumerated* types. The *default* case is optional and is for the case that the value of none of the constants equals the value of the *switch* statement expression. If none of the case constants matches the expression, and the *default* case is missing, no action will take place and control will transfer to the statement following the *switch* statement.

> **Note:**   You cannot write more than one *default* case within a *switch* statement. In addition, case constants must all be different.

The *default* case is normally put at the end of the *switch* statement. Although you may place it anywhere you want, it is good practice to write the *default* case at the end. While the ending *default* case does not need the *break* keyword, it is good practice to use it.

Note that you can place more than one case on the same line, as shown.

Example:
```
int number, StudentGrade
    .
    .
    .
number = StudentGrade /10; // a simple way to address a range of values
switch(number)
{
```

```
case 9: case 10: // two cases on the same line or on different lines
          LetterGrade ='A';
          break;
case 8:
          LetterGrade ='B';
          break;
case 7:
          LetterGrade ='C';
          break;
default:
          LetterGrade ='D';
          break;
}
```

The *break* keyword causes an immediate exit from the *switch* and transfers control to the statement following the *switch* statement. Note that cases of the *switch* statement serve just as labels. As a consequence, after the code for each case is done, execution falls through to the next case unless you use a *break* statement to leave the *switch*. This should not be seen as an oversight by the language designer. There are circumstances that require the program to execute several consecutive cases. In order to understand the subject better, assume that a programmer has forgotten to use *break* statements in the above code segment. Examine the code above, without a *break* statement, and see what the letter grade will be for a student whose mark is 95 in a course.

Now, consider the following piece of code and see what it does. Try to complete it as a short program.

```
int       first, second;
long int  result;        // long integer to hold the answers
int       ok;            // for a Boolean value of 0 or 1
char Operator;           // operator with small letters is a keyword.

cin >> first  >> second;
cin >> Operator;

ok = 1;                  // a Boolean flag for data validation purpose
switch (Operator)
{
          case '+':
                  result = first + second;
                  break;
          case '-':
                  result = first - second;
                  break;
          case '*':
                  result = first * second;
                  break;
          case '/':
                  if ( second == 0 )
                        ok = 0;
                  else
                        result = first / second;
```

```
                break;
        case '%':
                if ( (first < 0)  || (second <= 0) )
                        ok = 0;
                else
                        result = first % second;
                        break;
        default:
                        ok = 0;
}

if ( ok == 1 )// or if (ok)
        cout << result;
else
        cout << "\nData or operand is invalid!";
```

Self-Check Questions 1

1. What is meant by *conditional execution*?
2. Summarize the rules associated with the if statement.
3. How are nested *if* statements interpreted?
4. What is meant by a *compound statement*?
5. Write an *if* statement to implement the following expressions. The variables *first*, *second*, *third*, and *result* are assumed to be three integer values. (Do *not* use the the logical operator && in your statements.)

   result = first, if first is greater than second and second is greater than third

   result = second, if first is greater than second and second is less than or equal to third

   result = third, if first is less than or equal to second

6. A digital thermostat displays the following messages according to the temperature in your house, in Celsius, of your house.

Cold	Chilly	Good	Warm	Hot
10–14	15–19	20–24	25–29	30 and higher

   a. Write a paired *if-else* statement to implement the above conditions.
   b. Write a nested *if-else* statement for question 6a.
   c. Write a *switch* statement for question 6a. Remember that the *switch* constants must contain ordinal values only.

7. The following program computes the number of hours elapsed since Monday, assuming each day of the week, starting on Monday, is represented by a digit from 1 to 7. Does the program do the job? Notice that the *switch* statement does not use a *break* at all.

```
#include <iostream.h>
void main()
{
  const int   DayHours = 24;
  int day;        //  for a number between 1 to 7
  int total = 0;  // for total hours

  cout << "\nEnter a day code <1..7>: ";
```

```
cin  >> day;

switch ( day)
{
  case 7:    sum += DayHours;    //   Sunday
  case 6:    sum += DayHours;    //   Saturday
  case 5:    sum += DayHours;    //   Friday
  case 4:    sum += DayHours;    //   Thursday
  case 3:    sum += DayHours;    //   Wednesday
  case 2:    sum += DayHours;    //   Tuesday
  case 1:    sum += DayHours;    //   Monday
  default: ` sum += 0;
}  // end of switch statement

cout << "\nThe number of hours elapsed since Monday is: "
     << total;
}
```

Repetition Statements

Earlier we said that there are steps of a program that may be required to be executed more than once. In other words, there are programming situations that often require you to process a statement, either simple or compound, repeatedly. For example, to compute the sum of the first 100 integers, you will not write 100 addition statements. Instead, you can write one statement and repeat it 100 times as shown here. This type of statement is generally called a **loop.**

```
sum = 0;
num = 1;
while (num < 101)
{
   sum += num;
   ++num;
}
```

There are three different statements that control a loop. They are:

- The **while statement**
- The **do while statement**
- The **for statement**

The While Statement

The general form of the *while* statement is

```
while ( expression )
{
   statement;
}
```

The expression is evaluated to true or false. If it is nonzero (true), then the statement that follows is executed and the expression is re-evaluated. This process continues until the expression evaluates to false (zero), at which point the program proceeds to the next statement following the loop. In other words, the *while* statement will be executed repeatedly while the expression evaluates to true (nonzero). When the expression is false, control transfers to the statement following the *while* statement.

Consider the following example, which encodes a desired portion of the letters of the alphabet into numeric format using the sum of its ASCII value and the ASCII value of its successor. For example, the code for letter *A* with its ASCII value of 65 will be 65 + 66 = 131. If the portion limit hits letter *Z*, the encoding process will wrap around to use the code of the first letter, which is *A*. Learn the encoding process and write a short program to decode the numbers into their related letters.

```
Char    first, last;  // first and last letters of the portion
 int code;            // to be encoded

  cout << "\nThis program encodes alphabetical letters";
  cout << "\n\nEnter the beginning letter: ";
  cin >> first;
  cout << "\nEnter the last letter to be encoded: ";
  cin >> last;

while ( first <= last )
{
        code = (int)first; // uses casting
        if (first == 'Z')
            code += (int)'A';
        else
        {
            first++;
            code += (int)first;
        }

        cout << code << '\t';
}
```

Now examine the following code segment to see what it accomplishes. Try to guess why the variable *p* was declared as *long* integer.

```
int m, n; // Two arbitary numbers
long int p = 1L;  // letter L indicates a long integer
cout << "\nType two separate positive numbers: "
cin >> m >> n;

while( n > 0 )
{
   p *= m;
   --n;
}

cout << p;
```

The code segment listed below displays a table of numbers as shown. The code consists of two *while* statements, one within another. This type of loop is called a **nested loop.**

```
1    2    3
4    5    6
7    8    9
```

```
const int size = 3;   // for a 3 x 3 matrix of numbers
int row = 1;
int column = 1;
while ( row <= size )
{
   while ( column <= size )
   {
      cout << column +  size * (row - 1);
          << '\t';    // causes tab
      ++column;
   }
   column = 1;
   ++row;
}
```

Exercise

Write a nested loop using the *while* statement to display the multiplication table shown here.

1	2	3	4	5	6	7	8	9	10
2	4	6	8	10	12	14	16	18	20
3	6	9	12	15	18	21	24	27	30
				...					
				...					
				...					
10	20	30	40	50	60	70	80	90	100

The Do While Statement

The general form of the *do while* statement is

```
do
   statement;
while (expression);
```

The *do while* statement is similar to the *while* statement. In *do while,* the statement within the *while* loop is executed first and then the expression is evaluated. If the expression evaluates to false (zero), then the loop is terminated.

Note the important difference between the *while* statement and *do while* statement. In a *while* statement, since the conditional expression is evaluated first, if the result is zero, the statement within the loop will not be executed and control will transfer to the statement after the loop. On the other hand, since the conditional expression of the *do while* statement is evaluated at the end of the loop, the statements within the loop will be executed at least once. The following piece of code illustrates the *do while* statement. It asks the user to enter a valid small letter.

```
char  letter;
cout << "\nType in a small case letter and press enter: ";
do
{
    cin >> letter;
    if ( (letter < 'a')   || (letter > 'z') )
        cout  << "\nIt is not a small letter, try again!";
} while ( (letter < 'a') || (letter > 'z') );
```

Consider the following short program that uses the *do while* statement. The program uses the *getch()* function from *conio.h* header file to read characters without an echo. It then displays their uppercase equivalent on the screen. Also notice that *getch()* allows you to use the escape sequence ('\r') to indicate a carriage return or the ENTER key.

```
#include <iostream.h>
#include <conio.h>
void main ()
{
      const int diff = (int)'a' - (int)'A'; // 97 - 63 = 34
      char  letter;
      cout << "\nType in a short sentence and "
           << "press the ENTER key";
do
{
      letter = getch();
              // If a lower-case letter, convert to
              // upper case.
      if ( (letter <= 'z') && (letter >= 'a') )
          letter = letter - diff;
      putch (letter);
} while (letter != 'r');// getch() converts the ENTER key
                        //  to '\r'
```

Exercise

Re-do the examples and exercises at the end of the *while* statement discussion (pages 51–53) using *do while*. Note that conversion between the two is not straightforward.

The For Statement

The general form of the *for* statement is

```
for (initial expression; conditional expression; expression)
      statement;
```

The *for* statement of the C++ is more powerful than that of other programming languages. It works according to the following algorithm:

```
FOR variable  <--  initial value  DO
    IF (variable does not exceed the limit set by the conditional expression)
          loop statement
          increment/decrement variable
    ELSE
          exit loop
ENDFOR
```

In C++, the above algorithm is divided into two parts, the heading part, including the keyword *for* along with the parentheses, and the loop statement. The parentheses include the initial value of the variable that controls the loop, the conditional expression that checks the limit, and the increment or decrement statement. Note that all three expressions within the parentheses are optional; however, the two semicolons are always required.

Examples:

```cpp
// A program to produce a Fahrenheit-Celsius table
void main()
{
    const float factor = 5.0/9.0;
    const int lower = 0;
    const int upper = 200;
    const int step  = 20;
    const int zero = 32; // 32 degrees Fahrenheit is equal to
                         // 0 degrees Celsius
    int fahr;

    for ( fahr = lower; fahr <= upper; fahr += step )
    {
       cout.width(5);    // field width of 5: -----
       cout << fahr;
       cout.precision(2);   // two decimal points: ---.--
       cout << (5.0/factor) * float(fahr - zero)<< endl;
    }
}
```

You may rewrite the previous loop in different forms by removing the statements from the parentheses. In the following example, since the control variable of the loop was initialized before the *for* statement, the items in the parentheses start with a semicolon (;) only.

```cpp
int fahr = lower;
for (; fahr <= upper; fahr += step)
{
    . . .
    . . .
}
```

In the following example, the conditional expression has been moved to the body of the loop. Therefore, there is no need for a conditional expression within the parentheses. A semicolon (;) without expression signifies this.

```
int fahr = lower;
for ( ; ; fahr += step)
{
    if (fahr > upper)
        break;
        . . .
        . . .
}
```

We may also move the last expression in the parentheses to the loop body, as shown here.

```
int fahr = lower;
for(;;)
{
    . . .
    fahr += step;
    if (fahr > upper)
        break;    //   Terminate the loop.
}
```

Exercise

What does the following piece of code do?

```
for (int index = 1; index < 1001; index++)
{
    if ((index % 2) == 0)
        continue; // Continue means: skip next statement(s).
    cout << index << endl;
}
```

The *continue* statement in the above *for* statement instructs the program to skip the rest of the loop statement(s) in the body of the loop and go back to the beginning of the loop.

Notes:
1. You may declare a variable within the *for* loop. When you declare such a variable, it will not go out of scope after the loop. For example:

   ```
   for (int i =  1; i < 11; ++i)
       sum += i;
   ```

   From now on, the new variable *i* is available for use anywhere in the function block.
2. A *break* statement terminates the enclosing *switch*, *while*, *for*, or *do while*. It transfers control to the statement following the innermost *switch*, *while*, *for*, or *do while* statement that contains the break statement. Note that a break statement anywhere else outside those control blocks causes an error.
3. A *continue* statement causes the next iteration of the innermost enclosing *while*, *for*, or *do while* loop, skipping the statements after the *continue*.

Self-Check Questions 2

1. What is meant by *repetition?*
2. What are the repetition statements in C++? Explain the syntax rules associated with each one.
3. How does the *for* statement of C++ work? Can you use the *for* statement for any type of repetition?
4. What is the minimum number of times the *while* statement will be executed? What about the *do while* statement?
5. Write a *do while* statement that prompts the user to enter a valid digit from 0 to 9. The loop will not be terminated until a valid digit is entered.

2.3   ARRAYS

An array is a data type with four attributes:

1. It is a structure using a contiguous representation.
2. It has a fixed number of values.
3. All of the values are of the same type.
4. It has one common name for the entire set of values.

    To access a desired component of an array, use the name of the array followed by the index or subscript of the component. The subscript is also called the **selector** or **index expression.** In C++, the subscript starts from zero and as a result, the subscript in this language specifies an offset value from the beginning of the array, as shown in Figure 2.1.

    We normally use an array as a container for a certain number of data items that are to be kept available for repeated access during the program's operation. An array is also a random-access structure that allows you to manipulate its cells in any desired fashion. Furthermore, arrays help you to increase clarity of the program by reducing the number of variables of the same type.

    Arrays are divided into two forms; one-dimensional and multidimensional. Although all types of arrays are stored in the main memory in a linear format, one-dimensional arrays and multidimensional arrays have different shapes from the user's perspective. A **one-dimensional array** is a linear structure, whereas a **two-dimensional array** has a rectangular configuration. In C++ an array may have virtually as many dimensions as desired. Think about a book on the shelf of a library: each page of the book is a two-dimensional array of characters; the book itself is three-dimensional, with the pages being the third dimension; the place of the book on a shelf gives a new dimension—shelf—giving us four dimensions; and the floor of the library on which the shelf has been installed is the fifth dimension.

Figure 2.1 Sample Array

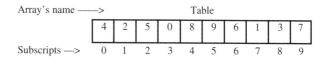

Declaration of Arrays (Arrays with One Dimension)

```
int  RandomData[1000];    //  Random Data is an integer array
                          //  of 1000 elements.
double YearSales[12];     //  YearSale is an array of 12
                          //  values of type double.
char   Name[32];          //  Name is a character array of
                          //  32 elements.
```

Conceptually, the elements of a C++ array can be of any type, including an object or even a *void* type (typeless) or a template. (We will cover these topics later.) Moreover, the size of the array must be established at declaration time, and, once it is declared, the size cannot be changed during its lifetime. In other words, the size of the array must be constant.

Similar to primitive data types, you may initialize an array with declarations such as those shown here. In such cases, you may omit the size of the array. The compiler will determine the exact size of the array based on the number of the elements specified at declaration time. (For the time being, do not worry about the keyword *static*. Just remember that all initialized arrays should be declared *static*.)

```
static short exams[] = {88, 82, 79, 90, 75, 80};  // a short integer array
static char block1[] = {'a', 'b', 'c', 'd', 'e', 'f', 'g' }; // a character array
static char block2[] = "abcdefg";  // a character array ended with the
                                                     // null character
```

Note that there is a difference between the last two declarations. In the first one, *block1,* a memory block of 7 bytes are allocated for 7 characters, while in the second one, *block2,* a memory block of 8 bytes is allocated, 7 bytes for the string and an extra byte for the null character used to signal the end of the string.

Remember: When you use double quotes around characters, you specify a C++ string. Moreover, all C++ strings end automatically with the null character.

Operation on Arrays

The basic operation on an array is selecting an element or a reference to the value of an array component. This is usually denoted either by a bracketed expression following the array name or using a pointer. (We will cover pointers later in this chapter.) For example, the following piece of code shows how an array is loaded with data.

```
const  int MaxSize = 10;
    . . .
    . . .
int  table [MaxSize];

for (int index = 0; index < MaxSize; ++index)
{
    cout << "\nType in an integer and press ENTER: ";
    cin  >> table[index];
}
```

The following code segment determines the number of characters, excluding the spaces, in a name.

```
const char space = ' ';
const int   length = 32;

char  name[length];
int   count = 0;

cout << "\nType in your full name and press ENTER: ";
cin.width(length); // longest name can have 31 letters
cin >> name; // You may also use getline(name, length, '\n').

for ( int index = 0; name[index] != NULL;  ++index)
    if ( name[index] != space )
    count++;

cout << "\nWhat a beautiful name you have "
    << name
    << ",  it has "
    << count
    << " letters!";
```

Exercise

The model numbers of some merchandise with their related prices are stored in the two arrays shown in Figure 2.2. Write a piece of code to obtain a model number, as input, and display its price on the screen.

Figure 2.2   Array Exercise

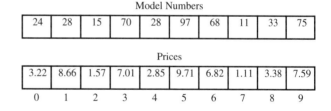

Model Numbers

24	28	15	70	28	97	68	11	33	75

Prices

3.22	8.66	1.57	7.01	2.85	9.71	6.82	1.11	3.38	7.59
0	1	2	3	4	5	6	7	8	9

Self-Check Questions 3

1. "An array is a structured data type." What is meant by this statement?
2. What is an array subscript? Why do we need a subscript?
3. What is an array element?
4. What is the relationship between an array element and an array subscript?
5. What is unique about the C++ array subscripts?
6. Can an entire array be read in or written out with a single I/O statement?
7. Define an array for each of the following specifications:
   A numeric array, called *Sales,* for monthly sales of a company (12 elements)
   A character array to hold alphanumeric (a . . . z and 0 . . . 9) characters (36 elements)
   A string to hold a full name (32 elements)

8. Write a piece of code to fill the array *Sales* from the keyboard. Then, write another code fragment to print out the largest and the second largest sales amounts of the year.

Multidimensional Arrays

Multidimensional arrays are declared by specifying each dimension with a bracket pair. For example, the following declarations show how an array with two dimensions is declared.

```
int two_d[3][4]; or
```

```
static int two_d[ ][ ] =  { {1, 2, 3, 5},{1, 0, 8, 7},{5, 4, 1, 6}};
```

or

You may initialize an array as follows:

```
static int two_d[3][4] = {1,2,3,5,1,0,8,7,5,4,1,6};
```

To reference the value of an element in a multidimensional array, know the order in which the elements are stored in the memory. This is particularly important in C++, where using pointers has a significant role in array operations. C++ is a row major order language; that is, the successive rows are stored linearly, row after row, in adjacent memory locations. Multidimensional arrays are viewed as arrays of array type. Let us illustrate this concept by showing a real-life shape (graphical representation) of an array with two dimensions (Figure 2.3), as declared, and its linear memory storage.

```
static int    The Box[][] = {    // The compiler determines sizes based
                                 // on the shape of initialized values.
                            {20, 25, 30},
                            {35, 40, 45},
                            {50, 55, 60},
                            {65, 70, 75}
                 };
```

The linear storage of the above two-dimensional array, using a row major order concept, will look like the one shown here. The successive rows are stored *one after another* in a linear format. The different shades in Figure 2.4 identify each row.

Figure 2.3   Two-Dimensional Array

20	25	30
35	40	45
50	55	60
65	70	75

The Box

Figure 2.4   Linear View of a Two-Dimensional Array

20	25	30	35	40	45	50	55	60	65	70	75
0	1	2	3	4	5	6	7	8	9	10	11

> **Remember:** All multidimensional arrays are stored linearly in the main memory. The example is an array with two dimensions. If you have an array with three dimensions, such as page, row, and column, like a book, it will also be stored linearly with successive pages.

Self-Check Questions 4

1. What does the following do? Briefly explain why the row index of the array has been used before its column index in the following *for* statements.

```
const int Rows    = 5,
          Columns = 4;

int Two_D[Rows][Columns];

for (int RowIndex = 0; Row Index < Rows; RowIndex++)
   for (int ColIndex = 0; ColIndex < Columns; ColIndex++)
      cin >> Two_D[RowIndex][ColIndex];
```

2.4   POINTERS

The ability of C++ to manipulate memory locations is one of the powerful characteristics of this language. It allows you to access variables of different types through their addresses, a method known as **indirection** or **pointer addressing.** Using pointers increases the efficiency of your programs, through faster operation, and facilitates direct access to computer hardware and peripherals. To understand the concept of a pointer, you should understand a memory location. A memory location is a named place in the memory that holds data and has an address. In other words, every variable has a location in the memory with three attributes:

- Name
- Contents
- Address

If you declare an integer, i.e., *int* number = 100; its memory location will look like the box in Figure 2.5 at the arbitrary address of 4688 in the main memory.

Most of the high-level languages provide facilities to manipulate the names and contents of program variables. C++ allows you to work directly with the third attribute, the hardware address, also called a *pointer.* We may define a pointer variable as a memory location whose contents is the memory address of another variable. For example, in Figure 2.6, the pointer variable *p* contains the address of the variable *number.*

Figure 2.5   Pointer Example I

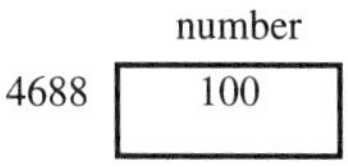

number

4688 | 100

Figure 2.6 Pointer Example II

Before being used, a pointer must be declared. Declaring a pointer variable is similar to declaring a normal variable, except that a pointer's name is always preceded by an asterisk (*). For example,

```
int   *p;    // Declares p to be a pointer to an integer.
float *q;    // Declares q to be a pointer to a float.
char  *ch;   // Declares ch to be a pointer to a character.
```

Note that the pointer is not of the given type but merely points to one (which might not exist). In other words, the pointer variable declarations *do not create* data of the specified type and *do not assign* values to them. They just allocate memory for them.

To connect a pointer to a variable address, use the address operator (&) as shown below:

```
int number = 100;    // Create an integer.
int *pointer;        // Create a pointer to an integer.
pointer = &number;   // Point the pointer at the integer.
```

The declaration of the variable *pointer* preceded by the character * tells the compiler that *pointer* is a pointer variable whose content is the address of an integer variable. Furthermore, the last assignment statement connects the pointer *pointer* to the variable *number* by placing the address of *number* into the contents of location *pointer*. The result of the noted declarations and assignment statement is shown in Figure 2.7.

Note that the following output statements have the same results.

```
cout << number;
cout << *pointer; // Display what is pointed to by the pointer.
```

The first one is the normal way used in other high-level programming languages such as Pascal and Modula-2. The first statement fetches and displays the contents of the location *number*. On the other hand, the second statement fetches and displays the value to which the pointer *p* is pointing. Therefore, the asterisk in front of a variable specifies a value to which the pointer is pointing. The value may be of any type, depending on its declaration. Let's see another example with a different type declaration and illustrate the effect of the code (Figure 2.8).

```
float radius = 2.80;
float *ptr;    // ptr points to a floating-point value

ptr = &radius; // Assigns the memory address of radius to p.
```

Figure 2.7 Pointer Example III

Figure 2.8 Pointer Example IV

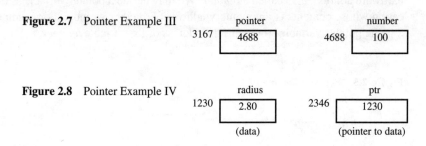

The statement *ptr = &radius* can also be written as *ptr = (float*)&radius*. We use the cast operator *(float*)* to make sure that the address is a pointer to float data. It is considered good practice to use casting.

Now we can write: *cout << *ptr;* or *cout << radius*. Both have the same results and both will display the number 2.80.

Important Considerations

Note the following important information about pointers:

- The address operator *&* gives the memory address of an object. It can be applied only to variables and array elements, and not to expressions. Examine the following for illegal C++ statements.

```
int *p;
p = &5;            // Number 5 is not a variable.
p = &(index + 10);  // (index + 10) is an expression.
```

- Pointers can be assigned to each other. For example,

```
int index, *p;
int *q;
int n = 5;
p = &n; // Assigns the address of n to p.
q = p;// Now both p and q are pointing to location n.
```

- Address arithmetic on pointers is allowed. This means that you may subtract two pointers from each other, or you may add a constant or subtract a constant from a pointer. However, you cannot add two pointers together. For example,

```
int *p, *q;
...
...
p = p + 1;
q--:
int n = p - q;  // correct
p = p + q;      // incorrect! You may not add two pointers together.
```

Notice that when you subtract two pointers from each other, the result is an integer value, not an address. To understand this concept better, consider a real-life example: Suppose that you are standing in front of your house at 907 Prospect Avenue and a person asks you for the location of the address 927 on your avenue. You would probably tell the person to go up the road twenty houses from your current location. In fact the number you gave the person is the difference between the two addresses (927 – 907 = 20). The answer is an integer and not an address any more. The same principle applies to pointers. The increment or decrement of a pointer, by any integer value, causes the pointer to be scaled by the size of the variable or object pointed to. The increment or decrement process produces another address. That is, if you add 2 to your house address of 907 Prospect Avenue, you will get the address of another house at 909 Prospect.

- Comparison of pointers using <, >, <=, >=, ==, and != work properly. For example, the following statement is a legitimate one. You will see more examples later in this book.

```
f ( p < q )
    cout << *p;
```

- A pointer can be compared with zero or *NULL* using == and !=. The keyword *NULL* is a symbolic name for the character \0 (the null character whose value is zero). For example,

```
while ( p != NULL )  // Null is a keyword.
                     // It has an ASCII value of 0.
{
      . . .
      . . .
}
```

- A pointer is not an integer. It is a variable whose contents or value is an address, not typed data like an integer.

The Application of Pointers

You can use pointers in C++, a high-level language, to do almost anything that assembly language can accomplish for you. Using pointers is considered to be one of the major strengths of C++. You can use pointers to

- Speed up the execution process by manipulating large blocks of memory with pointers
- Interface with the system's run-time library functions
- Return addresses of structures from functions
- Call functions using their addresses
- Pass simple and structured parameters
- Access and process strings
- Access the computer's memory and hardware peripherals

Self-Check Questions 5

1. What are the three attributes associated with every memory location?
2. Why is it necessary in C++ to be able to have access to a particular memory location?
3. Describe the effect of the following statements.

```
int     number = 125;
int     *FirstPtr, *NextPtr, *ThirdPtr;

FirstPtr = &number;
cout    << *FirstPtr;
```

4. With reference to question 3, which of the following statements are incorrect? Write your answers as comment lines.

```
const int value = 100;
FirstPtr = number;
FirstPtr = NextPtr;
cout << *NextPtr;
NextPtr = FirstPtr;
cout <<   *NextPtr;
cout << FirstPtr - NextPtr;
(*FirstPtr)++;
```

```
cout << *NextPtr;
ThirdPtr = &value;
cout << *ThirdPtr;
```

Pointers and Arrays

There is a close relationship between arrays and pointers. The relationship starts with the fact that the name of an array is a pointer to the array itself. As a result, one may conclude that pointer variables and array names do the same job when they are used to access memory. Is this conclusion correct? The answer is yes and no! Recall that a pointer variable takes an address as its value and a pointer variable, as its name implies, is subject to change. On the other hand, an array name evaluates to a fixed address that is not changeable. Therefore, we should modify our conclusion and say an array is a pointer to constant and an ordinary pointer is a pointer to variable. A pointer to a constant, like any constant, is not changeable.

To better understand this concept, consider the following code segment. The array name, *data,* is a pointer to the base address of the array, which is a fixed or constant address. We cannot perform address arithmetic on it. On the other hand, both *p* and *q* are pointer variables and can have their values changed. In order to be able to reference the elements of the array using pointers, we have assigned the base address of the array to pointer variable *p* and its ending address to pointer variable *q*. Now both *p* and *q* are variables, and as such they are changeable.

```
const int MaxSize = 100;
int data[MaxSize];
int *p, *q;

p = data; // data is pointer
q = data + MaxSize;    // point to the end of data
while (p < q)
{
   cin >> *p;
   ++p;
}
```

Let us have another example. Examine the following declarations. The name of the first array, *FixedArray,* defines a fixed pointer to a fixed address. The name of the second one, *VarArray,* specifies a variable pointer (a pointer to a variable address).

```
char FixedArray[] = "Hello World!";   // pointer to constant
char *VarArray = "Come down!!";       // pointer to variable
```

The statement *FixedArray++;* is invalid because the pointer to constant FixedArray cannot advance to the next array component. On the other hand, the statement *VarArray++;* is a legitimate statement. What about the following statements? Are they correct?

```
cout << *(FixedArray + 1);
cout << *(VarArray + 1);
```

Yes, both statements are correct. Each of them references an element of an array without changing its base address. Examine the comparisons in Table 2.2, which show the similarities and differences between an array name as a pointer and as a pointer variable.

Table 2.2   Array Notation vs. Pointer Notation

Array Notation[1]	versus	Pointer Notation
table[5]	==	*(table +5)
&table[0]	==	table

[1] The [ ] operator indicates an offset value from the beginning of the array.

Now consider the following code segment:

```
const int Size = 10;
int MyTable[Size];
int *Start,  *End;

Start = &MyTable[0];   // Identical to Start = MyTable;
End   = Start + Size;  // point to end of the table.

for ( ;  Start < End;  ++Start )
        cin >> *Start;
```

The close relationship between arrays and pointers allows us to define **string constants** and **arrays of character strings** or **arrays of pointers.** To declare a string constant you may have a declaration such as:

```
const char* message = "If you can't stand the heat, get out of the kitchen!";
```

To declare an array of character strings, also known as an *array of pointers* to *char,* do the following. The square brackets define an array and the asterisk denotes a pointer. Together, they declare an array of pointers, each of which points to a particular day of the week, which in turn is an array of characters.

```
static char *DaysOfWeek[] =
{
    "Sunday",
    "Monday",
    "Tuesday",
    "Wednesday",
    "Thursday",
    "Friday",
    "Saturday"
};
```

The array of pointers, addresses, can be illustrated as follows: The array contains the addresses of the strings representing the days of the week. The numbers are arbitrary memory addresses.

The array of pointers, addresses, is illustrated in Figure 2.9. The array contains the addresses of the strings representing the days of the week. The numbers are arbitrary memory addresses.

Notice that "Sunday" would actually require 7 bytes, 6 for the alphabetical characters and 1 for the null character. The same address calculation applies to other entries as well.

To access a desired day, such as Wednesday, at address 1022, write the following:

```
cout << DaysOfWeek [3];
```

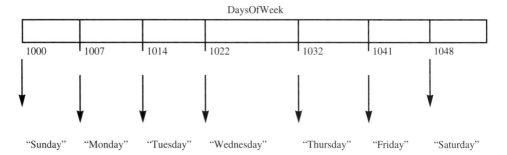

Figure 2.9   An Array for Days of the Week

Exercise

---

* Write a short program, using pointers, that obtains a line of text, up to 80 characters. Then use pointers to determine the size of the text and the number of spaces in the text.
* What does the following piece of code do?

```
const int n = 1024;

char *p, *q, *s;
        . . .
        . . .
        . . .

for ( s = p;   s < p + n; s++,   q++ )
        *q = *s;
```

* Declare an array of pointers to the following messages and write suitable statements to use them.
     File not found
     Write protected
     Read error
     Access denied
     Command not known

As noted previously, a matrix is stored in the main memory linearly, row after row. As a consequence, you may view the matrix as an array of pointers to the rows of the matrix. The related code in this case will look like this:

```
for (int RowIndex = 0; RowIndex < rows;   ++ RowIndex)
   for (int ColIndex = 0; ColIndex < columns; ++ ColIndex)
       cout << *(*(matrix + RowIndex) + ColIndex);
```

The code may seem a little difficult to understand. To help explain the pointer view of the matrix, consider Figure 2.10 and subsequent discussions. This figure consists of two parts:

* The array *matrix* has three components, each of which is an address (or a pointer) to a matrix row in the memory. The arbitrary addresses are 1230, 1233, and 1236.
* The linear storage view of data with three rows of the matrix at the noted addresses.

Figure 2.10   A Pointer View of a Matrix.

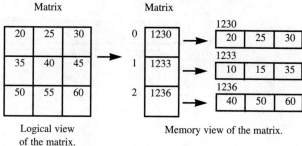

Logical view
of the matrix.

Memory view of the matrix.

Notice the above illustration of the *matrix*. It can be viewed as a single-dimensional array of three elements; therefore, we can say that **matrix == 1230,* which is in turn the address of number 20, the first element of the matrix. Moreover, we can say that **(1230) == 20* or **(*matrix) == 20.* Similarly, **(*matrix + 1) == 25,* and **(*matrix + 2) == 30,* and so on. Try to access the other rows of the matrix using the same method. Hint: **(matrix + 1) == 1233* and **(matrix + 2) == 1236.*

Examine the code segment below and its result. Complete the code for displaying the elements of the second and third rows.

```
int *ptr;               // a pointer to an integer

ptr = matrix[0];        // Assigns to pointer ptr the address of
                        // the first row (1230): similar to
                        // ptr = *matrix.
cout << *(ptr + 0);     // first element of the first row
cout << *(ptr + 1);     // second element of the first row
cout << *(ptr + 2);     // third element of the first row
cout << *(ptr + 3);     // fourth element of the first row

ptr = *(matrix + 1);    // Assigns to pointer ptr the address of
                        // the second row (1233).

ptr = *(matrix + 2);    // Assigns to pointer ptr the address of
                        // the third row (1236).
```

As was illustrated earlier, the first subscript of a two-dimensional array, *matrix[0],* is the address of the first element of the array. Examine the following code fragment:

```
const int rows    = 3,
          columns = 4;

int matrix[rows][columns];
int *low,   *high;
```

We may assign the base address of the matrix to the pointer variable *p,* followed by the statements shown here. The code takes advantage of the linear storage concept of multidimensional arrays in the memory.

```
int  size = rows * columns;  // total number of elements
low = &matrix[0][0];         // the address of the first element
high = low + size;           // end of matrix in the memory
```

```
while (low < high)
{
    cout << "\nType in an integer and press ENTER: ";
        cin >> *low;
        low++;
}
```

Note that in the above code fragment we obtained the base address of the matrix, the address of its first element, by using the statement *low = &matrix[0][0]*. You can achieve the same result by writing another statement (see the illustration for the memory layout of the matrix and the related discussions):

```
low = *matrix;
```

Self-Check Questions 6

1. Comment on the following statement:

    An array of two dimensions can be thought of as a single-dimensional array.

2. What do the following declarations and statements do? Show your answers as comment lines.

```
float     Wage[MaxSize];
    float     *left, *right;
    left =    &Wage[0];
    right = left + sizeof(Wage) / sizeof(float);

while ( left < right )
    cin >> *left++;
```

3. Declare a two-dimensional integer array and write a piece of code to read the elements of the array. Write your code in three different ways, using indices, a single pointer variable, and the array's name as an array of pointers to the rows of the structure.

Pointers to Void

Aside from the formal data types of C++, there is also another data type called *pointer to void*. It is a generic pointer that may be converted, with cast operation, to a pointer of a desired type. As a very useful feature of the language, this data type offers a lot of flexibility and power to programs. New versions of C++ have a new type called *template* that behaves similarly to this feature. Templates are easier to use and are more common in software development. The following short program demonstrates the use of pointer to void:

```
#include <iostream.h>
void main ()
{
    void *p, *q;         //  pointer to void: generic type
    void *array[2];      //  an array of pointers to void
    char ch = '!';
    int number = 1234;

    p = &number; // p now points to an integer.
```

```
q = &ch;        // q now points to a character.
cout << *(int*) p  << '\t' // Use cast.
     << *(char*)q << endl; // Shows the values of *p and *q.

array[0] = p;          // Assigns the pointer p to the first
                       // component of the array.
array[1] = q;          // Assigns the pointer q to the
                       // second component of the array
                       // to display the elements of the array.
cout << *(int*)array[0] << '\t'
     << *(char*)array[1]   << endl;
}
```

Notice the explicit type conversion by using a *cast*. The notations *(int*)* and *(char*)* coerce the pointers into the integer and character respectively. (We will discuss this subject further in subsequent chapters.)

2.5   REFERENCES

One of the strong features of C++ is its use of references. A reference is an alias or synonym for another variable name to which it is initialized. For example:

```
int Robert;
int &Bob = Robert;
```

The example suggests that both Robert and Bob are the same entities. Any attempt to modify Bob will affect Robert to which Bob is referenced. It also tells that references need initializers. Consider the next code segment. It has an initialized reference, *Bob,* and a normal variable, *Robert.* It works perfectly.

```
int Robert;
int &Bob = Robert;
Robert = 25;
Robert++;
cout << Robert << Bob;   // 26   26
Bob++;
cout << Robert << Bob;   // 27   27
```

To declare a reference, use the & (ampersand) character in front of it in the same manner that you use an asterisk in a pointer declaration. The difference between the two declarations is that a reference must always be *initialized* with a variable name of the same type.

The main use of references is to move large structures, including objects, around in memory. They optimize a program by eliminating the overhead associated with passing structures between functions. (We will address this topic in the next chapter.)

Exercise

Write a program to test the behavior of references and print out the addresses of the variables referenced.

Initialization Issues

A reference must always be initialized with a variable name of the type referenced. This is done at compile time. When a reference is initialized, it cannot be changed to another variable during the program run. If the initializer is of a different type or is a constant, you may be faced with problems. In such cases, Borland C++ automatically creates a temporary object for which the reference acts as an alias. For example,

```
int &first= 5;// Reference first becomes an alias for value five
int next = 10;

float &other = next;    // different types: does not work.
other++;                // The value of next will not change!

cout << first << '\t'
     << next  << '\t'
     << other;          // displays 5     10      11
```

There is no need to initialize a reference under the following conditions. (If you do not understand these conditions, do not be alarmed as they will be discussed later in this text.) Do not initialize if the reference is

• Declared with *extern;* or
• Declared as the return type of function, or
• The parameter of a function, initialized by the caller's argument(s), or
• The member of a class, initialized in the constructor function of the class.

Pointers and References

Though C++ references are closely related to pointer types, they have obvious differences. A reference is neither a pointer to the variable to which it refers nor a copy of that variable. It is simply another name for the variable to which it refers. Therefore, when you assign a value to a reference, you are assigning the value to the variable for which the reference acts as an alias.

2.6   STORAGE MANAGEMENT

C++ offers two operators for allocating and de-allocating memory. They are called the **new** and **delete operators.**

The new operator, when used with a pointer to some data type such as an integer, an array, or a structure, allocates memory for the desired item and assigns its memory address to the pointer. The delete operator returns the memory to the system. The following example shows how you can use the new and delete operators to set up a dynamic (run-time) array, which can also be a variably dimensioned array.

```
#include <iostream.h>
#include <stdlib.h>
void main()
{
```

```
    unsigned int size;
    int *table;
    cout << "\nEnter the array size: ";
    cin >> size;
    table = new int[size];
    for (int index = 0; index < size; ++index)
    table[index] = rand();   // random numbers from stdlib.h
    delete []table;          // Returns the memory to free store.
}
```

Note that the *delete* operator in the above program used empty brackets before the name of the pointer variable. The brackets indicate that there is more than one item to delete. In other words, if you used brackets with the *new* operator, then use brackets with the *delete* operator. Try writing a piece of code using the *new* and *delete* operators without brackets.

```
int     *ptr;
ptr =   new int;  // Allocates memory for a single integer.

cin >> *ptr;
        . . .
        . . .
delete ptr;       // Uses delete without brackets.
```

Furthermore, in the previous program, we assumed that the memory would not be exhausted. Obviously, this is not a safe assumption and there are many real-world situations in which the system reaches the out-of-memory state easily. Test the following piece of code and see what happens:

```
#include <iostream.h>
#include <stdlib.h>      // for function exit(int) to terminate
                         // when an abnormal situation happens
void main ()
{
   const int TenKBytes = 10240;  // 10 K of memory
   long int total = 0L;

   while (1)             // Loop forever
   {
      char fetch = new char [TenKBytes ];
   if (fetch != 0)       // we could also write  if(!fetch)
    {
         cout << "\nNo memory left";
         exit( 1 );      // terminates the program
    }
   total += TenKBytes;
   cout <<"\nReceived 10 K for a total of "
        << total << endl;
   }
}
```

To ensure that the memory was allocated, test your pointer each time you use the *new* operator. If the request can be satisfied, the *new* operator returns a normal pointer. If not, it returns a null pointer indicating that no space is left. In C++ a pointer that does not validly point at data returns a value of zero or null, so it can be used to signal an abnormal event, or in this case, no space.

C++ has a facility called *assert()* for handling a potential failure of the operator *new*. It is a part of the *assert.h* library header. Therefore, you should include this header file in order to make use of assertions. For example,

```
#include <assert.h>
void main ()
{
        const int size = 1024;  // an arbitrary size
        int *ptr;               // pointer to integer
        ptr = new int [size];   // Assigns the address of the
                                // allocated memory to ptr.
        assert( ptr != 0 );     // Tests if memory is allocated.
                                // Note: Assert checks the
                                   validity of any logical
                                   expressions.

        ...
}
```

If the assertion evaluates to false, the program terminates with an error message. Whenever there is a likelihood of getting an undesired null pointer, you should always use assertion.

Last but not least, when you do not need the assigned memory any more, return it to the operating system, through C++ run-time facilities, using the *delete* keyword. Failure to do that causes memory problems and sometimes sudden stoppage in execution of your program. One of the reasons for the message *null pointer assigned* or *dangling pointer* is that memory has been assigned but never returned.

Self-Check Questions 7

1. What is the purpose of the C++ *new* operator?
2. What is the purpose of the C++ *delete* operator?
3. What does the following program do?

```
include <iostream.h>
void main()
    {
    int    *Time  =  new int[3];
    Time[0] = 22;       // hours
    Time[1] = 10;       // minutes
    Time[2] = 25;       // seconds
    cout  << "\nThe time is: " << Time[0]  <<  " : "
                               << Time[1]  <<  " : "
                               << Time[2]  <<  " : ";
    }
```

4. What is missing in the program in question 3? (Hint: Be sure that the requested memory was allocated and it was released when there was no longer a need for it.)

SUMMARY

- C++ offers programmers rich facilities to specify the order in which the statements of programs are to be executed. They allow you to direct the execution of statements in the following ways:

    Sequentially

    Conditionally using the *if* statement and the *switch* statement

    Repetitively using the *for* statement, *while,* and *do while* statements

    As an exit from a loop or a *switch* statement using the keyword *break*

- A *break* statement is used with loops and the *switch* statement. It transfers control to the statement following the block of loop or *switch* statement in which it appears.
- C++ supports arrays of various dimensions with certain rules and regulations:

    The lower bound of any dimension is fixed as 0. Therefore the valid indices for a one-dimensional array are between zero and *the number of elements* minus one. C++ allows you to alter the lower bound of the arrays by using templates. (We will cover this in Chapter 5.)

    Array indices are enclosed in square brackets; the index of each dimension in a multidimensional array should be enclosed in separate paired brackets.

    Arrays may be initialized at declaration time.

    The name of a one-dimensional array is also a constant pointer to its base address in memory. The name of the array may not be used like a normal pointer. It is not a variable pointer; it is a constant pointer.

    To access an element at indices *i* and *j* of the two-dimensional array, *x,* using pointers, you should use the notation *(*(x + i) + j).

- Using pointers is very common in C++ for passing parameters between functions, string processing, memory access, and interface with peripheral devices.
- Pointers are variables that hold the addresses of other objects such as variables and functions. However, a pointer may be declared as *void,* in which case it will point to nothing.
- Pointers are declared in a manner similar to other ordinary variables. The only difference is that pointer variables are preceded by the asterisk character (*). A pointer is initialized by assigning the address of a variable to it.
- C++ referencing is another feature that reduces the overhead involved in copying large structures around in memory. A reference is neither a pointer nor another copy of a variable. It is an alias for another variable of the same type.
- Storage management is possible through the C++ *new* and *delete* operators. The *new* operator allocates the amount of memory requested and returns it to a designated pointer. The *delete* operator de-allocates the previously assigned memory. When you do not need the allocated memory any more, be sure to use the operator *delete*, otherwise, you may get into trouble.
- Beware of the *null pointer assigned* message. Another name for the *null pointer* is *dangling pointer.*

STYLE TIPS

- When you write a group of *if else if else* statements, also known as an *if else if* ladder, you should come up with a suitable scheme to avoid marching off the page. A common scheme is:

```
if(expression)
          statement;
else if (expression)
          statement;
else if (expression)
          statement;
...
...
else
          statement;
```

- When you have multiple *if*s and *else*s, as shown below, indentation as well as matching up the *if*s and *else*s helps clarity of code. Match the *if*s and *else*s starting from the innermost statement toward the outermost one. A common style scheme is:

```
if (expression1)
        if (expression2)
              if (expression3)
                    if (expressionx)
                            statementx1;
                    else
                            statementx2;
              else
                            statement3;
        else
                    statement2;
else
              statement1;
```

- Be sure to separate the keywords *while* and *for* from the subsequent parentheses.
- A loop body may consist of a compound statement, a single statement, or even a null statement (nothing). When you have a compound statement in a *while* loop or a *for* loop, use a suitable blocking style as illustrated. As with a single statement or a null statement, write these statements on separate lines. The same style applies to the *switch* statement.

```
while (expression)
{
        statement;
}

for  (...;...;...)
{
        statement;
}
```

- When writing *do while* statements, regardless of the number of statements in the loop body, use braces to enhance clarity.
- The *default* statement of the *switch* statement does not necessarily have to be placed as the last label. It can be placed anywhere. However, it is good practice to write it as the last case of the *switch* statement using the *break* statement to follow it.

SAMPLE PROGRAMS

The following programs focus on some of the major concepts and material in this chapter. They emphasize good programming style as well.

1. Write a program to implement the specification of its problem. This program gives you a chance to practice conditioned statements. A series of digits (each having a value between 0 to 9) is available as input. There is no indication regarding how many digits there are and the number of digits may vary from run to run. They are to be categorized into three groups (Table 2.3).
   Output should consist of the following:
   The number of input values examined
   The number of values in each group
   For each group, the number of pairs (A pair consists of two adjacent digits that belong to the same category.)

   For example, given twelve digits as shown: 0 3 5 4 7 2 1 6 6 9 8 2, the output will be as:
   Twelve digits read in;
   Four digits belong in the first group;
   Five digits in the second;
   Three digits to the third;
   One pair(s) in the first;
   Three pair(s) in the second;
   One pair(s) in the third group.

```
// Purpose:        To classify a group of digits
// File name:      digits.cpp
// Author:         Arthur Unknown
// Date:           31 July, 1998

#include<iostream.h>
```

Table 2.3 Random Digit Classification

Classifications
0–2
3–6
7–9

```
void  main()
{
            // Declaration part
    int digit, previous;
    unsigned int group_one, group_two, group_three;
    unsigned int pair_one, pair_two, pair_three;
    unsigned int count;

            // initializations
    count = group_one = group_two = group_three = 0;
    pair_one = pair_two = pair_three = 0;

    cout << "\nPlease enter  a group of single digits (0 to 9).  "
         << "To terminate, just enter a number bigger than 9 ---> ";
    cin >> digit;

    while ( (digit <= 9) && (digit >= 0) )
    {
       ++count;
       previous = digit;

       switch (digit)
       {
          case 0 :
          case 1 :
          case 2 :
                      group_one++;
                      break;
          case 3 :
          case 4 :
          case 5 :
          case 6 :
                      group_two++;
                      break;
          case 7 :
          case 8 :
          case 9 :
                      group_three++;
                      break;
       };// end of  the switch statement

       cin >> digit;
       if ( ((previous < 3) && (previous >= 0)) &&
            ((digit < 3) && (digit >= 0)) )
              ++pair_one;
       else if ( ((previous < 7) && (previous > 2)) &&
                 ((digit < 7) && (digit > 2)) )
                   ++pair_two;
       else if ( ((previous <= 9) && (previous > 6)) &&
                 ((digit <= 9) && (digit > 6)) )
```

```
                        ++pair_three;
      }              // end of while


                     // The program's output
      cout << count << "digits read in" << endl;
      cout << group_one << " in the first group" << endl;
      cout << group_two << " in the second group" << endl;
      cout << group_three << " in the third group" << endl;


      cout << pair_one << " pair(s) in the first group"  << endl;
      cout << pair_two << " pair(s) in the second group" << endl;
      cout << pair_three << " pair(s)in the third group" << endl;

    } //end of the program
```

2. C has been developed as a replacement for assembly language. In assembly language, the beginning of a table has an offset value of zero. C++ also follows the same rules. Therefore, all array subscripts in C++ start from zero. While this is good for system programming, it is not convenient in real-life applications.

Write a program, using an array with a suitable index, to store the annual sales data of XYZ Company for the period of 1992 to 1996. Therefore, you will use meaningful references to your array, i.e., *Sales[1992]* instead of *Sales[0]*, when necessary. Hint: An array subscript or index is an offset distance from the beginning of the array. Also, an array's name is a pointer to the beginning of the array in the memory. Therefore, given the following declaration,

```
int table[n];
int index = 3;
int *ptr = table;
```

we can say that:

```
table[index] == *(ptr+index) == *(&table[0]+3)
```

The following sample program displays the use of natural indexing of arrays:

```
// Purpose:     To demonstrate natural indexing of arrays
// File name:   natural.cpp
// Author:      Arthur Unknown
// Date:        31 July, 1998


#include<iostream.h>


const int     start = 1992,
              end   = 1998;




void  main ()
{

  long int SalesData[5];  // sales data for five years
```

```
                        // in a company
    long int *Sales;          // pointer to long integer

    Sales = SalesData - start; // The content of the pointer
                               // variable Sales is the address
                               // of SalesData—1992.

            // Now read in sales data into the array Sales
                for (int year = start; year < end; year++).
                    cin << Sales[year];  // Sales[year] ==  *(Sales+year)
}
```

3. Write a program that reads in a positive integer as input and converts it into a series of words and displays the result. For example, this program would convert 567 and display it as "five six seven." This program uses several important C++ features discussed in this chapter. It also uses the conditional operator (?:) to print spaces between words. Note that when you initialize an array, you should use the keyword *static* in front of its type. The keyword *static* causes the array to persist during the life of the program. (We will discuss this more in the next chapter.) Also, remember that a formal C++ string ends with the null character. Therefore, the maximum size of the longest word, i.e., seven, is six characters including the extra null character.

```
// Purpose:       To convert numbers into words
// File name:     convert.cpp
// Author:        Arthur Unknown
// Date:          31 July, 1998


#include<iostream.h>

void  main ()
{
    // Declaration
    const int digits = 10; // ten digits
    const int WordSize = 6;// maximum size of the words
    const char space = ' ';
    static char words[][WordSize] =
            {
                "zero", "one", "two", "three", "four",
                "five", "six", "seven", "eight","nine"
            };
    int DigitTable [digits];        // to hold the digits
    int index = 0;
    int number, digit;

    cout << "\nEnter a positive integer and press Enter: ";
    cin >> number;
    while (number != 0) // Single out each digit and place it in
    {                        // DigitTable.

            digit = number % 10;     // Get the last digit.
            DigitTable [index] = digit;
```

```
        ++index;
        number = number / 10;     // Shed the last digit.
    }
    --index; // Adjust the index.
    for ( ; index >= 0; --index )  // Pick up each digit.
    {
        cout  << words[DigitTable[index]];    // Convert it to a
                                              // related word.
(index > 0) ? cout << space : cout << '\n';  // Uses conditional operator
    }
}
```

4. Rewrite the above program using pointer variables instead of ordinary indices. Remember all the rules and regulations discussed in the chapter and in the summary as well.

```
// Purpose:     To convert numbers into words
// File name:   convert.cpp
// Author:      Arthur Unknown
// Date:        31 July, 1998

#include<iostream.h>

void main ()
{
    // Declaration
    const int digits = 10; // ten digits
    const char space = ' ';
    static char *words[] =
            {
                "zero", "one", "two", "three", "four",
                "five", "six", "seven", "eight","nine"
            };
    int DigitTable[digits]; // to hold the digits
    int *ptr = DigitTable;
    int number, digit;

    cout << "\nEnter a positive integer and press ENTER: ";
    cin >> number;

    while (number != 0)// Single out each digit to place it in
                        // table.
    {
        digit = number % 10;
        *ptr = digit;
        ++ptr;
        number = number / 10;
    }

            // Pick up each digit from the DigitTable.
    --ptr;  // Adjust the pointer.
    for ( ; ptr  >= DigitTable; --ptr )  // Pick up each digit.
```

```
    {
        cout << words[*ptr];// convert it to a related word.
        (ptr > DigitTable) ? cout << space : cout <<  "\n";

    }
  }
```

PROGRAMMING ASSIGNMENTS

The following programming assignments will apply what you have learned in the major topics of this chapter. They are intended to establish a thread among the material you have learned so far. This strategy will be followed throughout this book. You should also observe the rules of good programming style.

Read the following requirements carefully, develop an algorithm for each one, and put your knowledge to work by writing viable programs. A viable program is one that works under all possible conditions and is maintainable as well.

1. Write a program that will take seven-digit phone numbers and generate possible character sequences for each number so that a more powerful program can select those that make sense. Assume the phone numbers cannot contain the digits 0 or 1, as they do not correspond to letters on the phone. Therefore, the input stream must be validated for correct digits. For example:

   754–7669 might generate ski–snow

   Note that the program should produce a lot of output.

2. The next program is about index sorting. One of the major inefficiencies of array structures happens when large records are to be moved around in memory as a result of sorting requirements. One possible solution to this problem is moving the record indices rather than the records themselves. The process is called *index sorting*. For example, if a list of numbers looks like Table 2.4, the output of the program will look like Table 2.5. The places of the data are unchanged; the old indices have been sorted, and a new index column has been added. By doing index sorting, you have access to both the unsorted and sorted data.

Table 2.4 Index Sorting Sample Data

Index	Number
1	17
2	14
3	25
4	12
5	10

Table 2.5 Index Sorting Result

Old Index	New Index	Data
1	4	17
2	3	14
3	5	25
4	2	12
5	1	10

Write a program using the system's random generator, *rand()*, from the *stdlib.h* library to generate up to 100 pseudo-random numbers, sort them based on index sorting, and display the output according to the illustrated format. Use the following algorithm for this program. (You may use other algorithms, too.) Use the keyword new to create a run-time array based on a desired size given by the user.

```
Algorithm BubbleSort
Start
Input   size
Input   table[size]
Do
        set OkFlag to True
        For index  from 0 to  size - 2  DO
            IF ( table [index] > table [index + 1] )
                       hold = table [index]
                       table[index] = table [index + 1]
                       table [index + 1 ] = hold
                       set OkFlag to FALSE
            Endif
        Endfor
While   (OkFlag is FALSE)
Output headings
Tabulate old index,  new index, data
End BubbleSort
```

3. Write a short program, using pointers, that obtains two strings *S1* and *S2* and looks up *S1* in *S2*. Your search leads to three possibilities:

Substring *S1* is found somewhere in the target string.

Substring *S1* is not found in the target string.

Substring *S1* occurs more the once.

Depending on the result of the search, the program should display one of the following messages:

The substring . . . was found starting at the . . . character.

The substring . . . was not found.

For example, if *S1* is "cat" and *S2* is "concatenate," the message will be:

The substring cat was found starting at the 4th character.

3   Functions

3.2   GENERAL INFORMATION

Subroutines or sub-programs in high-level programming languages such as C++ provide the basic tools of procedural abstraction. In C++, subroutines are called **functions.** Functions allow you to break up a large job into smaller components, some of which may be useful in other programs. They allow the program to be split up among various source files that can be compiled separately and linked together, along with other library functions. Furthermore, functions hide irrelevant details from other parts of the program that do not need to know about them.

As we discussed earlier, a C++ function is the basic building block of any C++ program. This means that functions have a fundamental role in this language. Functions have proved themselves useful for building libraries, and flexible for developing system software and interfaces. Being a functional language, C++ makes it simple to build an application and easy to maintain it.

A function is an autonomous program unit that has its own heading, local variables, and statements. The format of functions is similar to that of the *main ()* function with which you are already familiar. The general form of a C++ function is:

```
type name(formal parameter list)// function heading
{
             Local Declaration
             statements;
             return statement;
}
```

In the declaration, the parts that are bold are optional.

- *type* specifies the type of the returned value from the function.
- *name* is an identifier for the name of the function.
- The *parameter list* or argument list contains one or more variables that the function needs to communicate with other functions. These variables are also called **formal parameters.** A function may have no parameters.
- The *local declaration* section may be used for declaring the local variables of the function.
- The *return* statement is an optional statement to send the end result of the function's operation back to its caller. The end result may be typed data, a simple or structured datum, an object, a pointer, or a reference.

3.3   CONSIDERATIONS

Note the following information before attempting to use a function:

- Communication of data values to the function is done via the arguments or parameters; communication from the function is done with values returned by the functions and/or external variables.
- Function calls can occur in any order depending on the logic of the program.
- C++ functions may be prototyped before being used. A prototype is simply the function heading followed by a semicolon. Declaring prototypes informs the compiler of the coming function(s) ahead of time.
- A C++ program consists of one or more functions. C++ functions cannot be nested; that is, functions cannot be defined inside other functions.
- The *return* statement does two things. It specifies the value to be returned to the calling function and also terminates the execution of the function. Any expression may follow the *return* statement. If there is no *return* statement, the returned type will be specified by the type keyword *void* at the beginning of the function heading line.
- Functions that return typed values can be viewed as variables, and as a result, they are often used in expressions (with the = sign). On the other hand, *void* functions are considered procedures and are to be called in an imperative way. For example:

```
area = function(length, width);      // It returns a typed value.
display(length, width);              // It does not return a typed value.
```

Carefully examine the following programs using functions. Program 3.1 displays a simple message. Since the function *output* in this program does not generate any data at all, it has been declared as *void*. Program 3.2 uses a function to compute the value of m^n, where both *m* and *n* are assumed to be positive integers.

Program 3.1

```
#include<iostream.h>
void output();     // C++ prototype
void main()
{
    output();
}

void output()      // a function that does not return anything
{
    cout << "Hello world!  How do you function so well?\n";
}
```

Program 3.2

```
// a function to compute p = mⁿ

#include<iostream.h>
int power(int, int);     // function prototype
void main()
{
    int m = 5, n = 4;     // for m raised to the power of n
    int answer;

    answer = power(m, n);
    cout << "the result  of m raised to power n is: " << answer;
}

int power(int base,  int exponent)
{
    int temp = 1;          // for intermediate calculations
    for (int index = 1; index <= exponent;  ++index)
        temp *= base;
    return temp;
}
```

3.4   FUNCTION PARAMETERS OR ARGUMENTS

Parameters provide a means of communication between program functions. There are two families of parameters that interact with each other. The parameters of the called function are known as **formal parameters** and those of the calling function are **actual parameters** or **arguments.** The formal parameters constitute the parameter list of a function and become place-holders for actual parameters. Therefore, the individual formal and actual

Figure 3.1   The Function *main* and Function *power* Parameters

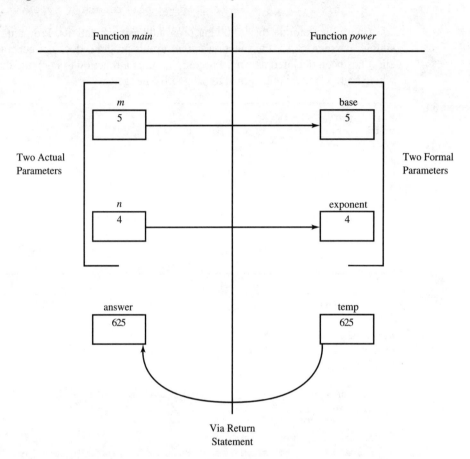

parameters must match in order, type, and number. Their identifiers, however, may or may not be the same. Consider Figure 3.1, which shows the relationships between the function *main()* and function *power()* parameters. The function power computes m^n.

When a function is called, the values of the actual parameters are transferred to the corresponding formal parameters. This is called **passing** parameters. There are three kinds of information transfer between functions of a C++ program:

- Pass-by value: value parameters
- Pass-by reference: reference parameters
- Pass-by pointer: pointer parameters

Lets's take a look at each of these parameter types.

Value Parameters

Value parameters should be thought of as local variables of the called function. Upon call, the values of the actual parameters are assigned to these variables. Then the relationship between the actual parameters of the calling function and the value parameters of the called function is disconnected. As a consequence, value parameters become independent and they may later be assigned new values without any side effects on the calling function or on other functions. Side effects normally alter the value of a variable outside of the function and may create unwanted results.

Examine the following example using value parameters to compute the perimeter of a rectangle. Obviously, there is a simpler way to compute the premeter. The specific algorithm was chosen to show you that value parameters do not cause any side effects at all. Note that it is not required that you write the identifiers (italicized words) in the heading of a function prototype, but to do so shows good programming style.

```
#include <iostream.h>
int Perim(int len, int  wide);                // function prototype
void main ()
{
        int length = 100,  width = 50;        // initialized variables
        int perimeter;
        perimeter = Perim(length, width);     // function call
        cout << length << '\t'
             << width  << '\t'
             << perimeter << '\n';
}


int Perim(int len, int wide)
{
        len *= 2;     // no side effect
        wide *= 2;    // no side effect
        return len + wide;
}
```

The output of the program is: 100   50   300

Reference Parameters

While value parameters are useful in situations in which information is to be transferred from the calling function to the called function in one direction only, in many applications, information must be transferred in both directions between the two functions. That is, the called function must be able to accept input from and be able to return output to its calling function. **Reference parameters** are generally used in such situations.

When a function containing a reference parameter is called, an actual parameter in the function is substituted for the formal parameter within the function itself. Thus the actual parameter will be used during the execution of the function. This contrasts with the use of a value parameter, where the value of the actual parameter is assigned, or copied, to the formal parameter. Notice the distinction between *assignment* and *substitution*. It is this substitution process that allows a two-way transfer of information between the functions. Note that when the actual parameter is substituted for the formal parameter, we say that the formal parameter has received the *lvalue* (pronounced "ell-value") of the actual parameter. The term *lvalue* is derived from the variable's position to the left of the assignment operator; it names a location to which new values can be assigned.

A reference parameter is preceded by the ampersand (&) character in both the prototype and function itself to signify that the called function is allowed to have direct access to the location of the related actual parameter. Thus the reference parameters become **aliases** of actual parameters. In other words, each referenced location can be accessed by two names.

To understand this concept, let us begin with a simple example:

```
#include <iostream.h>

void swap(int&  first, int&  next);   // function prototype

void main()
{
     int FirstNumber = 5,
         NextNumber  = 6;

     swap(FirstNumber, NextNumber);
     cout << FirstNumber
          << NextNumber;
}

void swap(int& first, int& next)      // Uses reference parameters.
{
     int temp;
     temp  = first;
     first = next;
     next  = temp;
}
```

The output of the program is: 6 5

In this example, the values of the reference parameters, *first* and *next,* are changed and the new values are assigned to their corresponding actual parameters, *FirstNumber* and *NextNumber.* Remember that a reference parameter is an alias for the actual parameter to which it is initialized. This means that references are not pointers and it is incorrect to use the asterisk character (*) in front of it. As a matter of fact, C++ offers references (as an improvement from C) to make your programming job easier by not having to use a lot of pointers and addresses in the functions.

Pointer Parameters

Pointer parameters are similar to reference parameters because they receive data and transmit a computed result to the calling function. The difference between passing the two is that you have to manually create pointers and pass the addresses of the arguments, whereas for reference parameters, the address connection is automatically done by the compiler. Therefore, to use pointer parameters, you should declare your arguments as pointer type and use the asterisk (*) character in both the prototype and the function itself.

Consider the following example. It behaves similarly to reference parameter passing except that you use the asterisk (*) character instead of the ampersand (&) character in front of the variable names. However, the calling function uses the ampersand character (&) in front of its actual arguments to signify their addresses.

```
#include <iostream.h>
void swap(int    *first, int   *next);    // prototype
void main()
{
   int FirstNumber = 5,
       NextNumber   = 6;

   swap (&FirstNumber, &NextNumber);    // via addresses
         cout << FirstNumber
               << NextNumber;
 }

void swap(int *first, int *next)
{
   int temp;

   temp    = *first;          // Copy the data of first to temp.
  *first = *next;             // Copy the data of next to
                              // what is pointed at by first.
  *next = temp;               // Assign the value of temp to location
                              // addressed by the pointer variable next.
}
```

A single-dimensional array may be used as an argument of a function. In this case, since the name of the array is a fixed pointer too, the identifier for the array argument can be used either as an ordinary array name or as a pointer variable in the function. The examples given here are two versions of the same function. The first version uses an array in its ordinary structure and the second one uses the same array as a pointer.

Example:
```
void display (int table[], int size)
{
        int index = 0;
        while (index < size)
        {
                cout << table[index];
                ++index;
                }
        }
}
```

Example:
```
void display(int *table, int size)
{
    int *low    = table;       // Get the start of the table.
    int *high  = low + size; // Get the end of the table.

    while (low < high)
    {
            cout << *low;
            ++low;
    }
}
```

Now, consider a function for copying one string into another. The function uses the names of the strings as pointers. Also, note that a C++ string is terminated by the *null* character.

```
// to copy one string into another
   void   CopyStr(char *source, char *target)
{
   while (1)  // This loop terminates by the
             // break statement.
   {
           *source = *target;    // Assigns target to
                                 // source, one character at a time.

           if (*source == NULL)  // End of the string?
                     break;      // Stop the loop.
           ++ source, ++target;  // Uses comma operator.

   }
}// end of function
```

The last example compares two strings. Comparison of strings is done character by character from left to right until either:

- A pair of unequal characters has been reached. The process is stopped at this point, and the difference between the ASCII values, *int(character),* of the two unequal characters is computed and returned. The returned result can be negative or positive, depending on the alphabetical order of the two characters. For example, the comparison of the two strings "James" and "Jamie" will stop at letters 'e' and 'i' and the function will return −4 as a result of the subtraction of *int('i')* from *int('e'),* which is 101 − 104. A negative result indicates that the first name ("James") is alphabetically lower than the second name ("Jamie").
- Both strings are exhausted and the *null* characters have been reached. This means that both strings are identical and as a result, the function will return 0. For example, the comparison of the strings "John" and "John" will result in a zero being returned.

Exercise

The ASCII values of letters 'A' and 'a' are 65 and 97, respectively. What will be displayed as a result of the following code?

```
cout << CompStr("JOHN", "John");

int CompStr(char *source, char *target)
{
                // The following single-statement loop continues
                // as long as the characters of the two strings
                // are identical

for(; *source == *target;  source++, target++)
   if (*source == '\0')    // End of both strings?
       return 0;           // Indicates two identical strings.

                // Otherwise do the following:
```

```
return *source - *target; // returns the difference
                          // between the ASCII values of the
                          // the first unequal characters.
}
```

Exercise

Write a function, *strlookup,* which accepts two strings, *source* and *target,* and returns the first location in the string *source* where any character from the string *target* occurs, or –1 if *source* contains no characters from *target.*

Constant Parameters

Formal parameters of a function may be declared as constants. For example, the prototype of function *CompStr* of the previous example is written as:

```
int CompStr(const  char*,  const  char*);
```

The prototype calls for a function to compare two strings and return an integer value based on the outcome of the comparison. The keyword *const* in front of the formal parameters of the function header tells the compiler that the function does not modify the parameters and leaves item intact. This provision of the language lets the compiler generate better code and makes the program more readable as well.

Self-Check Questions 1

1. Describe the grammatical structure of a C++ function. How and where is the function prototype written? How does this grammatical structure differ from that of a function definition?
2. Write a function that will accept, as input, an integer value to determine and return its sign as –1 for negative numbers and +1 for positive values.
3. Comment on the following statement:

   Parameters or arguments provide interface between two functions.

4. What is meant by *pass-by-value* parameter (argument) passing? When is it used?
5. What is meant by *pass-by-reference* parameter passing? When is it used?
6. What is meant by *pass-by-pointer* parameter passing? When is it used?
7. Write a function called *ProcessTime* that will accept, as input, the number of minutes a person has worked in a day. The function is to convert the minutes into hours and fractions of an hour, in minutes, and pass them to its calling function. The following piece of code shows how the function is called.

   ```
   int   minutes = 385;
   int   hours,  fraction;
   ProcessTime(minutes,  hours,  fraction);
   cout <<  hours  << "hours and "
                   << fraction << " minutes\n";
   ```

8. Rewrite the above function using pointer variables (pass-by-pointer).

9. Write the appropriate function prototypes for the functions written in this question.
10. The following function prototype represents a function that copies one string to another. Explain how the arguments are passed, by value or by pointer?

```
void  strcpy (char source[],  char  target[]); // copy target
                                               // to source
```

3.5   CONSTANT FUNCTIONS

A function may be declared as constant. This is one of the features of C++ primarily used in data abstraction and object-oriented programming. (This topic will be covered in Chapter 6.) Following is an example of a constant function:

```
void display () const
{
    cout << member;    // The statement does not change
                       // anything.
}
```

Note that a constant function indicates that nothing in the function can change. Furthermore, keep in mind that a constant function is different from a constant parameter function: in the latter the parameters are declared as constant whereas in the former the function itself is constant.

3.6   FUNCTIONS RETURNING A POINTER

A function may return a pointer to a simple, as well as a structured, data type. The example shown below is a function that returns a pointer to a character string. The function receives an integer in the range of 1 to 7, each representing a day of the week. It then converts the number into the name of the related day and passes it back via a pointer. If the number is out of range, the message *illegal day* will be displayed.

```
char *WeekdayName(unsigned int  n)
{
    static char *name[] =  // Initialized arrays are declared as static.
    { "illegal" "Sunday", "Monday", "Tuesday",
      "Wednesday", "Thursday", "Friday",
      "Saturday"
    }
    return ( (n < 1 || n > 7) ? name[0] : name[n] );
}
```

The calling function will call the function *WeekdayName* as follows:

```
unsigned int number;

cout << "\nEnter a number between 1 and 7: ";
cin  >> number;
cout << WeekdayName(number);
```

The next function requests memory from the C++ run-time memory manager routines.

```
char* GetMem(int n)
{
    // The following local variable ptr
    // does not go out of scope due to static declaration.
        static char* ptr = new char[n];
        return ptr;
}
```

> **Note:**   It is important to understand that any function's local variables do not exist upon termination of the function. Therefore, any attempt to return the address of a function's local variables causes a memory addressing error known as a **dangling pointer.** The keyword *static* prevents the destruction of a variable once the function has terminated. Variables declared as *static* remain "alive" and retain their contents throughout the life of the program.

Examine the following short program. Function *SumOfDigits* returns a pointer to its calling function. The *static* declaration of local pointer variable *ptr* guarantees the correct transfer of an answer. Test the program without using the *static* declaration and see what happens.

```
#include<iostream.h>
        // Computes sum of digits of the variable num
        // and returns it via a pointer variable.
int*  SumOfDigits( int num ); // function's prototype

void main()
{
        int number, sum;

        cout <<"\nEnter a number: ";
        cin >> number;
        sum = *SumOfDigits(number);
            // Notice the function's call
        cout << sum;
}


// This function computes the sum of digits of a positive
// number and returns it via a pointer variable.  The
// static declaration of the local pointer variable ptr
// guarantees the correct transfer of answer.

        int*  SumOfDigits( int num)
        {
          static int *ptr;   // stays permanently
          ptr = new int;
          *ptr = 0;
          while( num != 0 )
              {
```

```
                    *ptr += num % 10; // get a digit
                    num /= 10; // shed the digit
            }
        return ptr; // the static declaration allows this
    }
```

Exercise

Write a function, *SentLoc,* that will accept a pointer to a character string and an integer *n* as parameters. It will find the place of the *nth* sentence in the text and return a pointer to that location. A sentence is terminated with a full stop (.). If the text has one sentence only, or does not have a full stop at all, the function will return a null pointer.

3.7   FUNCTIONS RETURNING A REFERENCE

A C++ function can return a reference type. This is a new concept in the history of developing programming languages. It changes the behavior of a function and makes it a flexible tool for solving some of the programming problems that in the past needed extensive coding. (The major application of this feature is in object-oriented programming, which is covered in Chapter 6.) We can show some clear examples to demonstrate the use of functions that return references. The first example is a simple one; consider it carefully. In essence, what it does is make the function a right value *(rvalue);* that is, the function can be used on the left side of the assignment statement. As a consequence, the returning value of the function can be modified, because the function returns a pointer to its own returned value and the function itself becomes an alias for its returned value.

```
#include <iostream.h>
int& f(); // function f returns a reference type.
int first = 10;

void main()
{
int next = 20;
next = f();     // Assigns the value of function f
                // to variable next.
cout << first  << '\t'        // displays 10    10
     << f()    << '\n';
next++;
f() = next;     // Assigns the value of
                // variable next to first.
cout << first  << '\t'        // displays 11    11
     << f()    << '\n';
}

// definition of function f
int& f()
{
 return first;
}
```

We can take advantage of fact that the function creates a pointer to its own returned value, becoming an alias for its returned value. This is useful in overloading the subscript operators ([]) in data abstraction in order to define a new meaning for these operators. The following simple example illustrates this application of a function that returns a reference.

```
#include <iostream.h>
static int table[] = { 1, 5, 4, 6, 7, 8 };
int& select(int index);   // Selects an element of
                          // the array specified
                          // by index.

void main
{
      const int max = 6;
      const char space = ' ';
      select(1) = 4;    // Changes array[1] to 4.
      select(2) = 5;    // Changes array[2] to 5.

      for (int index = 0; index < max; ++index)
      {
            cout << table[index];
            cout << ((index > 0) ? space : '\n');
      }
}


// definition of function select
   int& select(int index)
{
   return table[index];
}
```

3.8   POINTER TO FUNCTIONS

A C++ function is not a simple variable to be used directly as a parameter of other functions. In addition, functions cannot be inside each other. As a consequence, the question arises: How can you use a function as a parameter of another function? The answer lies in the fact that a function name, similar to an array name, is a constant pointer to its base address in the memory. Therefore, you can assign a function name to a pointer variable and manipulate it in a desired manner, i.e., as a parameter of another function. A pointer to function has the following basic form:

```
type (*function name)(parameter list)
```

Consider the following function:

```
double power( float first, int second )
{
      double result = 1.0;
      for (int index = 0; index < second; index++)
```

```
         result *= first;
      return result;
}
```

It may be called by another function as x = (*power)(p, q); where p and q are supplied by the expression.

The following program demonstrates the use of a pointer to a function name as parameters of other functions. The program is written to sort a series of integer values using a suitable sorting algorithm. (The program uses the bubble sort technique.) Examine the program carefully. Look especially at the prototype of the *sort* function: it does not use the names of functions in the parameter list. Also, in the definition of the function, the code segment does not use any identifiers with pointers to functions in the parameter list.

```
// function prototypes
void swap (int   *first,   int   *second);
int compare ( int first, int second);
void sort ( int  t[], int  n, void (*exchange)(int*,
            int*), int (*relation)(int, int) );

void main()
{
   static int table [] = { 10, 13, 8, 49, 6, 53, 12};
   int size = sizeof(table) / sizeof(int);   // size == 7
   sort( table, size, swap, compare );

   for (int index = 0; index < size; ++index)
            cout << table[index];
}

void swap(int* first, int* second)
      // swaps the value of two variables
{
   *first  = *first   - *second;
   *second = *second  + *first;
   *first  = *second  - *first;
}

int compare(int first, int second)
{
     return  (first - second); // Returns zero, or a negative or a positive
                         // value.
}


      // In the following function, the pointers exchange
      // and relation correspond to functions swap and
      // compare respectively.

      void sort(int t[], int n, void (*exchange)(int*,
            int*), int (*relation)(int, int) )
      {
         int flag = 1; // a Boolean value to control the process
```

```
        int index;
        --n;
        while (flag)    //  similar to while (flag ==1)
        {
                flag = 0;
                for (index = 0; index < n; ++index)
                    if (relation(t[index], t[index+1]) > 0)
                    {
                        exchange (&t[index], &t[index+1]);
                        flag = 1;
                            }
                }   // end of while
}
```

Notice the use of the pointers to function in the prototype declaration of the above *sort* function. The pointer to function, as parameters, may be used with the original names of the function associated with, or completely with, different names. What matters is the type and order of their related parameter list. In our example, we used different names, as shown here:

```
void (*exchange)(int*, int*)
```

and

```
int (*relation)(int, int)
```

You may declare a pointer to function to represent the address of a function by pointing to that function. The basic pointer to function declaration may be written as:

```
type    (*pointer name) (parameter list);
```

or:

```
int   (*process) (int, int);
```

The above declaration statement declares the pointer to function (whose name is *process*) to be a pointer to a function with two integer parameters and returning value of integer type. Similar to other pointer variables, you may also declare an array of pointers to function(s) such as:

```
int   (*table[2]) (int, int);
```

Consider the following sample program, which uses an array of pointers to functions. Written to perform basic arithmetic, it prompts the user to enter a code for a desired operation. Then the code will be read in and used as a subscript of the array to call an appropriate function. As an exercise, complete the program by writing two functions to perform addition and subtraction operations. Then run the program.

```
// function prototypes
int add(int, int);
int subtract(int, int);

// declaration of a pointer to function
int (*process)(int, int);

// a table of pointers to functions
int (*table[2])(int, int); // Each table element points to a function.
```

```
void main()
{
    int FirstVal = 10,
    NextVal  = 5;

    int code;
    process = add;          // Assigns the address
                            // of function add to process.
    cout << process(FirstVal, NextVal);//Displays sum.

        // Assigns the address of function add to table[0].
        table[0] = add;

        // Assigns the address of subtract to table[0].
        table[1] = subtract;

    // now an application example
    cout << "\nEnter 0 to add two numbers and 1"
             << " to subtract: ";
        cin >> code;

        // function call
        cout << table[code];   // Will perform addition or
                               // subtraction based on the
                               // user's choice.
}
```

To analyze the program, look at it from the top to bottom. The first two lines represent the prototypes for the two functions, *add* and *subtract*. The third line is a pointer to function pointing to a function with the same specifications as functions *add* and *subtract*. The last one is an array of pointers to functions, each of which has the same attributes as functions *add* and *subtract*. This means that each component of the array can point to either function. In the program itself, we assigned the address of function *add* to *process,* a pointer to function, and used the pointer as an ordinary function. We also assigned the addresses of the two functions, *add* and *subtract,* to the two cells of the array and used each cell's content as an ordinary function.

Self-Check Questions 2

1. The following function computes the square of an integer value.

```
    int  square (int number)
    {
        return number * number;
    }
```

Write a function called *sum* of squares to compute the sum of the squares of the first *n* numbers as follows:

$$1^2 + 2^2 + 3^2 + 4^2 + ... + n^2.$$

The function will receive as input the value of *n* and a pointer to function *square.*

2. Write a function prototype for function *sum* of squares.
3. Write a statement to call function *sum* of squares.
4. Write another function to compute the cube of an integer value. Then call function *sum* to compute the sum of the cubes of the first *n* numbers.
5. Write the necessary declaration for the pointer to function called *DoIt* to be used with the following function prototype:

```
void   swap(float, float);
```

3.9   STORAGE CLASSES

Storage classes or modes determine when storage is allocated and when it is de-allocated. Storage classes of C++ are:

- *Automatic*
- *Static*
- *Extern*
- *Register*
- *Dynamic* using the new and delete operators (covered earlier)

Let's look more closely at each class.

The Automatic Class

Local variables within a function are classified, by default, as ***automatic* variables** because they are allocated automatically when the function is called. They are de-allocated automatically when the called function terminates. This implies that automatic variables do not maintain their value from one invocation of the function—in which they are defined—to the next.

The Static Class

In contrast to ordinary local variables, the ***static* local variables** of a function come into existence when the function is called and continue to exist until the entire program terminates. This means that *static* variables, unlike ordinary local variables that are de-allocated when a called function terminates, remain in existence for the duration of the program. Thus, upon a function call, the *static* local variables of that function are allocated permanent memory and initialized. When the function terminates, the value of *static* variables persists for subsequent function calls. To declare a *static* variable, write the keyword *static* in front of the data type.

    Static variables are very useful for handling large data structures as local variables and for returning pointers and references by functions as well. An example of this is using the keyword *static* with initialized arrays. You are already familiar with this example. *Static* variables are also useful in recursive functions where access to the previous value of each function call is necessary. To understand how this class of variables work, consider the following program:

```
#include<iostream.h>
void display();                 // prototype

void main()
```

```
{
    int i;                      // local variable

    for (i = 0; i < 5; i++)    // five times
        display();
}

void display()
{
    static int i = 1;   // a permanent variable initialized only once
    int j = 1;   // Local variables are temporary.
    cout << i << '\t'
         << j << endl;
    i++, j++;       // increment variables
}
```

Program output:

1	1
2	1
3	1
4	1
5	1

The next example shows a local pointer variable declared as *static*. This pointer variable is a local variable and unless it is declared *static*, goes out of scope upon termination of the function. Lack of *static* declaration causes a dangling pointer or *null* pointer assignment error.

```
#include <iostream.h>

// function prototype
// Receives an integer in the range (0 to 10).
// Return the name of the related digit.

char* alpha(int);

void main()
{
    int number;

        // ...
        // ...

    number = 5;

    cout << alpha(number);
}

// function alpha
char* alpha(int n)
{
```

```
static char* name[] = {"Zero", "One", "Two", "Three", "Four",
                       "Five", "Six", "Seven", "Eight", "Nine",
                       "Ten", "illegal"};

return (n <11 || n >= 0)? name[n] : name[10];
```

}

The Extern Class

If a variable is to be used in one file while defined in another, it must be declared ***extern*** or external. An *extern* variable directs the compiler in how to resolve the address issues of these variables during the linkage phase. *Extern* variables are needed for large projects composed of several source files.

Example:
```
extern int m; // Indicates that m has been declared in another file.
    void main()
    {
        int n;
        cin >> m
            >> n;
        ...
        ...
    }
```

Note the following information about extern variables:

- External arrays can be initialized at the time of declaration.
- *Extern* variables are permanent (static), while *automatic* variables exist only within the block they are defined.
- External *static* variables can be seen (i.e., are available) in files where they are defined, but not in any others.

The Register Class

We declare a variable as a **register** if it is intended to be used intensively, such as a control variable in a *for* loop. C++ has inherited this feature from the C language, which was originally developed for systems programming in which speed was critical. To achieve speed of execution, the *register* storage class was added to the language because they facilitate manipulating data in the CPU registers much more quickly than if the same data resides in the main memory. You can use the *register* storage class with characters, integers, and pointers. It is normally used for control variables of *for* loops and as array indices. Keep in mind that declaring a variable as register is just a suggestion to the compiler, which may or may not be implemented. For example,

```
int sum = 0;
for (register int index = 1;
    index < 1001;
    ++ index)
    sum + = index;
```

3.10   SCOPE OF VARIABLES

The portion of the program in which a variable is declared and maintains its original definition is called the **scope of the variable.** In other words, scope refers to areas of a program from which a variable is accessible. We can define three types of scope in C++:

- Block scope
- File scope
- Function scope

Let's take a closer look at each.

Block Scope

Block scope is a code segment enclosed in braces ({...}). An identifier declared within a block is visible within this block only. This means that the identifier is confined to the code segment between the two braces. Block declarations allow you to reuse identifiers. Consider the following example: The identifier *index* is a local variable within its defined block and is undefined after the closing brace.

```
if ( response == 'y' )
{                            // beginning of the block
     int index = 0;          // a local block variable

     for ( ; index < 12; ++index)
          cout << Sales[index];
}// end of the block; index no longer available
```

Blocks may be nested inside each other, and when this occurs, they hide identifiers with the same name defined in enclosing blocks. This means that you may declare and use the same identifier in different blocks. For example, the identifier *index* in the following nested blocks refers to different data objects.

```
{
     int index;
     ...
     ...
     {
          int index;   // a different variable from the previously
          ...           // declared one
          ...
     }
}
```

The identifiers defined within a function may also have block scope that is local to that function. The local variables of a function can be referred to within the function and not outside it. The lifetime of local variables is the duration of the block or function in which they have been declared. Note that value parameters of a function are also considered local variables of that function and as such they occupy their own memory storage and are de-allocated when the function terminates.

We can extend the lifetime of a local variable from the duration of its associated blocks to the duration of the program by placing the keyword *static* before its data type.

Such a local variable behaves similarly to a global variable in that it does not perish after the execution of the function. However, it is not accessible to any other block in the source file except the block in which it has been declared. When a block is called for the second time, its *static* variables "wake up" and remember the values they had when their parent function went out of scope.

File Scope

An identifier that does not belong to any block or function of a program has a **file scope;** that is, a scope from the point of declaration to the end of the source file. A file scope identifier is said to be a global identifier and can be referred to from anywhere inside the source file. In C++ global variables are declared before the *main* function. For example:

```
int x = 5;              // global variable
void main(void)
{
      int x = 10;       // local

      cout << x;        // local  x

      // global x with address resolution operator
      cout << ::x;      // See the note following.
      ...
      ...
}
```

Note that when a global identifier happens to have the same name as a local one, the global identifier can be differentiated by using the scope resolution operator (::) before it.

It is good programming practice to declare identifiers locally, that is, to confine their lifetime to the smallest scope in which they have been declared. By doing so you can hide the details of data manipulation among different parts of the program and thus reduce the possibility of undesired side effects. Also, localizing the data objects allows programmers to choose local identifiers without the knowledge of those existing in the surrounding scope. This is important in the case of large projects.

Function Scope

While C++ defines two levels of data, global and local, it has only one level of functions. C++ functions are autonomous program units that cannot be nested inside each other. Therefore, functions have a global scope and their lifetime is the duration of the program. This is also known as **function scope.** Functions are also visible in the entire source file and can be called by other functions or used in expressions as long as they are defined before being called or prototyped.

Self-Check Questions 3

1. What is meant by the term *storage class?*
2. What is meant by the *scope* of a variable?
3. What is the difference between a *global* variable and a *static* variable?

4. How is a block variable defined? Write an example.
5. What is a *dangling pointer?*

SUMMARY

- C++ is a function-based language. A C++ program is a collection of single level functions, one of which must be called *main*. Functions can be used in their traditional mathematical form to compute and return a single value or no value at all. In the latter case, a C++ function will do what a procedure does in other high-level languages. A function that returns a value is used as a part of an expression or assignment statement using the equal (=) sign. A function that avoids returning a value is used alone in a statement.
- The *return* statement does two things:

    It returns the end result of the function to its caller.

    It terminates the function to which it belongs.

- Calling functions can pass a value to the called function using three different methods:

    By value, in which the value becomes the property of the function and is stored in a local variable.

    By reference, in which the associated formal identifier establishes a two-way relationship with its actual identifier in the memory. Any change to the variable in the function side will affect its counterpart from the calling side. Remember that a reference is never been considered a pointer. Instead, it defines a second name or an alias for another identifier.

    By pointer, in which associated formal and actual parameters are connected with each other using addresses. Pointer parameters have their own memory storage that points to the memory locations of their actual parameters (arguments).

- When a parameter is passed to a function with the intention that it remains unchanged at the end of the operation of the function, you may declare it as constant using the keyword *const*. It provides protection against undesired side effects. In this case, the compiler will trap any attempt to modify the value as an error.
- Functions may return a reference to a value. This is a new feature in programming and often solves complex problems in a simple way. Remember that the function cannot return a reference to a locally declared automatic variable.
- Functions may return a pointer. This attribute helps in moving large structures around in memory without overhead.
- Using pointers to functions allows you to build generic code and use functions as variables.
- Storage classes determine the lifetime of variables. C++ supports:

    The *automatic* class. This includes local variables of a block and/or functions. These variables are created when the block is entered or the function is called; they are terminated when the block or the function goes out of scope.

    The *static* class. Here, variables are initialized once upon the first call of the function and retain their value for the duration of the program. When the function goes out of scope, they go to "sleep" and when the functions are called, they wake up and re-member their previous value.

The *extern* class. These include variables that have been defined in another source file. The keyword *extern* tells the compiler how to resolve the address allocation during the linking phase.

The *register* class. Variables of this class are normally intended to be used inten-sively. It is a suggestion to the compiler which may or may not be implemented.

The *dynamic* class. Here, the C++ run-time system, using the *new* operator, creates new objects for the program. The *delete* operator de-allocates memory; that is, the memory is returned to the system.

- The scope of a variable is the code region or program portion in which that variable is accessible. The scope of C++ variables are either global or local. The scope of func-tions is always global. C++ defines three types of scopes:

  Block scope

  File scope

  Function scope

STYLE TIPS

- Write functions that are clear, short, and cohesive. The screen size of your computer is possibly a good criterion for the maximum size of a function. A cohesive function per-forms a single job and no more. Cohesion helps fault isolation and software mainte-nance and also makes the function reusable. Remember that a function is not a closet into which you stuff code.
- Side effects can lead to difficult debugging problems. Be sure to limit the number of global variables and that you have full control of them. Improper use of pointer vari-ables may also cause side effects and cases of dangling pointers.
- Localizing the program variables is a good practice. It enhances clarity and is good for teamwork and testing individual functions of a project.
- Functions should have no coupling effects. This means that you should limit the inter-action between two functions.
- All function interfaces must be documented properly. Interface documentation should include purpose, the condition(s) upon function call, and the post-condition result when the function goes out of scope. Write the interface documentation in front of their pro-totypes as shown below. The function is to look up a search target in an array. If the target is found, its position will be returned; otherwise, a null pointer will be sent to the calling function. The alternative commenting method of C, using /*.. */, is clearer for large pieces of documentation where the size of comments is more than a single line.

```
// Interface for function lookup
// PURPOSE:  To search an array for a target value
// GIVEN:    An array of type integer with low <= high
//           that defines the index range of the array.
```

```
// RETURN:   A pointer to the position of the target
//              item, if found, otherwise, a null pointer.
int* lookup(int*, int, int, int);//array, target, low, high
```

SAMPLE PROGRAMS

1. Write a structured program to sort a list of numeric values, using selection sort. This sort is modelled on sorting cards and simply selects successive items and places them into their desired sorting position. The given sorting algorithm sorts a list of integer data into ascending order. Let's look at the mechanism of this technique as shown in Figure 3.2.

Figure 3.2 Unsorted List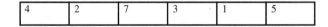

a. Select the largest value of the list and place it at the end:

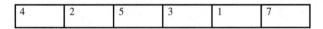

b. Select the next largest and place it in its proper position toward the end:

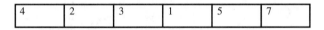

c. Continue the process until the list is exhausted. The result will be:

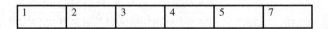

This program is a possible solution to the problem; it uses pointers to functions in the parameter list of its functions. It can also work without pointers to functions; however, it demonstrates how to use them when a need arises. Remember that pointers to functions in the parameter list use empty parentheses only.

```
// Purpose:    This program uses the selection sort
//             algorithm to sort a table of integer
//             values.
// File Name:   select.cpp
// Author:      Author Unknown
// Date:        August 5, 1998


// Interface for function  MaxIndex
// PURPOSE:    To find the index of the highest value in
//             the table.
// GIVEN:      The table address, and an index value other
//             than zero.
```

```
// RETURN:    The index of the highest value.
int MaxIndex(int* table, int high, int(*compare)(int,int));

// Interface for function compare
// PURPOSE:    To determine if one value is equal to , less
//             than, or greater than the other.
// GIVEN:      Two values
// RETURN:     A zero, or a negative, or a positive number
int compare(int m, int n);

// Interface for function swap
// PURPOSE:    To exchange two values that are not in
//             proper order, i.e., ascending order.
// GIVEN:      Two reference parameters.
// RETURN:     None.
void swap(int& p, int& q);

// Interface for function SelectSort
// PURPOSE:    To sort a table of integer values.
// GIVEN:      The tables, table size, a pointer to
//             function swap.
// RETURN:     The same table of integers but sorted.
int*  SelectSort (int *table, int TblSize,
              void (*swap)(int&, int&));

    #include<iostream.h>
    void main()
{
    static int table[] = { 6,1,5,3,2,4 };      // for test purpose
    int TblSize = sizeof(table) / sizeof(int);  // to size of 6
    int* TblPtr = table;
    TblPtr = SelectSort(table, TblSize, swap);

    // display the sorted list
    for (int index = 0; index < TblSize; index++)
            cout << TblPtr[index];
}
int compare(int m, int n)
{
    return m - n;  // Returns zero, or a negative or a
                   // positive value.
}
void swap(int& p, int& q)  // Uses reference parameters.
{
    int temp;
    temp = p;
    p    = q;
    q    = temp;
}
  // The following function is using a pointer to function.
int MaxIndex(int* table, int high, int (*compare)(int, int))
```

```
            {
                int LoIndex, HiIndex;
                HiIndex = 0;
                LoIndex = 1;
                while (LoIndex <= high)
                {
                    if (compare(table[HiIndex], table[LoIndex]) < 0)
                        HiIndex = LoIndex;
                    LoIndex++;
                }
                return HiIndex;
            }


            // selection sort using pointer to function
            int*  SelectSort (int *table, int TblSize,
                                void(*swap)(int&, int&))
            {
                int index = TblSize - 1;
                int j;
                while (index > 0)
                {
                    j = MaxIndex(table, index, compare);
                    swap(table[j], table[index]);
                    --index;
                }
                return table;
            }
```

2. One of the major restrictions of digital computers is their hardware limitation for storing numbers larger than a certain size. We can, however, solve this problem either through changing their base from 10 to a bigger one, i.e., 50, or just simply by storing them as character strings. We will implement the latter approach. First we will read large numbers up to twenty digits, and then we will perform the addition operation. Note that we normally read the numbers from left to right but we use them in arithmetic operations from right to left. This requirement imposes a shifting process on the data in order to align unequal size data. The problem can be solved without shifting with two functions, *sum* and *subtract*. Function *subtract* is in prototype only. Write the definition of the function as an exercise.

```
// PURPOSE:    This program obtains two values that might have
//             up to twenty digits, adds them, and displays the
//             result.
// FILE NAME:  largeint.cpp
// AUTHOR:     Author Unknown
// DATE:       August 5, 1998


// Interface for function length
// PURPOSE:    To find the length of a character string.
// GIVEN:      A character string.
// RETURN:     An integer representing the length of the
//             given string.
```

```
int length (char*);
// Interface for function copy
// PURPOSE:    To copy a target string into a source
//             string.
// GIVEN:      Two character strings.
// RETURN:     Source string with a copy of the target
//             string.
void copy (char*, char*);


// Interface for function get_data
// PURPOSE:    To read in a big integer in the form of a
//             character string.
// GIVEN:      A pointer to an empty character string.
// RETURN:     A character string representing input data.
void get_data (char *);


// Interface for function sum
// PURPOSE:    To add two character strings together.
// GIVEN:      Two character strings.
// RETURN:     The sum of the two given strings via a
//             pointer variable.
char *sum (char*, char*);


// Interface for function subtract
// PURPOSE:    To subtract two character strings from each
//             other.
// GIVEN:      Two character strings.
// RETURN:     The difference of the two given strings via
//             a pointer.

char* subtract (char*, char*);


#include <iostream.h>
const int size = 32;  // an arbitrary size for the program's strings
void main ()
{
    //      data declaration
    char string1[size],  string2[size];
    char  *first = string1, *second = string2;
    char *result;
    char  action;
    int  OK = 1; // a Boolean flag to terminate the program

        //      input data
    do
    {
    cout <<"\nCommands: Enter 1 to add,"
```

```
                << " 2 to subtract:";

          cin >> action;
          cin.ignore( 80, '\n' );// Skip rest of line.
          switch (action)
          {
                case 1:
                        get_data( first );
                        get_data( second );
                        result = sum( first, second );
                        break;

                case 2:
                        get_data( first );
                        get_data( second );
                        result = subtract( first, second );
                        break;

                default:
                        cout <<"\nInvalid command,"
                            << " try again";
                        break;
            }

     cout << "\nThe answer is: " << result;
     cout << "\nDo you want to continue?"
           << " Please enter <y> or <n>: ";
     cin >> response;
     if ((response != 'n') ||
         (response != 'N') ||
         (response != 'y') ||
         (response != 'Y') ||)
         {
              cout << "\nIncorrect response; program terminated!";
                  OK = 0;   // Turn off the flag.
    }
else if ((response = = 'n') ||
         (response = = 'N'))
      {
           cout << "\nBye!";
           OK = 0;
      }
  } while (OK);
}

void get_data (char *str)     // Reads in a string
                              // and shifts it to the right.
{
       char *low, *high;     // Pointers to the start and end
                             // of strings.
       char *temp;
```

```
            cout << "\nPlease enter a large positive integer";
            cin >> str;// read in the string
            high =  str + length( str );     // Get the address
                                             // of the end of the string.
            low = high;// Lets both pointers point to the end.
            high++;
            while (low >= str)
            {       /*  shift digits to the right */
                    *high = *low;
                    --low;
                    --high;
            }
            *high = ' ';
}

int length (char* s)   // Computes the length of a string.
{
            int index = 0;
            for (index = 0;   *s != NULL;   s++)
                 index++;
            return index;
}

void copy (char* s, char* t)
{
        while ( *t != NULL ) // Do the loop as long as there is data.
        {
            *s = *t;
            s++, t++;          // Comma operator guarantees left to right
                               // operations.
        }
        *s = NULL;             // Add the null character.
}

char *sum (char *s1, char *s2)
{
        char *index1 = s1 + length( s1 ) - 1;        // end of s1
        char *index2 = s2 + length( s2 ) - 1;        // end of s2

        char static s3[size];
        char *index3;
        int  temp, carry = 0;

        if ( (index1 - s1) >= (index2 - s2) )        // Checks for the longer value.
             copy ( s3, s1 );
        else
             copy ( s3, s2 );

index3 = s3 + length( s3 )  - 1;

while ( (index1 > s1) && (index2 > s2) )
```

```
{
     temp = *index1 - '0' + *index2 - '0';          // Converts characters to
     *index3 = (char)((temp % 10) + carry + '0');   // digits for arithmetic.
     carry = temp / 10;  // Holds the carry digit (if any).
     index1--;
     index2--;
     index3--;
}   // end while

while (index2 > s2)
{
     temp = *index2 - '0' + carry;
     carry = temp / 10;
     *index3 = (char)((temp % 10) + '0');   // Converts it back to character.
     index2--;
     index3--;
}   // end while

while (index1 > s1)
{
     temp = *index1 - '0' + carry;
     carry = temp / 10;
     *index3 = (char)((temp % 10) + '0');
     index1--;
     index3--;
}   // end while

     *index3 = (char)(carry + '0');
     return s3;
}
```

PROGRAMMING ASSIGNMENTS

1. A survey of thirty-six students at a college career program reveals the age distribution of the students shown here:

$$20 - 20 - 20 - 21 - 22 - 22 - 22 - 24 - 25 - 26 - 26 - 28$$

$$28 - 31 - 32 - 33 - 33 - 33 - 33 - 34 - 34 - 35 - 37 - 38$$

$$38 - 39 - 40 - 40 - 41 - 42 - 44 - 46 - 46 - 46 - 48 - 49$$

Write a structured program to analyze the age pattern of the students.

The output of the program consists of Table 3.1 and other information that follows:

The statistical measures of this requirement have been defined here for your information.

Mean: An ordinary arithmetic average denoted as:

$$\frac{x_1 + x_2 + x_3 + ... + x_n}{n}$$

Table 3.1   Sample Program Output

Statistical Analysis			
Class	**Class Range**	**Absolute Frequency**	**Relative Frequency**
1	20–24	—	—
2	25–29	—	—
3	30–34	—	—
4	35–39	—	—
5	40–44	—	—
6	45–49	—	—
Mean	=		
Median	=		
Range	=		
Standard deviation	=		

Median: The midpoint of a distribution. To compute the median:

Arrange all observations in order of size, from smallest to largest.

If the number n of observations is odd, the median is the center observation in the ordered list.

If the number n of observations is even, the median is the average of the two center observations in the ordered list.

Mode: The observation with the highest number of occurrences. If two observations have the same number of occurrences, the list does not have a mode.

Standard Deviation: A measure of spread around the mean. It is the most common measure. It is denoted as the square root of the variance:

$$\sqrt{\frac{(x_1 - x)^2 + (x_2 - x)^2 + \dots + (x_n - x)^2}{n - 1}}$$

2. A set is an *unordered* collection of objects of the same type. A set can be viewed like an array except that a set is not considered an ordered structure and a set's elements are unique. We describe a set by enclosing its contents in braces:

$\{1, 3, 5, 7\}$ is a set containing the first four odd numbers.

$\{\text{'z', 'x', 'c', 'v', 'b', 'n', 'm'}\}$ is a set containing the letters on the bottom row of a computer keyboard.

We define some of the common terminology associated with the sets as follows:

Set Membership: Tells whether or not an item is an element of a set. For example, 3 is a member of set $\{1, 3, 5, 7\}$.

Set Equality: Two sets are equal if they have exactly the same elements. For example, sets $\{1, 3, 5, 7\}$ and $\{1, 3, 5, 7\}$ are equal.

Set Assignment:	The assignment of one set's elements to the other.
Set Union:	The union of two sets, +, is another set that contains all the elements of both sets: $s = s_1 + s_2$. For example, if $s_1 = \{1, 3, 5, 7\}$ and $s_2 = \{9, 11, 13, 15\}$, s, the union of the two sets, will be $\{1, 3, 5, 7, 9, 11, 13, 15\}$.
Set Difference:	The difference of two sets is a set that contains all the elements of the first set that are not also the members of the second set: $s = s_1 - s_2$. For example, if $s_1 = \{1,3,5,7\}$ and $s_2 = \{3, 5, 15\}$, then s, the difference of the two sets, will be $\{1, 7\}$.

Given the following function prototypes, develop a structured program to perform set operations. Assume that the number of elements in a set is restricted to 100. The parameters for each set consists of a pointer to the set and a value parameter for the actual number of elements in the set. The maximum size of the set may be defined as global constant.

```
int   AddElement (int*, int, int);        // Returns 1 for success and 0
                                          // for failure.
int   Remove (int*, int, int);            // Returns 1 for success and 0 for
                                          // failure.
int   IsEmpty (int*, int);                // Checks whether or not the set is empty.
int   IsFull (int*, int);                 // Checks whether or not the set is
                                          // full.
void  Assign (int*, int, int*, int);      // Assigns one set to another.
int*  union (int*, int, int*, int);
int*  difference (int*, int, int*, int);
int   equal (int*, int, int*, int)        // Returns 1 or 0.
void  display (int*, int);
```

3. We want to give a deck of cards a number of perfect shuffles until the deck comes to its original order. A perfect shuffle is one in which the whole deck is split exactly in half before the cards are interleaved. When you finish each shuffling, the first card is the first card from the first half, the second card is the first card from the second half, the third is from the first half, and so on.

   Write a well-structured program to simulate card shuffling in order to count and print out the number of shufflings required to bring a deck of cards to its original state. Perform the experiment at least three times to find the average number of shufflings. Use pointers in your functions.

   a. The initial order of a deck of new cards

AC	2C	3C	4C	5C	6C	7C	8C	9C	10C	JC
	QC	KC								
AD	2D	3D	4D	5D	6D	7D	8D	9D	10D	JD
	QD	KD								
AH	2H	3H	4H	5H	6H	7H	8H	9H	10H	JH
	QH	KH								
AS	2S	3S	4S	5S	6S	7S	8S	9S	10S	JS
	QS	KS								

b. The order of the deck after the first shuffle

AC	AH	2C	2H	3C	3H	4C	4H	5C	5H	6C
	6H	7C								
7H	8C	8H	9C	9H	10C	10H	JC	JH	QC	QH
	KC	KH								
AD	AS	2D	2S	3D	3S	4D	4S	5D	5S	6D
	6S	7D								
7S	8D	8S	9D	9S	10D	10S	JD	JS	QD	QS
	KD	KS								

4   Features and Facilities

4.1   PREVIEW

In this chapter you will learn:

- The Enumerated Data Type
- The Type Definition Construct: *typedef*
- Templates
- Types of Functions
- Common Libraries
- The Preprocessor
- Command-Line Arguments

4.2   THE ENUMERATED DATA TYPE

An **enumerated data type** is a new data type composed of a finite set of values named and ordered by the programmer. It is a convenient way of defining new data types based on particular requirements. Consider the following example. Each declaration line starts with the keyword *enum* followed by a template name or tag and a set of names for the values of the type.

```
enum Days {Monday, Tuesday, Wednesday, Thursday, Friday, Saturday, Sunday};

enum Furniture {oak, teak, maple, walnut, rose, veneer, douglas};

enum College {arts, math, phys, chem, comp, biol, busin};
```

The syntax of the enumeration type is:

```
enum enumeration-type {enumeration-list};
```

To distinguish user-defined enumerated types from the C++ lowercase data types, capitalize the enumerated types. Let's write a simple program using an enumeration type.

```
enum Days {Monday, Tuesday, Wednesday, Thursday, Friday, Saturday, Sunday};

void main ()     //to calculate the weekly wage of an employee
{
      const double  pay_rate = 7.72;
      double  wage;
      short hours_worked;
      short  total = 0;
      Days day; //enumerated data type

      for (day = Monday; day <= Sunday;  day++) // seven days
      {
            cin >> hours_worked;
            if (day == Sunday)
                  hours_worked = hours_worked * 2;
            total +=  hours_worked;
      }
      wage = (double)total * pay_rate;
      cout << "\nThe wage at the end of the week is:  "
            << wage;
}
```

Each enumeration type is internally stored as a constant alias with an integer value equal to its position in the list. Monday is 0, Tuesday is 1, and so on and so forth. You may also explicitly associate an integer value with any enumerated name, as shown below. In this case, the system will assign consecutive values until it encounters your assigned value. Then a new sequence will start from the point of the assignment.

```
enum Cars {Chevrolet, Chrysler, Ford = 3, Honda, Mazda, Toyota};
```

If you write *int n = (int)Mazda,* the value of 5 will be assigned to *n.* You can also write a piece of code to see the result:

```
Cars car;
car = Mazda;
cout << (int)car;      // Displays integer 5.
```

You should notice that the values of enumerated types in C++ are not tightly bound to the user-defined data type. This attribute of the enumerated types limits their use. This means that you cannot check if a value is of a desired type.

Remember:
1. The values of an enumerated data type, like other program constants, are right values *(rvalue);* that is, they are to be used on the right side of assignment statements.
2. Enumerated data types are not compatible with any other data types.

3. The enumerated-type data constants cannot be used in input and output operations; they may only be used in assignment, conditional, and repetitive statements. Therefore, the following statements result in errors:

```
cin >> car;   // Car is an enumerated-type data.
cout << car;
```

The following short program demonstrates the use of an enumerated data type. Try to run it and see the results. The program shows how to convert an integer value into an enumerated constant by type casting. It also shows how to print out the real-life name of an enumerated type through a conditional statement, i.e., the *switch* statement.

```
enum Cars {Chevrolet, Chrysler, Ford, Honda,
          Mazda, Toyota};
#include <iostream.h>

void main ()
{
      const double rebate = 0.01;
      int code;
      Cars car;
      cout << "\nEnter a code from <0 .. 5>: ";
      cin >> code;
      car = (Cars)code;      // Type conversion using cast.

      switch (car)
      {
         case Chevrolet:
            cout << "\nChevrolet, ";
         case Chrysler:
            cout << "Chrysler and ";
         case Ford:
            cout << "Ford have ";
            cout << "\n a rebate of "
                    << (rebate * 100)
                    << "% of the car price this week";
                       break;
         case Honda:
            cout << "\nHonda, ";
         case Mazda:
            cout << "Mazda and ";
         case Toyota:
            cout  << "\nToyota have no rebates"
                    << " this month!  ";
                    << "We have another discount"
                    << " instead!";
            break;
            default:
                    break;
      }
}
```

As a last note on this subject, since standard C++ does not support the Boolean values *true* and *false* directly at this time, the enumerated type is an ideal way to define Boolean types, as shown here:

```
enum  Boolean {false, true};
void main ()
{
     Boolean  flag = true;
     ...
     ...
     while (flag) // similar to (flag == true)
     {
          ...
          ...
     }
}
```

Self-Check Questions 1

1. What advantages are there in the use of enumerated-type data?
2. How is an enumerated-type data defined?
3. Which operators can be used with enumerated-type data?
4. Can enumerated-type data be used as

   a control variable in a loop statement?

   a selector in a switch statement, such as the following?

```
switch ( car)
{
   case Toyota:  ;
        ...
        ...
        ...
}
```

4.3   *TYPEDEF* OF C++

C++ has a special facility called *typedef* that defines new names or synonyms for the previously defined data types. For example, you can make synonyms for the *int, char,* and pointer to character data types as shown here. You may capitalize the new names to distinguish them from the C++ lowercase data types:

```
typedef int   Integer;
typedef char  Character;
typedef char* Pointer;
```

Then you may use the new types in the program as:

```
Integer number;
Character ch;
Pointer p;
```

The syntax of the *typedef* is:

```
typedef <data type> <new name> [size];
```

The optional part of the syntax, with the ([]), is used with array declarations. Consider the following example, which includes a short skeleton program to demonstrate usage. The *typedef* works well with other structured data types, too.

```
const int size = 80, rows = 5, columns = 5;
typedef char String[size];
typedef int Matrix[rows][columns];
...
...
void main ()
{
        String Address; // Address is a character array of size 80.
        Matrix matrix;  // Matrix is a two-dimensional array of [5][5].
        ...
        ...
}
```

You may also define a *typedef* declaration for *enumerated* types as follows:

```
typedef enum Boolean {false, true} BOOLEAN;
```

The *typedef* creates aliases of data types known to the compiler. They do not create new data types.

> **Note:** Since *typedef* declarations belong to the compiler, they are terminated with a semicolon (;).

The *typedef* definition may be used as a facility for clear documentation of programs. For many, using integer, character, or float is more convenient and readable than their C++ built-in type names. The same is also true with structured data types. (We will discuss them in the next chapter.) Another major use of the *typedef* is for solving code portability issues when you use the basic data types such as *integer, short,* and *long* of the language; basic data types are machine dependent. Therefore, you may write a *typedef* for a computer with a particular word size, such as 16 bits, and make your program portable to another machine with 32-bit words by just changing the *typedef* declaration. For example, on a 16-bit machine, you may use:

```
typedef short int Integer; // Identical to int for 16-bit integers.
```

On a 32-bit machine, however, the above *typedef* should be modified as:

```
typedef int Integer;       // Short and int are now different.
```

Self-Check Questions 2

1. Given the following *typedef* declaration, write a function that accepts the length and width of a rectangle and computes its area and perimeter for the calling function.

```
typedef unsigned int Cardinal;
```

2. Given the following *typedef* names, write two examples to show how they are used as type specifiers within the program.

```
typedef    char*    string;
typedef    string   DaysOfWeek;
```

4.4   TEMPLATES

You may remember from Chapter 3 our discussion about functions using *void* pointers for generic data types. Some people may find this feature a little awkward. Fortunately, Borland's version 3.1 and up of C++ offers a new facility called *template* to develop the same functions in terms of generic data types. It is a very simple and productive approach for handling applications with generic data types. By using *template,* there is no need for writing duplicate functions with different data types. For example, to be able to do a comparison on integers, floats, characters, arrays, and other structured data types, you need to write five functions, all of them doing the same task but using different data types. Templates are also used quite often in developing generic classes in data abstraction and object-oriented programming. The syntax of function templates is shown below. When there are several templates in an application, they should be placed in a header file so they can be used in different programs.

```
template <class user-defined type identifier>
```

The following example includes a function, using *template,* to perform comparison operations on different data types. Please note that the compiler will generate the appropriate code for each version of the template function.

```
#include <iostream.h>
template <class ItemType>
int  compare (ItemType x, ItemType  y);

void main ()
{
    int m = 5, n = 10;
    char ch1 = 'z', ch2 = 'Z';
    float p1 = 3.14, p2 = 3.1415;
    char *p = "John Browne", *q = "John Brown";

    cout << compare (m, n);          // Displays -1.

    cout << compare (ch1, ch2);      // Displays  1.

    cout << compare (p1, p2);        // Displays -1.

    cout << compare (p, q);          // Displays  1.

    cout << compare (*p, *q);        // Displays 0 for comparing the
                                     // first letters only.
}
template <class ItemType>
int compare (ItemType x,  ItemType  y)
```

```
{
    if (x == y)
         return 0;
    else if (x > y)
         return 1;
    else
         return -1;
}
```

Templates can support multiple types, too. Consider the following example, which includes two different types, *int* and *float.*

```
template <class type1, type2>
type1 add (type1 x, type2 y)
{
    return (type1)(x + y);
}
```

Exercise

Write a function *display* that accepts an array of generic type with its size as parameter and displays the contents of the array.

Self-Check Questions 3

1. What is the purpose of C++ templates?
2. Suggest a couple of algorithms that become very useful when combined with templates.

4.5   TYPES OF FUNCTIONS IN C++

We have already discussed C++ references and templates as major features of C++. Another substantial improvement of C++ over other traditional languages is its versatility in developing different types of functions tailored to different program requirements. C++ offers four types of functions:

1. Inline functions
2. Overloaded functions
3. Functions with default parameters or arguments
4. Functions with variable declaration placement

Let's take a look at each type.

Inline Functions

When a function is called, the following process happens:

* The address of the next instruction, in the calling function, is saved to be used after the function's termination;
* Memory for the value parameters and local variables of the function is allocated;

- Parameters of the calling function are passed to the called function; and
- Upon termination of the function, memory of the value parameters and local variables are de-allocated; the returning value is passed to the calling function; and the address of the next instruction, which was saved before function call, is retrieved to resume the suspended instructions.

Therefore, a function call involves investment of extra time and space, also known as **overhead.** This overhead is especially severe when the size of the function code is relatively small and the number of function calls is high. C++ has eliminated this problem by introducing the **inline function,** which does not involve any function call. Instead, it moves the code into the calling function, thus increasing the execution speed of the program.

A C++ inline function is like a normal function with the following exceptions:

- The function header starts with the *inline* qualifier.
- They do not require prototype; they must be fully defined.
- Inline functions do not accept repetitive statements. However, they don't mind recursion.
- Inline functions should be small; otherwise, they may cause run-time problems due to the code substitution requirement.

Consider the following inline function.

```
inline int sum (int m, int n)
{
        return m + n;
}
```

Whenever this function is called, it is literally replaced with the statements of the function. An inline function has type checking, block definition, and local variables. You may create a header file containing useful inline functions, which are often used in object-oriented programming when the function code is not large.

Overloaded Functions

Function overloading allows the programmer to create a family of functions with an identical name but different data types to perform a particular operation. Overloaded functions are used as a tool in object-oriented programming. Below is an example using the overloaded function *power* to compute *m* raised to the power of *n* where *m* and *n* can be of any type.

```
// prototypes
int     power(int, int);
double power(double, double);
double power(double, int);
double power(int, double);
#include <math.h>      // for library function pow as a helper
#include <iostream. h>

void main ()
{
        int a = 12; // base
        int b = 3; // exponent
```

```
        cout << power( a, b );

        double  c = 5.6;
        int d = 5;
        cout << power( c, d );
        ...
        ...
}

//  definition of functions
int  power (int base, int expo)
{
        int p = 1; // holds the answer
        while ( expo )
        {
                p *= base;
                -- expo;
        }
        return p;
}

double power (double base, double  expo)
{
        return pow (base, expo);   // Uses math.h library.
}

double power (int base, double  expo)
{
        return pow (double(base), expo);
}

double power (double base, int expo)
{
        double p = 1.0;
        while (expo)
        {
                p *= base;
                -- expo;
        }
        return p;
}
```

Note: The type and order of the function's parameters causes the system to choose the proper function.

Use an overloaded function when you want to perform a general purpose operation on a set of data that may have different types every time you use them. It eliminates the need for different storage names for functions that perform the same operation(s) but on different data types. To write functions for computing a power in other languages, you have to write different names for different data types. For instance, you might write *IntInt-Power, DblDblPower, IntDblPower,* and *DblIntPower* names for the functions. It seems very awkward and inconvenient. (Also, an overloaded function performs a table called *polymorphism* in object-oriented programming. It is an important attribute of this paradigm which we will cover in Chapter 6.) Note that the data type of at least one parameter of each copy of the overloaded function must be different.

During the linking phase, the C++ compiler has to generate a unique name for each function to be used. This name normally consists of the function name preceded by an underscore. When a function is overloaded—that is, several functions with identical names are created—the compiler still has to generate a unique name for each function; otherwise, you will encounter address resolution problems during the linkage process. The compiler does this through a process called **name mangling,** based on an encoding scheme that includes the function name, the scope of the function, and its argument types.

Functions with Default Arguments

In C++, you can specify default parameter values in a function. This feature provides you with the ability to write flexible functions in which you can omit one or more of the arguments or replace them completely. Let us look at the following examples.

Program 4.1

```
void display (int = 1, float = 2.5, char = 'm');
void main()
{
        display();                // Display all parameters.
        display(1, 3.4);          // Display 1 3.4 m.
        display(2, 3.8, 't');     // Display 2 3.8 t.
}

void display (int one, float two, char three)
{
        cout << one;
        cout << two;
        cout << three;
}
```

Program 4.2

```
void announce (char* message =
            "This is a message." );
            void main ()
            {
                char* message1 = "This is a testing.";
                char* message2 = "The test is over.";

                announce();
                announce(message1);
                announce(message2);
            }

            void announce (char* message)
```

```
        {
            cout << message;
        }
```

Program 4.3

```
int process (int, char = '*', int = 5);
void main ()
{
    int x = 5;
    char ch = '#';
    process( x );
    process( x, ch );
}



int process(int m, char c, int n)
{
    return ((c == '*') ? (m - n) : (m + n));
}
```

> **Note:** The parameter list of a function with default parameter values may contain both **ordinary** and **default parameters.** Ordinary parameters must be at the beginning of the parameter list, starting from the leftmost, followed by default parameters on the right side of the parameter list. In other words, there should be no ordinary parameters after defaults in the list. Also, default values can be provided either in the function prototype or function header, but not in both.

Functions with Variable Declaration Placement

There are situations in which the number of parameters of a function is not known until run time. Therefore, there should be a mechanism to handle these cases. This is not a new demand in programming, although the approach of C++ and ANSI standard C in solving the problem is new. In the past, before the ANSI standard was developed, the C language did not even have parameter checking. It could accept functions with a variable number of parameters as long as the function code could handle them. This is no longer possible because of the requirement for function prototyping in both ANSI C and C++. As a consequence, both languages tackle the issue of a variable number of parameters through a number of facilities that are in the header file called *stdarg.h*.

To write a function with a variable number of parameters, use an **ellipsis** in the parameter list. An ellipsis is three successive periods (...) with no spaces and must be on the rightmost of the parameter list. Let us look at an example:

```
void my_func(int n, char ch, ...);
```

The above declaration indicates that the function will be defined in such a way that it has at least two known arguments: an *int* and a *char,* but it can also have any number of additional arguments. In other words, the ellipsis can be interpreted as *et cetera* (etc.). One of the known parameters of the function normally acts as a flag or an indicator as to how many items follow. You can omit the comma before the ellipsis.

When using variable parameter functions, include the *stdarg.h* header file. It contains the necessary facilities as shown here.

va_list:	Creates a list, and assigns a name to it.
va_start()	Initializes arguments and fetches the first one.
va_arg:	Extracts the next argument.
va_end()	Closes the list.

The following example demonstrates the use of functions with a variable number of parameters as well as the application of the *stdarg.h* header file. The function is a simple one that extracts a number of integer values and displays them on the screen. The number of the integer values can be different from run to run. The function terminates either if a value of zero is extracted or when the *for* statement has completed its cycle.

```
#include <iostream.h>
#include <stdarg.h>          // Contains the necessary macros.
void display(int ...);       // function prototype

void main ()
{
   display(3,2,5,8);         // A call with four parameters in
}                            // which the first one (3)
                             // indicates the number of
                             // variables to follow.

void display (int n...)      // A known integer followed by an unknown
{                            // number of values.
   va_list args;             // Open the list of variables and
                             // from now on call it args.
   va_start( args, n );      // Fetches the first value.

   for (int index = 0; index < n;  index++)
   {
        int temp = va_arg(args, int); // extract
                                      // each parameter
        if (temp != 0)
             cout << temp << '\n';
        else  break;
   }
   va_end( args );           // Call the closing macros.
}
```

Self-Check Questions 4

1. When is it desirable to declare a function as *inline?*
2. What is meant by an *overloaded function?*
3. Suggest another alternative to function overloading.
4. Describe the rules that must be observed when

   writing a *default-parameter* function.

   calling a *default-parameter* function.

5. Write a function using variable declaration placement to be used for computing the area of a square, a rectangle, and a trapezoid. Use the following formulas and the function prototype:

$$Area_{(square)} = side * side$$
$$Area_{(rectangle)} = length * width$$
$$Area_{(trapezoid)} = (side\ 1 + side\ 2) * height\ /\ 2$$

int AreaOf(char flag ...); // function prototype

Flag characters of *s, r, t* for square, rectangle, and trapezoid, respectively, will indicate the type of operation required.

4.6   COMMON LIBRARIES

C++ has access to a rich library of entities such as utility functions, constants, and macros (discussed later in Chapter 6) for performing essential services such as I/O operations as well as efficient implementation of specialized and frequently used operations. All library entities are grouped and found in C++ header files and header files defined by ANSI C. There are more than fifty header files, most of which are beyond the scope of this text, following is a description of those header files that are the most commonly used. The complete list of these files, along with their specific considerations, can be found in the documentation of the C++ compilers.

<assert.h>	*<bios.h>*	*<ctype.h>*
<errno.h>	*<float.h>*	*<fstreram.h>*
<iostream.h>	*<limits.h>*	*<locale.h>*
<math.h>	*<mem.h>*	*<memory.h>*
<search.h>	*<setjump.h>*	*<signal.h>*
<stdarg.h>	*<stddef.h>*	*<stdio.h>*
<stdlib.h>	*<string.h>*	*<time.h>*

Now we will describe the commonly used header files and see how they are used in a program.

Header File	**Purpose**
<assert.h>	To diagnose logic errors in the program.

Example:

```
#include <assert/h>
#include <iostream.h>

void main()
{
   int first = 2,
       next = 3;

   assert (first == next);
}
```

In the above code, the assert tests the condition. Since it does not evaluate to true, it calls abort with the following message:

```
assertion failed: first == next, file xxx.cpp, line 9 (including blank lines)
```

The next example tests whether the required memory has been allocated.

```
char* ptr = new char[1024]; // 1 k of memory
assert(ptr ! = 0); // memory allocated?
```

Header File	Purpose
<conio.h>	Declares various functions used in calling the operating-system console I/O routines. The functions of this header file cannot be used in Graphical User Interfaces (GUI) applications.

Example:

```
#include <conio.h>
void main()
{
    char ch;
    clrscr (); // clear screen
    .

    .

    .
    ch = getch (); // Read a character.
    .

    .

    .

}
```

The routines in Table 4.1 reside in this file header. The list is by no means complete. Look up other routines in the Library reference of your compiler.

Table 4.1   The <conio.h> Header File

Function Name	Purpose
clreol()	Clears all characters from the cursor position to end of line in text window.
clrscr()	Clears the current text window and places the cursor in the upper lefthand corner at position (1,1).
cprintf() as in:	Writes formatted output to the screen; behaves like *printf ()* of the *stdio.h* header file (see Appendix A).
cputs(string);	Writes a string to the screen.
cscanf()	Scans and formats the input from the console; behaves like *scanf()* of the *stdio.h* header file (see Appendix A).
delline()	Deletes line in text window; moves all lines below it one line up.
getch()	Gets character from keyboard; does not echo to screen.
getche()	Gets character from keyboard; echoes to screen.
getpass	Reads a password from the console (should not be used in Win32s and Win32 GUI applications).
gettext(l,r,t,b, dest)	Stores the contents of an onscreen text rectangle defined by *left, top, right, bottom*, into the memory area pointed to by destination.

Table 4.1   (continued)

Function Name	Purpose
gotoxy(column, row)	Positions cursor in text window; e.g., *gotoxy (30,20)*.
insline()	Inserts a blank line in the text window.
kbhit()	Checks for currently available keystrokes.
lowvideo()	Selects low-intensity characters.
movetext(left, top, right, bottom destleft, destright)	Copies text onscreen from one rectangle to another.
normvideo()	Selects normal-intensity characters.
outp(port, integer))	Outputs a byte to a hardware port.
outpw(port, unsigned)	Outputs a word to a hardware port.
textattr()	Sets text attributes (foreground and background colors) in a single call (not usable with Win32s and Win32 GUI).
textmode(integer)	Puts screen in text mode.
textbackground(integer)	Sets new text background color (not usable with Win32s and Win32 GUI).
ungetch(character)	Pushes a character back to the keyboard buffer.
window(l,t,r,b)	Defines active text window.
wherex()	Gives horizontal cursor position within window.

Header File	Purpose
<ctype.h>	To test, classify, and modify characters.

The following *ctype.h* functions return a zero or nonzero value, depending on the result of the tests. The functions in Table 4.2 use the character *c* as an example.

Example:

```
char ch;
ch = 'a';
if (isalpha(ch))
    cout << "It is a letter";
ch = toupper(ch);
```

Table 4.2   The <ctype.h> Header File

Function Name	Purpose
isalpha(c)	Tests if *c* is an alphabetic character.
isalnum(c)	Tests if *c* is an alphanumeric character (a-z, A-Z, 0-9).
islower(c)	Tests if *c* is a lowercase letter
isupper(c)	Tests if *c* is an uppercase letter.
isdigit(c)	Tests if *c* is a decimal digit 0–9.
isprint(c)	Tests if *c* is a printable character, including space.
ispunct(c)	Tests if *c* is a space, endln, tab, etc.
iscntrl(c)	Tests if *c* is a control character (such as FF, HT, NL).
isxdigit(c)	Tests if *c* is a hexadecimal digit (a–f, A–F, 0–9).
isspace(c)	Tests if *c* is a white-space character (CR, FF, HT, NL, VT, SPACE).

Header File	Purpose
<float.h>	To determine the properties of floating-type representation.

There are many constants in this library. Some of the most commonly used constants are listed in Table 4.3.

Table 4.3 The <float.h> Header File

Constant	Representative Value
FLT_MAX	3.4E+38
FLT_MIN	−3.4E-38
DBL_MAX	1.7E308
DBL_MIN	−1.7E-308
LDBL_MAX	1.1E+4932
LDBL_MIN	−3.4E-4932

Exercise

Complete and run the following program to display the value associated with each constant of the header file float.h on your computer.

```
#include <iostream.h>
#include <iomanip.h>
#include <float.h>

void main()
{
    // Make room for up to 80 digits to be printed and
    // set precision of the fraction part to digits.
    cout << setw(80) << set precision(20); // <iomanip.h>

    //Display in normal form from left side of the screen.
    cout.setf(ios::floatfield | ios::showpoint | ios::left);
    cout << FLT_MAX; //maximum floating point number
}
```

Header File	Purpose
<limits.h>	To determine the properties of integer-type representation.

Some of the constants of this library are listed in Table 4.4. The table values are system dependent.

Modify your program written for floating-point numbers to display the representable values of integer type.

Header File	Purpose
<math.h>	To perform common mathematical operations on values of type *double*.

Some of this file's functions are listed in Table 4.5.

Table 4.4   The <limits.h> Header File

Constant	Representative Value
INT_MIN	–32768
INT_MAX	+32767
LONG_MIN	–2147483648
LONG_MAX	+2147483647
SCHAR_MIN	–128
SCHAR_MAX	+127

Table 4.5   The <math.h> Header File

Function Name	Purpose
fabs(double)	Returns absolute value.
ceil(double n)	Returns an integer greater than or equal to *n*.
floor(double n)	Returns an integer less than or equal to *n*.
exp(double)	Returns e^{real}.
log(double)	Returns logarithm (base e).
log10(double)	Returns logarithm (base 10).
pow(double, double)	*pow(m, n)* returns m^n.
sqrt(double)	Returns square root.
sin(double)	Returns the *sin* of an angle, which must be in radians.
cos(double)	Returns the *cosine* of an angle, which must be in radians.

Consider the following program, the purpose of which is to show the use of functions *log, exp,* and *pow* of the header file math.h. Expand it with more functions of the library entity.

```
#include <iostream.h>
#include <math.h>

void main()
{
   int m = 10;
   double n = 2.5;

   double temp = log(m); // logarithm of m in base e

   //Compute m to the n power using exp and log functions.
   cout << exp( n * temp);
   cout << '\t';
   cout << pow(m, n); // produces the same result
}
```

The output of the program is: 316.227266   316.227266

Header File	Purpose
<stdarg.h>	To provide facilities to handle functions with an arbitrary number of arguments.

Table 4.6 shows some of the common facilities of this library. (See Chapter 6 for an explanation of macros.)

Header File	Purpose
<stdlib.h>	Contains generic utilities, including functions, macros, and types to be used in programs.

Table 4.7 lists some of the functions in this file.

Consider the following program that validates the digits of a long integer in string format. Try to expand it with more functions from the header file stdlib.h.

```
#include <iostream.h>
#include <stdlib.h>

//function prototype
//Validates a number represented by a string of digits.
//Returns: -1 for invalid numbers; the number itself
//in numeric format otherwise.
long int validate( char []);
void main()

{
```

Table 4.6   The <stdarg.h> Header File

Macro	Purpose
va_list argp	Declares a variable as a pointer to the beginning of the unnamed additional arguments.
va_start(argp, x)	Extracts the first argument.
var_arg(argp, y)	Extracts the next argument.
va_end(argp)	Cleans up the *va_list* object; necessary if you have executed *va_start*.

Table 4.7   The <stdlib.h> Header File

Function Name	Purpose
abs(int)	Returns the absolute value of an integer.
atoi(string)	Converts a numeric string to a value of *type integer*.
atol(string)	Converts a numeric string to a value of *type long integer*.
atof(string)	Converts a numeric string to a value of type *double*.
exit(integer)	Closes all files and terminates the program; if *status* is zero or *EXIT_SUCCESS*, the program reports successful termination; if the status is *EXIT_FAILURE*, the program reports unsuccessful termination.
free(ptr)	De-allocates the data object whose address is *ptr*.
malloc(size)	Allocates memory of desired size for a desired data object and returns its address; for example, *char *p = (char*)*malloc(81 * sizeof(char));.
rand()	Generates a pseudo-random number.

```
      char *value = "123o345";// A number with an invalid digit
      cout << validate(value);
}

//function validate
long int validate( char number[])
{
    int index = 0;

    do
    if (number[index] < '0' || number[index > '9')
       return -1; // invalid digit encountered
    else
       index++;
    while( number[index] ! = NULL);

    return atol(number);
}
```

Header File   **Purpose**

<string.h>   To manipulate strings and other arrays of characters.

Table 4.8 lists the functions in this file.

Table 4.8   The <string.h> Header File

Function Name	Purpose
memcmp(s1, s2, n)	Compares successive elements of two arrays of unsigned *char*, beginning at the addresses s1 and s2 (both of size *n*), until elements that are not equal are found. If s1 equals s2, returns zero; if s1 is less than s2, returns a negative number; otherwise, returns a positive number.
memcpy(s1, s2, n)	Copies an array of type *char* beginning at the address s2 to another array of *char* beginning at the address s1 (both of size *n*) and return s1.
memmove(s1, s2, n)	Similar to *memcpy* function; however, if the arrays overlap, accesses each of the elements values from s2 before storing to avoid ending with a corrupted copy.
memset(s, c, n)	Stores unsigned *char c* in each of the elements of the array of unsigned char beginning at *s*, with size *n* and return *s*.
strcat(s1, s2)	Concatenates the strings.
strchr(s, ch)	Searches for the first element of the string *s* that equals *ch*; if successful, returns its address; otherwise, returns a null pointer.
strcmp(s1, s2)	Compares two strings; if both are identical, returns zero; if s1 is less than s2, returns a negative number; otherwise, returns a positive number.
strcpy(s1, s2)	Copies s2 into s1.
strncmp(s1, s2)	Compares *n* characters from s2 with s1.
strncpy(s1, s2)	Copies *n* characters from s2 into s1.
strrchr(s, ch)	Finds the last position of *ch* in the string; if not found, returns NULL.
strspan(s1, s2)	Searches for the first element in the string s1 that equals none of the string s2 and returns its subscript.
strcspan(s1, s2)	Returns the number of consecutive characters in s1 that do not occur in s2.
strlen(s)	Returns the length of *s*.

> **Note:**   Functions whose names start with "str," such as *strcat,* operate on C++ strings, and those whose names start with "mem," such as *memcpy,* operate on character arrays.

Consider the following program that validates a positive integer value. Assume that a positive integer value contains up to five valid digits and should not be more than the 32767.

```cpp
#include <iostream.h>
#include <stdlib.h>
#include <string.h>

//function prototype
//Validates a number represented by a string of digits.
//Returns: 0 for invalid numbers;
//number itself otherwise.
int validate(char number[]);

const char *MAXINT = "32767"; // assumption
const int size = 8, // maximum size of an entry
          ValidSize = 5; // maximum size of a good integer

void main()
{
   char value[size]; // string representing integers
   int ok = 1; // a flag for true and false results

   cout << "\nEnter a positive integer < 0 to 32767>:";
   cin >> value;

   if ( strlen(value) > ValidSize ) // invalid integer
      ok = 0;
   else  if(strlen(value) == 5) // may or may not be valid
         if(strcmp( MAXINT, value ) < 0 ) // Invalid case
            ok = 0;
         else // check individual digits
            ok = validate(value); // right size; what about digits
         else
            ok = validate(value);
         if (ok) // If everything is ok
      cout << atoi (value); // Convert it to numeric integer.
   else
      cout <<"\nAn invalid number ("
         << value <<") was entered!\n";
}

// Validate the number and return the result.
int validate(char number[])
{
   int index = 0;
   do
      if (number[index] < '0' || number[index] > '9')
```

```
          return 0; // invalid digit encountered
     else
          index++;
  while ( number[index] ! = NULL);

return atoi(number); // Convert and return the valid number.
}
```

As mentioned earlier, functions whose names start with "mem" such as "memcpy" are used to process character arrays, not strings. Character arrays, unlike strings, do not terminate with the *null* character. For example,

```
const int length = 4;

char first[] = {'a', 'b', 'c', 'd', 'e', 'f', 'g', 'h', 'i', 'j'};
char next [4];

memcpy( next, first, length); // Copies four characters from first
                              // to next.

for ( int index = 0; index < length; ++index)
   cout << next[index]; // displays: abcd
```

Note that character arrays cannot be printed out directly. You should use a repetitive statement to print it out character by character.

Header File	Purpose
<time.h>	To use the machine clock and date facilities. The functions share two static duration data structures, a time string of *type array of char* and a time structure of type *struct tm*.

Table 4.9 lists some of the functions of this file header.

Table 4.9   The <time.h> Header File

Function Name	Purpose
*asctime(*t)*	Converts date and time to ASCII; the pointer *t* in the function is of type *struct tm*.
*ctime(*t)*	Converts date and time to string; it is equivalent to *asctime(local time(t))*.
clock()	Determines processor time.
clk_TCK	Number of clock ticks per second.
difftime(time1, time2)	Computes the elapsed time in seconds of type *double* from time1 to time2. Both times are of type *struct time_t*.
*localtime(*ptr)*	Converts date and time to a structure and assigns it to a pointer of type *struct time_t* (see the *struct* data type in the next chapter).
NULL	Yields a null pointer constant that can be used as an address constant expression.
*time(*ptr)*	Gets time of day and assigns to a pointer of type *struct time_t*.

The following examples show some of the common applications of the functions of the *time.h* header file.

```
#include <iostream.h>
#include <time.h>
void display(time_t *);     // Displays date and time.
void main ()
{
    time_t  ThisTime = time(NULL);
    display(&ThisTime);
}

void display (time_t*  t)
{
    cout << "It is now " << ctime(t);  //  current time
}
```

The function displays something like: **It is now Fri October 25 11:42:20 1998**
The next function causes a delay of *n* seconds.

```
void pause (unsigned int n)
{
    long int start, end, timer;
    start = time( &timer );         // Get the start time.
    end = start + n;                // Set the end time.
                                    // Wait for n seconds.
    while (time( &timer ) < end);   // Repeats n seconds.
}
```

The following code segment measures the amount of time (in seconds) used by a function.

```
clock_t   start, end; // clock_t is a type
                      // Defined in time.h.
start = clock();      // Get the start time.
foo();                // function call
end = clock();        // Get the end time.
                      // Compute the time elapsed.
double elapsed_time = (((double)end - (double)start) /
                            CLK_TCK) / 100;
```

4.7   THE PREPROCESSOR

Many useful features of C++ are handled through a filter program called the **pre-processor.** Originally designed for the C language using multipass compilation, this software was designed to define constants and macros, include library files, and perform conditional compilation for the host program.

In modern implementations such as Borland C++, the functionality of the preprocessor is built into the compiler. Borland C++ performs the entire preprocessing and compiling operation in an integrated environment. The compiler pulls in the include files,

Table 4.10   C++ Directives

Directive	Use
#include	Include library files.
#define	Define a macro or a constant.
#undef	Undefine a macro.
#if	Denotes a test of a compile time condition.
#ifdef	Denotes if defined; tests if some status is defined.
#ifndef	Denotes if not defined; tests if a status is not defined.
#else	Denotes an alternative if test fails.
#elif	Combination of #else and #if.
#endif	End of conditional compilation statements.
#line	Give a line number to the object code at a desired point of the program.
#program	The # and ## preprocessor operators.

performs tests for the conditional compilations, expands macros, and produces an intermediate file for further compilation. As a holdover from C, Borland C ++ uses the same terminology, but it does not use the old process.

The traditional actions of the preprocessor are still determined by directives placed in the source file. Each directive is identified by the pound sign (#) in front of it. We have used *include* directives in all of our source files. The list of C++ directives and uses are shown in Table 4.10.

The C++ directives are used to perform the following:

- Definition of Constants
- Definition of Macros
- Conditional Compilation
- File Inclusion
- Special Operations

Let's take a look at each operation.

Definition of Constants

C++ allows you to define symbolic constants to enhance a program's readability using the following general form:

```
#define name replacement
```

Note these special considerations for the use of this operation:

- There should be at least one space between each entity.
- Directives do not need a semicolon(;). Traditionally, directives have not been treated as matters for the compiler, but rather for the preprocessor.
- A directive can appear anywhere in the program, and what it establishes will be effective for the remainder of the source file.

- The replacement for the symbolic names can be a string constant. For example:

```
#define message "Hello world!"
```

- The replacement may also be an expression such as:

```
#define CelsiusConv     5.0 / 9.0
```

The preprocessor will substitute the expression for its defined name in the source code without evaluating it.

```
int  Fahrenheit = 65;
Celsius =  CelsiusConv * (Fahrenheit  - 32);
```

with

```
Celsius  =  5.0 / 9.0 * (65 - 32);
```

Look at the following definitions. Some of the definitions create an appearance similar to that of Pascal or Modula-2. For example, the combination of the definitions for *if* and *then* allows you to remove parentheses from *if* statements and to use *then* with it.

```
#define max          100
#define is           ==
#define isnot        !=
#define integer      int
#define real         float
#define if           if(
#define then         )
#define begin        {
#define end          }
#define and          &&
#define or           ||
#define beep         "\007\007\007\007\007"
#define page         '\f'
#define line         '\n'
#define title        "Langara College"
#define procedure    void
```

We defined the word *then* as a left parenthesis for its replacement. You can also define it without any replacements at all. This means that the use of the word *then* in the program does not have any meaning for the preprocessor. Consider the following example, in which the replacement for the word *then* is blank.

```
#define then
```

Using this definition, you can write statements such as what is shown without any penalty for the word *then*.

```
if ( x > y ) then
sum = x + y;
```

Definition of Macros

A **macro definition** is similar to a constant definition except that the replacement for the symbolic name is one or more statements. They are used to make the programs more readable, compact, and fast. Inline functions, which you have already encountered, are similar to macros. In fact, they act the same way except that inline functions allow for more powerful structure and checking of data types. Inline functions are used quite often in data abstraction and object-oriented programming. However, since macros do not require type checks, they provide flexibility for situations in which the types of data may change from one call to another.

Consider the examples carefully. The considerations for constants also apply to the macro definitions. Furthermore, you should note that:

- Use of parentheses around the macro entities ensure proper evaluation. For example:

```
#define sqr(x) ((x) * (x))
```

- The preprocessor simply substitutes the expressions textually in the source code without evaluating them. For example:

```
int number = 10;
int next = sqr( number ); // will be replaced by next = 10 * 10
```

- A macro's formal parameter is local to the macro. It does not create conflicts with similar identifiers of the program. For example, given the following definition,

```
#define INC(x) (x++)
```

the program may use an identifier called *x* or anything else as shown.

```
int x = 5, y = 10;
INC(x);
INC(y);
```

Examine the following definitions carefully to understand how they work.

```
#define min(x,y)    ((x) < (y) ? (x) : (y)) // Use conditional operators.
#define even(x)     ((x)&1 ? 0 : 1)
#define odd(x)      ((x)&1 ? 1 : 0)
#define forever     while(1)
#define swap(type, x, y)
            { type temp = (x);(x) = (y); (y) = temp); }
#define until(x)    while (!x)
#define area(r)     (3.14 * r * r)
#define ConeVolume(area, height) (1/3 * area * height)
```

If the definition of the macro spans several lines, type the continuation line character (\) at the end of all but the last line. Look at the example:

```
#define swap(type, x, y) { \
                    type temp = (x); \
                    (x) = (y); \
                    (y) = (temp); \
                }
```

You may also use library functions in your macro definitions to improve a program's readability by hiding the functions and using more understandable terms in the source code. Examine the following definition:

```
#include <string.h>
#define length(s)  (strlen(s1))
```

There is no doubt that macros are useful and sometimes powerful in programming. However, be careful not to cause undesired results as a consequence of incorrect parentheses. Consider the following macro:

```
#define sqr(x) (x * x) // wrong parentheses
```

Say you call the above macro in the following statement:

```
int m = 5, n = 3;
int s = sqr(m + n);
```

We would expect the answer to be 64, but because the expression is expanded to 5 + 3 * 5 + 3, we get an answer of 23. By using parentheses around not only the macro, but also all of its elements, we can guarantee that

```
#define sqr(x)    (x) * (x)
int s = sqr(5+3);
```

expands to

```
int s = (5+3) * (5+3);
```

giving us the correct result of 64.

A statement such as $s = sqr(m++)$; will cause an erroneous answer. Why?

Finally, note that since a macro performs string substitutions if a macro call happens many times, the code substitution will occur many times, too. As a consequence, the size of the program may be increased accordingly. Therefore, limit the size of the macros to very few lines; otherwise, replace them by functions.

Built-in Macro Names

C++ has six predefined macro names:

__LINE__	Provides the line number of the current line of the source file being processed.
__FILE__	Provides the name of the current source file being processed.
__DATE__	Provides the date the processor began to process the current source file.
__TIME__	Provides the time the processor began to process the current source file.
__STDC__	An implementation-defined macro to provide ANSI compatibility. If it is defined, the compiler will accept only standard C/C++ code and nothing else.
__cplusplus	Another implementation-defined macro to specify the scope of operations of a compiler. If defined, the compiler is in C++ mode. Otherwise, it allows you to write a module that will be compiled sometimes as C and other times as C++. Through conditional compilation, you can control which C and C++ parts are included.

Now consider the following example to understand this type of macros better.

```
#include <iostream.h>
void main()
{
```

```
    cout << "\nThis program is saved under"
         << __FILE__
         << '.';

    cout <<"\nIt was compiled at"
         <<__TIME__
         << " on " << __DATE__ << '.';

    // Check if your compiler is in C++ mode.

    #ifdef __cplusplus
    cout << "\nThe compiler is in C++ mode.";
    #endif
}
```

Conditional Compilation

It is quite customary for software developers to write programs that can run on more than one type of platform or be used by a number of different users. Obviously, the easiest way to accomplish this is to develop different versions of the software. However, creating two versions is not an effective use of time and resources. Fortunately, C++ allows you to combine the code for all the versions into a single program file. It allows you to stop portions of the code from being compiled so as to customize the program for a particular specification. This process is called **conditional compilation.**

Conditional compilation is accomplished by using special preprocessor directives, including *#if, #else, #elif, #endif, #ifdef,* and *#ifndef:*

#if condition

   Compile these statements

#else

   Compile these statements

#endif

The simple example here shows how to use a single piece of software on two different C++ compilers by using conditional compilation. The code initializes a pointer to the EGA/VGA video of the system. (You do not need to know all the details about the hardware at this stage.)

```
#ifdef BORLANDC
     egabase = (char far*)(MK_FP(0xA000.0000);
#endif

#ifdef MICROSOFT
     egabase = (char far*)0xA0000000;
#endif
```

The programmer simply can write a definition such as:

```
#define BORLANDC
...
void main ()
```

```
{
      char far *egabase;
      ...
      ...
      #ifdef BORLANDC
            egabase = (char far*) MK_FP(0xA000.0000);
      #endif

      #ifdef MICROSOFT
            egabase = (char far*) 0xA0000000;
      #endif
      ...
      ...
}
```

and the preprocessor will compile only the code that is relevant for the Borland compiler.

The following example shows how you can declare a variable differently, depending on the size of the file to be used by the program.

```
#include <iostream.h>
#include <limits.h>
const int IntSize = INT_MAX;//maximum allowable integer

      #define FileSize      100000

      #if    FileSize <= IntSize
                  int    Employees;
      #else
                  long int Employees;
      #endif

      void main()
      {

                        .
                        .
                        .

          cout << sizeof(Employees)
                << " bytes" ;
                        .
                        .
                        .

}
```

The next example shows how to use conditional compilation to isolate a code region for the purpose of testing or debugging.

```
#define TEST
#include<iostream.h>

void main ()
{
      int sum = 0;
      for (int index = 1; index < 5; index++)
```

```
      {
            sum += index;
            #ifdef TEST
                  cout << i << sum;
            #endif
      }

      cout << "The grand total is: " << sum;
}
```

Furthermore, conditional compilation is also used to debug by isolating the desired regions of the source code for close scrutiny. For example:

```
#define DEBUG
    . . .
    . . .
#if defined   DEBUG
      debugging statements
#endif
```

File Inclusion

The file inclusion facility of the preprocessor allows you to create external files composed of related functions, constants, and macros to be included with different source files. Including files like this prevents unnecessary repetitions. It also facilitates program maintenance by allowing you to quickly correct and/or improve multiple projects by changing only the entities that need modification. The files containing the entities are called header files with their names traditionally ending with the suffix *.h*. To include a file, use the directive *#include <filename>* or *#include "filename"* for user-defined modules. As a result, the preprocessor replaces the line containing the directive *#include* with the contents of the header file. The best example of file inclusion is *#include <iostream.h>* for I/O operations. You may include any of the more than fifty header files provided by your compiler with this directive, and you may build your own library or toolbox for inclusion as well.

Remember that C++ does not allow multiple inclusions of the same file. This problem happens in projects that consist of different files, where a specific file header (for instance, *<iostream.h>*) has to be used in several file units. Fortunately, all header files have a built-in protection against multiple inclusions. For instance, if you examine one of the header files (e.g., *iostream.h*), you will see three lines of conditional compilation directives along with the source code, as shown here:

```
#ifndef IOSTREAM_H
#define IOSTREAM_H
```

body of the source code

```
#endif
```

Let us analyze the effect of the noted directives and see how they protect the project against multi-inclusion problems. When you include the *iostream.h* file for the first time, its entire code, including the conditional compilation directive, will be added to your source file. Next time, if you attempt to include the same file, it will not be included since the fist line of the file, *#ifndef IOSTREAMH,* evaluates to false due to the existing copy of *iostream.h.* The rest of the file is skipped and not included. All header files have the same built-in protection against multiple directives inclusion. Follow this approach when you build your own header files.

Special Operations

Other features of the preprocessor are:

*   #line directive
*   #pragma
*   The # and ## operators

The #line directive supplies line numbers to a program for cross-reference and error checking. For example, you may specify a line number to a section of the program as shown:

```
#include <iostream.h>

#line 100
void main()
{
    cout << "\nThe number of this line is:"
         << __LINE__; // displays 103
}
```

The #pragma permits implementation-specific directives of the form:

```
#pragma directive-name
```

It allows you to give specific instructions, with predefined meanings, to the compiler. If the compiler does not recognize the pragma's directive name, it simply ignores it without any problems. Note that each compiler has its own pragma directives. Consider the following example based on Borland C++ pragmas startup and exit using the syntax:

```
#pragma startup function-name <priority>
#pragma exit function-name <priority>
```

The pragma startup tells the compiler that a designated function should be called upon program startup (before the *main* function is called). In contrast, the pragma exit instructs the compiler that a designated function should be called upon program exit (just before the program terminates). Also, note that:

*   The function must be previously declared taking no arguments and returning *void.*
*   The optional priority parameters should be an integer in the range (64 to 255). The highest priority is 0. Functions with higher priority are called first at startup and last at exit. An unspecified priority defaults to 100.

```
#include <iostream.h>

// function prototypes
void salutation();
void goodbye();

#pragma exit goodbye // calls goodbye function upon program exit
```

```
#pragma startup salutation 64 // 64 is the highest parameter.
                              // It means a high priority call.
// Note: Although the program has not called functions
// salutation and goodbye, they are executed in that order
// through pragma directives.

void main()
{
 cout << "\nThis program uses the pragma directives."
}

void salutation()
{
    cout << "\nWelcome aboard."
         << "I teach you how to use the pragma directives.";
};

void goodbye()
{
    cout << "\nI hope you now understand the concept of the"
         << "pragmas of C++. For more information,"
         << "consult the programmer's guide of your C++"
         << "compiler. Bye!";
}
```

C++ supports two preprocessor operators # and ##. The # operator causes the argument it precedes to become a quoted string. For example,

```
#define text(s) #s
       . . .
       . . .
cout << text(This is a cool feature!);
```

The ## operator causes concatenation of two tokens. For example,

```
#define together(first, next) first ## next
       . . .
       . . .
void main()
{
    int MarysAge = 45;
    cout << together(Marys, Age); // similar to cout << MarysAge
}
```

> **Note:**   Both # and ## operators are used in conjunction with the #define directive.

4.8   COMMAND-LINE ARGUMENTS

The C language, the predecessor of C++, was originally designed for systems programming and was used for writing the UNIX operating system. Under UNIX, every command is a program and every program is a command. This means that when you type the name of a file containing a compiled program, it is executed. Moreover, a program name, like a command, can be followed by arguments called **command-line arguments** to specify a desired operation. With this operating system, when you want to delete a file or format a disk, you type the commands

```
C:>  del  xyz.c
C:>  format a:
```

The commands *del* and *format* are program names and *xyz.c* and *a:* are command-line arguments. By using command-line arguments, you can develop utility programs based on assumed data rather than actual data for different applications. For example, you may write a program to simulate a simple calculator called *calc.cpp* to perform basic arithmetic, as shown:

```
calc 123 + 456
```

The command *calc,* as the name for the calculator's source file, is a command that is given three arguments: an operand, an operator, and another operand.

To write a program using command-line arguments, you must use two arguments in the main of the program, as shown below:

```
void main (int argc, char *argv[])// *argv[] or **argv
{
      // Body of program goes here.
}
```

The arguments *argc* and *argv* are two traditional names commonly used as command-line arguments. The argument *argc* is an **argument counter;** it keeps track of the number of command-line arguments, including the program name. The argument *argv,* **argument vector,** is an array of pointers to strings, each of which representing a command-line argument, including the name of the program at the beginning. Consider the given example to demonstrate the use of command-line arguments with a simple function that computes m^n, e.g., 4^5. We will call the program (source file) *power.cpp.* Note that command-line arguments are stored in string format.

```
#include <stdlib.h>
#include <iostream.h>
void main (int argc, char *argv[])
{
    int base, exponent;
    long int result = 1L;   // Long int is more suitable.
    base = atoi(argv[1]);   // Convert the string to integer.
    exponent = atoi(argv[2]);

       for (int index = 0; index < exponent; i++)
           result = result * base;
       cout << result
}
```

We can now compile the program and use it whenever we need it, as shown:

```
C:>
    power   5   4
```

When the program is executed, the value passed for the argument *argc* is 3, and the argument *argv* contains three strings:

```
argv[0] == "power"
argv[1] == "5 "
argv[2] == "4 "
```

Note that all of the command-line arguments, including single digits are stored in string format, which means that they are an array of characters that end with the *null* character.

> **Note:**   When you click on an icon or select "Run" in the compilation environment, you invoke a program from the command line.

Exercise

What does the following program do?

```
void main (int argc, char *argv[])
{
    int index = 1;

    for ( ; index <argc; ++index)
    {
     cout << argv[index];
     (index < argc - 1) ? cout  << ' ' : cout << '\n';
    }
}
```

Self-Check Questions 5

1. Why are the preprocessor directives not terminated with a semicolon(;)?
2. How does a macro work?
3. Describe the grammatical structure of a macro.
4. C++ offers its own alternatives to using C macros and constant definitions. What are they? Briefly describe their significance.
5. Write a program using command-line arguments to convert miles to kilometers. Assume that 1 mile is equal to 1.68 kilometers.
6. Explain what is achieved by using conditional compilation.

SUMMARY

- The enumerated data types of C++ allow you to deal with program elements in practical human-oriented ways rather than in rigid computer-oriented methods.
- The *typedef* construct is used to assign new names to data types and to define new types. It is used to enhance readability and as better documentation.

- C++ templates are used to define generic functions and classes. In the case of functions, a template function can replace several overloaded functions.
- Types of functions in C++ are:

  Inline functions for short and frequently used functions. They are mainly used in object-oriented programming. They can reduce a program's overhead by eliminating function calls that are to be executed frequently.

  An overloaded function, used as one that has the same name as one or more functions but has a parameter list with different data types. Overloaded functions are used to perform a general-purpose operation on a set of data that have different types from time to time during the execution.

  Functions with default parameters or arguments, which enable you to specify default values for function parameters.

  Functions with variable declaration placement, which allow you to write functions with an arbitrary number of arguments. The header file *stdarg.h* containing several macros has to be included to handle these functions.

- C++ has access to a library of more than fifty header files containing very useful functions, constants, and macros. They are used in both systems programming and application development.
- The preprocessor of C++ is a piece of software in charge of dealing with the operations specified by the program's directives. The directives are used primarily for constant definition, macro definition, conditional compilation, and file inclusion. The preprocessor of modern single-pass compilers is an integrated part of the compiler.
- Command-line arguments are powerful features of C++ that allow you to develop programs to be called with arguments at the command line.
- C++ supports six predefined macro names.
- C++ programs are inplementation-specific directives to issue special instructions to the compiler.

STYLE TIPS

- When you use function templates, use two separate lines for the function heading to increase readability, as shown here:

```
template <class AnyType>
void swap (AnyType x,  AnyType y)
{
    AnyType temp;
    temp = x;
    x = y;
    y = temp;
}
```

- The default values of the parameter list of default parameter functions can be either in the function prototype or in its definition, but not both. Specify the default values with the prototypes. If you do otherwise, be consistent throughout the application.
- With respect to the preprocessor:

If you intend to use one or two functions of a header file, write them yourself; don't import them.

Beware of macro pitfalls. They have to be properly parenthesized; otherwise, you'll see incorrect results. If type checking is a consideration, use an inline function instead.

When you develop your own header file, be sure to enclose the entire code in appropriate conditional compilation directives to guard against the multiple inclusion error.

Documentation of the preprocessor directives plays an important role, particularly when you are dealing with conditional compilation under different system specifications.

SAMPLE PROGRAMS

1. Using a function with a variable number of parameters, write a program to calculate the areas of circles, rectangles, and squares. The function will include a flag of type enumerated *shapes* to indicate the desired shape. For example, the flag *Circle* will indicate a circle, *Rectangle* will signal a rectangle, and *Square* will specify a square.

```
// Purpose:            To compute the area of a circle, or a
//                     rectangle, or a square.
// File name:          shapes.cpp
// Author:             Arthur Unknown
// Date:               10 August, 1998

#include <iostream.h>
#include <stdarg.h>
#include <ctype.h>

enum shapes { Circle, Square, Rectangle };

//
// Interface for function DisplayArea
// GIVEN:      An enumerated flag representing a circle, or a
//             rectangle, or a square.
// RETURN:     The area of the desired shape using the header
//             file macros.
// *****************************************************
void display_area(shapes, ...);

void main ()
{
        int Radius, SideOne, SideTwo;
        shapes chosen_shape;
        char Response;

        // Display prompt and get input.
        cout << "\nThis program calculates the areas of "
            << "circles, squares, and rectangles" << endl;
        cout << "\nEnter 'C', 'S', or 'R' for each shape: ";
        cin  >> Response;
```

```
                    // Ensure that response is in uppercase letters.
                    if (islower(Response))
                        Response = toupper(Response);
                    switch (Response)
                    {
                        case 'C':
                                cout << "\nEnter Radius: ";
                                cin >> Radius;
                                chosen_shape = Circle;
                                display_area(chosen_shape,Radius);
                                break;

                        case 'R':
                                cout << "\nEnter two sides: ";
                                cin >> SideOne >> SideTwo;
                                chosen_shape = Rectangle;
                                display_area(chosen_shape,
                                        SideOne, SideTwo);
                                break;

                        case 'S':
                                cout << "\nEnter side: ";
                                cin  >> SideOne;
                                chosen_shape = Square;
                                display_area(chosen_shape,
                                        SideOne);
                                break;
                    }
                }

        void display_area(shapes designator, ...)
        {
            const float pi = 3.14;
            int first, next, area;

            va_list   args;                 // Open macros.
            va_start(args,  designator);    // Extract first variable.

            switch (designator)
            {
              case Circle:
                    // Extract first variable.
                        first = va_arg(args, int);
                        area = (float)(first * first) * pi;
                        break;

                case Rectangle:

                    // Extract first and second variables.
                        first = va_arg(args, int);
                        next = va_arg(args, int);
```

```
                        area = first * next;
                        break;

                // Extract one variable.
                case Square:
                        first = va_arg(args, int);
                        area = first * first;
                        break;
        }
        cout << area;
        va_end(args);                          // Close macros.
}
```

2. Using command-line arguments, write a program to compute and display the roots of a quadratic equation in the form of $ax^2 + bx + c = 0$. It should return the number of roots calculated: 2 in the normal case, 1 in the linear case ($a = 0$), and 0 in the complex case ($b^2 - 4ac < 0$). Use single digits for the coefficients

   For example, if a user enters *calcroot 2x – 3,* the program displays:

```
One root as follows:
root = 1.5
```

   If the user enters *calcroot x^2 – 2x – 3,* the program displays:

```
2 roots as follows:
first root = -1
second root = 3
```

   If the user enters *calcroot $2x^2$ + 2x + 4,* the program displays:

```
No real roots!
```

   Note that the discriminant of the equation $(d = b^2 – 4ac)$ determines the status of the equation. That is, if $d > 0$, there are two real roots, if $d = 0$, there is only one root, and if $d < 0$, there are no real roots.

```
//  Purpose:     To compute and display the roots of
//               a quadratic equation.
//
//  File name:   quad.cpp
//  Author:      Arthur unknown
//  Date:        10 August, 1988


#include <iostream.h>
#include <stdlib.h>
#include <math.h>

enum Boolean{ false, true};

//*************************************************
//   Interface for function main                  *
//                                                 *
//   GIVEN:   A quadratic equation in the form of  *
```

```
//              ax2 + bx + c or ax2 + bx or ax2 + c    *
//   RETURN:   None.  Displays the roots (if any) in *
//             notation.                               *
//****************************************************
void main(int argc,  char*    argv[])
{
   int a, b, c;  // coefficients: aX^2 + bX + C
   int d;  // discriminant of the equation

   int first, second, // roots of the equations
       sign;  // sign of coefficients

   Boolean   complex, SingleRoot, quadratic;

   complex = SingleRoot = quadratic = false;  // initial values
   if (argc < 4 || argc > 6) // check the format
     {
       cout << "\nError in data entry. Bye Bye!";
       exit(1);
     }

   if ( argc == 4 )  // ax^2 + bx or ax^2 + c or bx + c
   {
      // check if the equation is quadratic
      for ( int i = 0; argv[1][i] != '\0'; ++i)
          if ( i > 0 && argv[1][i] == '2' )
            {
              quadratic = true;  // flag it
              break;
            }
       }

      if (quadratic)  // if quadratic equation
       {
           // determine the sign of the first coefficient
           sign = argv[1][0] == '-';
           if (sign) // if the sign is negative
             {
           if ( argv[1][1] <= '9' && argv[1][1] > '0' )
                 a =  -( argv[1][1] - '0' );  // get the first coefficient
                else
                  a = -1;
             }
          else // positive first coefficient
              if ( argv[1][0] <= '9' && argv[1][0] > '0' )
                  a =   argv[1][0] - '0';
                else a = 1;

           // check if the equation is in the form of ax^2 + bX
           if( argv[3][1] == 'x' || argv[3][0] == 'x' )
             {
                 if ( argv[3][0] <= '9' && argv[3][0] > '0' )
```

```
                    b = argv[3][0]  - '0';  // get the second coefficient
                else
                    b = 1;

                first = 0;
                sign = argv[2][0] == '-';  // check the sign
                if ( sign )  // if negative sign
                    second = b / a;
                else
                    second = -b / a;
            }
            else  // is in the form of aX^2 + c
            {
                c = atoi( argv[3] );  // convert to integer: uses stdlib.h
                sign = argv[2][0] == '-';
                if (sign)  // if negative sign
                    c = -c;
                if ( c / a  > 0 )    // no real root
                    complex = true;    // flag it
                else
                {
                    first = sqrt( -c/a );
                    second - -first;
                }
            }
        }
    }
    else // the equation is not a true equation.
        // it is in form of  bX + C with a single root
    {
            sign = argv[1][0] == '-'; // check the sign
            if ( sign )  // if negative
                if ( argv[1][1] <= '9' && argv[1][1] > '0' )
                    b = -(argv[1][1] - '0');  // get the first coefficient
                else
                    b = -1;
            else if ( argv[1][0] <= '9' && argv[1][0] > '0' )
                    b = argv[1][0] - '0';  // get the first coefficient
                else
                    b = 1;

            c = atoi( argv[3] );
            first = c / b;
            SingleRoot = true; // flag it
    }
}
else // it is a true quadratic equation
{
    sign = (argv[1][0] == '-');  // determine if the sign of
        if (sign)                // the first coefficient is negative
        {
            if ( argv[1][1] <= '9' && argv[1][1] > '0' )
```

```
            a =  -( argv[1][1] - '0' );   // get the first coefficient
        else
            a = -1;
     }
    else // non-negative coefficient
        if ( argv[1][0] <= '9' && argv[1][0] > '0' )
            a =   argv[1][0] - '0';
        else a = 1;

    if ( argv[3][0] <= '9' && argv[3][0] > '0' )
        b = argv[3][0] - '0';   // get the first coefficient
    else
        b = 1;
    sign = argv[2][0] == '-';
    if (sign)  // if negative sign
        b = -b;
     c = atoi( argv[5] );
     sign = argv[4][0] == '-';
     if (sign)  // if negative
        c = -c;

    d = b * b - 4 * a * c; // compute discriminant
    if ( d < 0 ) // no real roots
        complex = true;   // flag it
    else
    {
        first  = ( -b + sqrt( d )) / ( 2 * a);
        second = ( -b - sqrt( d )) / ( 2 * a);
    }
}

if (complex)
   cout << "\nNo real roots!";
else if ( SingleRoot)
        cout << "\nOne root only: " << first  << endl;
    else
    {
       cout <<"\nThere are two roots as follows:";
       cout <<"\nfirst root = " << first;
       cout <<"\nsecond root = "  << second;
    }
}
```

PROGRAMMING ASSIGNMENTS

1. The time zones in the continental United States, from east to west, are as follows:

Zones:	Eastern (EDT)	Central (CDT)	Mountain (MDT)	Pacific (PDT)
Example:	04:00	03:00	02:00	01:00

Using command-line arguments, write a program that finds a time based on one of the above zones and then determines its equivalent in Pacific time.

The input to the program consists of the time of the day, in military format, and the desired designator of the time zone from which the time is to be converted, such as 1435 EDT. This input requests the equivalent in Pacific time of 2:35 p.m. Eastern time.

The output of the program is similar to the format of the input. However, if the time is invalid, the output is an appropriate message. For example, if the program's name is *pacific.cpp* and you type

```
PACIFIC 1435 EDT
```

the program will display:

```
1135 PDT.
```

If you type

```
PACIFIC 1435 PDT
```

the program will display:

```
The time is already in PDT!
```

If you type

```
PACIFIC 1435 NOT
```

the program will display:

```
Invalid Time Zone Entered. Bye!
```

2. Using command-line arguments, write a program to convert an alphanumeric phone number to its equivalent numeric format. For example, if the name of the program is *phone.cpp* and you enter *phone ski-snow,* it will display 754–7669. If you type *phone 22-print,* it will display 227 – 7468. Each digit is assigned three letters:

Digit	Letter	Digit	Letter	Digit	Letter
2	ABC	3	DEF	4	GHI
5	JKL	6	MNO	7	PRS
8	TUV	9	WXY		

Use as many features from Chapter 4 as you can.

5   Structures, Classes, Unions, and Files

5.1   PREVIEW

In this chapter you will learn:

- Structures
- Classes
- Unions
- Files

5.2   STRUCTURES

The C++ language has been designed so that it can effectively communicate a real-world model to the computer through the data abstraction process. **Data abstraction** is one of the major fundamental concepts in software development and software engineering. The support of C++ for data abstraction is available through a rich set of built-in or intrinsic data types as well as special constructs, including *array, structure, union, class,* and *enumeration* as shown in Figure 5.1.

Note that there is a declaration qualifier in C++ called *unsigned* that may be used with *char, int, short,* and *long* data types. We use this qualifier both in low-level operations and calculations where you do not need to be concerned about representing negative values. For example,

```
unsigned long     seconds;
unsigned          total, index; // shorthand notation: unsigned integer
unsigned char     byte;
unsigned short    years;
```

Figure 5.1   Structures

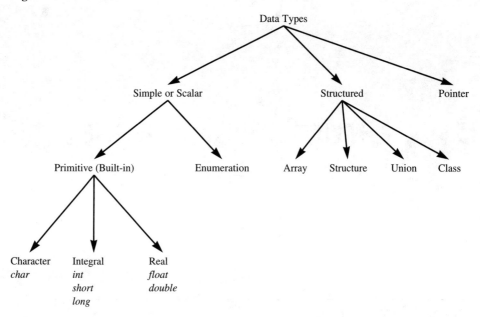

We have so far covered the family of simple or scalar data types as well as the enumeration and array types. We defined an array as a structured type, the elements of which are all of the same type. While arrays satisfy a particular spectrum of data objects, there is a wide range of real-world models where their abstractions may need a variety of different types of elements. The following examples (Figure 5.2–5.5) show these models of data.

A bank record may look like this:

Figure 5.2   Bank Record

Name	Address	Phone	Account	Sex	Balance	Type
Mary Lou	100 W. 49th Ave	323–5362	12345	F	123.75	Saving

A student record may look like this:

Figure 5.3   Student Record

Name	Address	Phone	ID	Sex	GPA	Major
Arthur	100 W. 49th Ave	323–5362	12345	M	3.21	Arts

A desk record may look like this:

Figure 5.4   Desk Record

Name	Measures	Model	Manufacturer	Price	Date Purchased	Purchase No.
Classroom desk	8 x 4 x 6	M1Q2345	Acme	234.55	10/9/96	123

A date record may look like this (with identical data types):

Figure 5.5   Date Record

Day   Month   Year

10	9	1995

C++'s **structure,** abbreviated as *struct,* is a vehicle for defining such abstract objects that may contain a group of data of different or identical types. A structure is an aggregate data type that contains a collection of related data items whose types can differ but which is referenced under one common name.

Declaration of a Structure

To declare a struct, you must create a template describing a structure and its related elements. The form of a structure template is shown below. The keyword *struct* names and identifies a structure. The optional *tag* word (hence the brackets) provides a way to refer to the structure later in the program. The declaration also describes individual items or members of the structure. Once again, notice that the *tag* name is optional and can be omitted when there is only a single reference to the structure at the end of the template.

```
struct [tag]
{
        type      member1;
        type      member2;
        type      member2;
             . . .
             . . .
        type      memberN;
}[structure variable(s)];
```

As shown in Table 5.1, the first example or method declares a structure, *PersonType,* to be used as a new type for the entire source file. The second method defines the same structure, *PersonType,* and two variables, *person* and *people,* immediately at the end of it. The last method uses *typedef* facility of C++ and is a more formal way of declaration.

> **Note:**   Do not assume that the fields within a structure are stored contiguously. They are often padded for alignment reasons, so such an assumption may lead to portability problems.

Accessing Structure Fields

As said earlier, in an array all elements are of the same type and the same size. As a consequence, an offset value or an index is used to reference the *i-th* element of the arrays. In contrast to an array, the type and size of members of a structure may or may not be identical. Although this attribute relaxes the type restriction and allows you to use different types, it does not permit you to use an index any more. Instead, you would use another access method called *dot* or *period* notation with C++'s *member* operator (.). The *dot* notation is comparable to using the apostrophe in English to denote possessive form, such as *John's book* or *the man's car.* We use *dot* instead of apostrophe to show the relationship. For example, if the

Table 5.1 Declaring a Structure

Method 1	Method 2	Method 3
``struct PersonType
{
char name[32];
char sex;
unsigned age;
unsigned weight;
};```	```struct PersonType
{
char name[32];
char sex;
unsigned age;
unsigned weight;
} person, people[100];```	```typedef struct
{
char name[32];
char sex;
unsigned age;
unsigned weight;
} PersonType;```
A new template, *PersonType*, will be used in the program: PersonType Person;	A new template, *PersonType*, will be used in the program with *person* and *people* as structure variables.	Using *typedef*, identifier *PersonType* specifies the new type.

variable *person* is of type *PersonType,* as shown in the table, the following statements show how to access members of the variable *person*.

```
cout << person.name << '\t'
     << person.sex  << '\t'
     << person.age  << '\t'
     << person.weight;
```

Table 5.2 shows how to use different methods of declaration in your programs. While the first and third methods are common in programming, the second one is used to create global variables for the entire source file. Using *typedef,* especially in a large project, is very helpful for changing structure members. This means that if you create a single header file of *typedef*s for the whole application, you will be able to update a *typedef* in one place and propagate it across the software without a need for locating the places that need changing.

Table 5.2 Accessing Structure Fields

Method 1	Method 2	Method 3
``struct PersonType
{
    char name[32];
    char sex;
    unsigned age;
    unsigned weight;
};

void main ()
{
    PersonType person;``` | ```struct PersonType
{
    char name[32];
    char sex;
    unsigned age;
    unsigned weight;
} person, people[100];

void main ()
{
    person.age = 20;``` | ```typedef struct PersonType
{
    char name[32];
    char sex;
    unsigned age;
    unsigned weight;
};

void main ()
{
    PersonType person;``` |

Table 5.2   (continued)

Method 1	Method 2	Method 3
`person.age = 20;`	`people[5].age = 40;`	`person.age = 20;`
—	—	—
—	—	—
`}`	`}`	`}`
Identifier *Person* is a structure variable of type *PersonType*.	*Person* and *people* are global structure variables of type *PersonType*.	Identifier *PersonType* is a new type and *person* is a structure variable of type *PersonType*.

The next example shows that members of a structure, *struct,* may themselves be structured (Figures 5.6 and 5.7). Similarly, structures may be elements of arrays or other structures. This means that you can construct embedded structures, and as a result, the dot notations to access desired members will be sequenced:

```
typedef struct
{
      int day, month, year;
}DateType;


typedef  struct
{
      char Name[32];
      char Address [64];
      . . .
      . . .
      DateType DateHired;
} PersonType;
```

Figure 5.6   A Structured Structure (1)

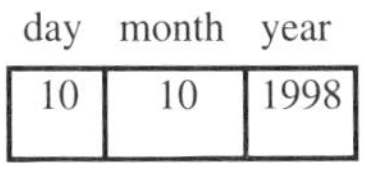

Figure 5.7   A Structured Structure (2)

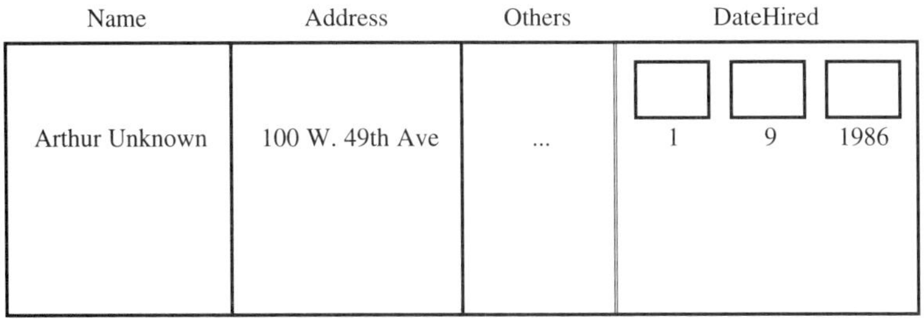

The structure *PersonType* includes another structure called *date*. To access the members of this structure, use sequenced dot notations:

```
PersonType person;      // variable declaration of type PersonType
person.DateHired.day = 1;
person.DateHired.month = 5;
person.DateHired.year = 1978;
```

An Array of Structures

As we said, structures may be elements of an array. Consider the following example to create 1000 instances of the *Personnel* structure.

```
PersonType person[1000];
```

To access a particular member of the elements of the array, use the following:

```
cout  << "\nEnter the age";
cin   >> person[index].age;  // Index has a value between 0 to 999 inclusive.
```

Structure Member Initialization

A structure may be initialized during the declaration of the structure variable if it is of the internal *static* or external *extern* storage class. For example:

```
static PersonType person =
{
        "Cyrus Kashani",
        'M'
        18
        124
};
```

Each individual member of a structure may also be initialized:

```
strcpy( person.name, "Cyrus" );
person.sex = 'M';
person.age = 19;
person.weight = 124;
```

Pointers to Structures

A pointer may be established to a structure in a similar way to other data objects. For example, in the following declaration, the variable *ptr* points to a structure of type *PersonType*.

```
PersonType *ptr;        // pointer to structure
PersonType person;      // a variable of type structure
strcpy( person.name, "Cyrus" );
person.sex = 'M';
person.age = 17;
person.weight = 124;
ptr = &person;          // Assigns the address of the variable person
                        // to the pointer variable ptr.
```

Table 5.3 Accessing Notation

Normal Accessing Notation	Shorthand Accessing Notation
(*ptr).name	ptr->name
(*ptr).sex	ptr->sex
(*ptr).age	ptr->age
(*ptr).weight	ptr->weight

After the last statement *(ptr = &person;),* the *ptr* variable points to the variable person. Thus you may access the structure members as:

```
(*ptr).name
(*ptr).sex
(*ptr).age
(*ptr).weight
```

Please note that the parentheses around the pointer variable are required because the selection operator (.) has a higher precedence than the indirection operator (*). If you did not use the parentheses, it would be as if you wrote **(ptr.name)* instead of *(*ptr).name,* making *ptr.name* the name of the structure.

In C++ there is a shorthand notation for accessing structure members through pointers. Examine the notation in Table 5.3.

Shorthand notation is more convenient. It uses the "->" operator composed of two keyboard characters, the hyphen (-) and the angle bracket symbol (>). This operator (->) has the same precedence as the selection operator (.).

Pointers to structures are normally used for passing parameters between functions efficiently and for returning this type of data objects by the functions. Therefore, the shorthand notations are a more convenient and equally effective way for accessing structure members. Let us now write a short program using functions with a pointer to structure.

```
* Interface for function GetData                    *
* Purpose: To read in the structure elements.       *
* Given:    A pointer to the structure              *
* Return:   None.                                   *

void GetData(PersonType*);

void main ()
{
    const int TableSize = 1000,
              NameLength = 32;
              PersonType   personnel[TableSize];  // with 1000 cells
    int count;
    int command = 1;      // controls data entry

    count = 0;// Keeps track of the number of active cells.
    while (command == 1)
    {
        GetData( &personnel[count] ); // Passes member's address count++;
        cout << "\nIs there any more? If yes enter 1;
            << " otherwise, 0 and press Enter key:  ";
```

```
        cin  >> command;
    }
}


//  function GetData to read in the structure's elements
void  GetData(PersonType*  ptr)    // Uses pointer.
{
    cout << "\nEnter name: ";
    cin.get( ptr ->name, NameLength );
    cout << "\nEnter sex: ";
    cin  >> ptr ->sex;

    cout << "\nEnter age: ";
    cin  >> ptr ->age;
    cout << "\nEnter weight: ";
    cin  >> ptr ->weight;
}
```

Notice that a call by pointer requires the address operator (&) before the variable name:

```
GetData( &Personnel[count] );
```

If you had another variable, such as *person,* of type structure *PersonType,* you would use:

```
GetData( &person );
```

Remember that structure names, unlike array names, are not pointer types. As a consequence, we passed the structure variable *person* <u>by pointer</u> to function *GetData* in order to achieve efficiency in the above program. We could also pass it to the function by value, which is the default mechanism in C++. The latter approach involves overhead in terms of time and space and affects the efficiency of your code. C++ allows you to use references for passing structures to functions. This is simpler and more convenient. For example, the prototype of function *GetData* will be:

```
void GetData ( PersonType& employee);
```

It will be called as:

```
GetData(Person)
```

Assignment of Structures

All the members of one *struct* variable can be collectively assigned to another *struct* variable as long as both variables are of the same type.

Exercise

Write two functions for the above program for the following requirements. Try to use both *pass-by-pointer* and *pass-by-reference* methods for function parameters.

1. To display the information about the entire personnel.
2. To modify the age of the *i-th* member in the table, such as to change the age of the third person from 25 to 35. Note that if the *i-th* member does not exist in the table, the function should return 0 to indicate failure; otherwise, it should return 1.

Bitfields

C++ structures may also be used to implement bitfields. A **bitfield** is a collection of bits (one or more) that provide compact storage for items that have a limited range of possible values. A bitfield member is declared just as any other but with the following considerations:

- A bitfield cannot span an integer boundary. This means that the bitfield type must be *int* or *unsigned int*.
- A bitfield does not have an address of its own; that is, you cannot use the & operator to get the address of a bitfield. Furthermore, a bitfield cannot be referenced by a pointer.
- Bitfields are machine dependent.
- Bitfields are accessed similar to ordinary structure members.

You may declare a bitfield using the following template. Note that each field has a name and an associated width specifying the number of bits in that field.

```
struct tag
{
     unsigned field1 : width1;     // bits
     unsigned field2 : width2;     // bits
          ...
          ...
     unsigned fieldN : widthN;     // bits
};
```

Bitfield implementation is not common in C++ programming. However, it is a neat feature that allows you to economize on memory by better utilizing the machine's hardware in your application. A structure may contain both bitfields and regular members. Bitfields do not affect regular members. Finally, note that bitfields might affect portability.

Consider the following example, in which a bitfield structure is created to represent a date. We selected 5 bits to represent days of a month $(2^5 - 1 = 31)$, 4 bits to represent months of the year, and 7 bits to represent the year in a two-digit format.

```
typedef struct
{
    unsigned int day : 5;    // 5 bits to represent 32 - 1 = 31 days
    unsigned int month : 4;  // 4 bits to represent 12 months
    unsigned int year : 7;   // 7 bits to represent up to  99 years
} DateType;
```

Now our program can reference a date such as 8/25/98 as:

```
DateType date;
date.month = 8;
date.day   = 25;
date.year  = 98;             // two digits only
cout << date.day   <<'\'
     << date.month << '\'
     << date.year  << "\n";
```

Notice we used a bitfield structure to represent date because the fields of a date, *month, day, and year,* lend themselves to a specific format that are suitable for the bitfields. It is a neat feature because each field has an associated meaning, and it saves memory too.

Self-Check Questions 1

1. What is the major difference between an array and a structure?
2. Describe the grammatical form of a structure.
3. How is a *struct* used in the program?
4. How can an individual structure element be accessed?
5. Can an entire *struct* be assigned to another structure?
6. Can an entire structure be read into the computer with a single input statement?
7. Is the structure name a pointer to the start of the structure?
8. How are structures passed to functions? (Hint: There is more than one way.)
9. Declare a structure, *weather,* to represent weather conditions, including temperature and pressure.

Functions as Structure Members

C++ allows you to bundle your variables and their associated functions together as structure members. For example, the following declaration demonstrates a structure that contains data and functions as members:

```
struct PartType
{
    long int PartNo;
    char name[32];
    double price;
    double GetPrice ()
    {
        return price;
    }
    void DisplayInfo ()  // an inline function
    {
        cout << '\n' << PartNo << '\t' << name;
    }
}part;  // a global variable for structure PartType
```

Note that when a function is relatively small, such as five or six lines, you may define the function either within the *struct* itself as an inline function or outside of it. We defined function *GetPrice* and *DisplayInfo* as inline outside the *struct*. To define a function outside of the *struct,* you have to identify the function by preceding its name with the *struct* name and the **address resolution operator (::),** or double colons. The *address resolution* operator tells the compiler to which *struct* the function belongs. Address resolution is one of the critical issues of compilation and the compiler must know precisely the association between functions and classes. Let us rewrite the previous example defining its two functions outside of the structure.

```
struct PartType
{
    long int PartNo;
```

```
    char name[32];
    double price;
    double GetPrice ();
    void DisplayInfo ();
};

// Function GetPrice uses the scope resolution operator (::)
// to indicate its affiliation with structure PartType.
inline double PartType::GetPrice ()
{
    return price;
}

inline void Part::DisplayInfo ()
{
    cout << '\n' << PartNo << '\t'
         << name << '\t' << GetPrice();
}
```

Now we can use one of the above structures in a short program. Notice that both data members and function members are accessed via the member or *dot* operator.

```
#include <iostream.h>
...
void main ()
{
    PartType  AutoPart;
    AutoPart.PartNo = 1237654L;
    AutoPart.price = 23.65;
    strcpy( AutoPart.name, "Vanity Mirror" );
    AutoPart.DisplayInfo();
}
```

As mentioned earlier, C++ also allows you to initialize the structure variables together using braces. The values within the braces will be assigned to their related variables according to their type and declaration order.

```
PartType   AutoPart = {1237654L, "Vanity Mirror", 23.65};
AutoPart.DisplayInfo();
```

Examine the following example:

```
struct NoticeType
{
    char TheMessage[128];
    void display () { cout << TheMessage; }
};

void main ()
{
    NoticeType   Note = { "May you always be an object treated
                           with respect!" };
    Note.display();
}
```

The ability to use data and functions together under the umbrella of a structure is the cornerstone of the data abstraction concept. Due to the critical role of data abstraction in software development, Chapter 6 is devoted to this concept.

Another point that is worth stating is that by default—unless otherwise specified—all the members of a *struct* (data and functions) are considered **public domain.** This means that both data members and function members are accessible to all functions within the user's source file (client program), as you saw in the above examples. In other words, we cannot hide our members from the rest of the program, and as such we cannot impose any restrictions on accessing certain structure members if the application requires. (Since **data hiding** plays an important role in data abstraction, C++ offers a new construct called *class* as a vehicle for data abstraction and object-oriented programming. We will discuss the C++ *class* in the next section of this chapter.)

Exercise

Given the following structure declaration, write the necessary definition for the function *convert* that converts a numeric date notation to its equivalent alphanumeric format and displays the result. Then write a short program to test your work. For example, if today's date is 8/24/98, the function will display its alphanumeric format as August 24, 1998. Hint: You may use either an initialized array of month names or a suitable *switch* statement for your function definition.

```
typedef struct
{
      int day, month, year;
      void convert ();
} DateType;
```

Finally, the C++ compiler allows you to use pointers to functions as structure members. This feature facilitates a connection to the system library and user-defined functions that already exist and thus helps code reusability. Consider the following program which implements a structure containing an integer type data and a pointer to function as its members. The function pointer can be pointed to different functions, albeit of the same types. In the case of this example, the function points to either function *add* or function *subtract,* depending on the value of its flag member.

```
#include  <iostream.h>

// structure declaration
typedef struct
{
    int first, second;       // two numbers for arithmetic
                             // operations
    int (*func)(int, int);   // Represents a function with two
                             // integer parameters.
} ArithType;                 // for arithmetic operations

// function prototypes
int add(int, int);
int subtract(int, int);
```

```
void main ()
{

int option;   // option for a desired operation

ArithType   Record;       // an array of two structures

    // GetData
cout << "\nEnter two separate integers (e.g., 23 45) :";
cin  >> Record.first  >> Record.second;

    // Process data.
cout << "\nEnter <0> for addition, "
     << " or <1> for subtraction"
     << " and <99> to terminate: ";
cin  >> option;

if ( option == 0 )
  Record.func = add;
else if (option == 1 )
  Record.func = subtract;
  else
        cout << "\nThank you and good bye now!";

// Output the result.
(option == 1 || option == 0)?
cout << Record.func(Record.first,  Record.second): cout << "Bye!";
}

// function definitions
int add (int m, int n)
{
    return m + n;
}

int subtract (int m, int n)
{
    return m - n;
}
```

The above program shows that similar structures may be used in menu-driven programs to control the flow of logic based on different choices.

5.3   CLASSES

As mentioned earlier, a **class** is a means of extending C++ to create new data types. They let you restrict the scope or accessibility of selected members in the rest of the program. The general format of a class declaration is similar to that of a structure except that a class declaration starts with the keyword *class* and with a level of information hiding before its selected members. Moreover, all the members of a *struct* are public by default and all the members of a *class* are private by default. This means that if you want to use a *class* instead of a *struct,* you must use the keyword *public* followed by the colon (:) character before declaring the *class* members. Let us look at an example of a *class* declaration and compare it to a structure with similar effects.

```
class Part                          struct Part
{                                   {
  public:                             long int PartNo;
    long int PartNo;                  char name[32];
    char name[32];                    double price;
    double price;                     double GetPrice ();
    double GetPrice ();               void DisplayInfo ();
    void DisplayInfo ();            };
};
```

These two declarations are identical and their members are accessible by other parts of the program. If the two are identical, why does C++ use the *struct* construct? The answer lies in the portability issue of the applications produced by the C and C++ languages. Otherwise, you can handle all types of structures easily by using C++ *classes.* Moreover, you may call a structure a *class* subset or a *class* as a structure extension. Both statements are correct; each construct simply describes an aggregate and neither one allocates memory. (However, the keyword *class* is more powerful than the keyword *struct,* as you will see in Chapter 6.)

5.4   UNIONS

A **union** is a construct that can store values of different types in a single location. In other words, the same block of bytes, declared as *union,* can be used in different ways, giving the programmers an overlay capability in memory. The syntax, declaration, and accessing methods of the *union* fields are almost the same as those for structures except that its declaration uses the key word *union* instead of *struct.*

Consider the following program, which has a *union* construct called *UnionType* with three components. It can accommodate at any time a double, a long integer, or a normal integer value. Toward this attribute, a *union* is assigned the amount of memory equal to the size of the largest component. Now, run the program and see what happens.

```
typedef union
{
    double m;
    long n;
    int d;
} UnionType;

#include<iostream.h>
void main ()
{
    UnionType  data;
    data.m = 4.14;
```

```
   cout << data.m;              // Displays  4.14.
   data.n = 654321L;            // The member operator (.) allows access.
   cout << data.n;              // Displays 654321.

        // declaring an array of unions
        // The implicit assignments may cause incorrect output.
        UnionType table[5] = { 2, 2.5, 5697874L, 234, 90000L };

        cout << table[0].d    // integer
             << table[1].m    // double
             << table[2].n    // long
             << table[3].d    // integer
             << table[4].n;   // long
}
```

Notice that access to the members of a variable of type *union* is possible through either the member operator (.) or (->), depending on whether you use a variable name or a pointer variable, respectively. The concept is similar to that of structures.

The second example picks apart an integer value as it is stored in the memory. We assume that an integer value takes up 16 bits of memory or 2 bytes. Note that we use a bitfield structure, similar to what we discussed before, to represent the bytes of an integer data.

```
        typedef union
        {
            int number;
            struct ByteType
            {
               unsigned int FirstByte  : 8;
               unsigned int SecondByte : 8;
            }Bytes;      // Represents the bytes of the integer.
        } IntType;       // Represents an integer value.
```

Now you can use the above declaration in a program and see exactly what is stored for an integer number. Complete the following piece of code and run it on your own computer to see the output.

```
void main()
{
IntType  data;
data.number = -1; // stored as 1111 1111 1111 1111

cout << hex << data.Bytes.FirstByte << '\t' //displays ff in hexadecimal format
     << hex << data.Bytes.SecondByte;  // displays ff
}
```

Application of Unions

Some common applications of unions are representing a single data item in alternate ways, and processing record variants or variable-length records. The following examples demonstrate these applications. The first example shows how to use a *union* construct to represent a single data item in different ways. Each computer on the Internet is identified by a unique address called an IP address. It is used to track down and reach a desired computer on the network. An IP address contains four numbers separated by periods such as 234.33.5.1. Working from left to right, an IP address takes us from a broad domain to more specific network-linked organization. IP addresses are usually stored internally as *unsigned long integer* (32 bits), each integer taking a single byte. For example, the IP address 129.11.5.4 is stored internally as 10000001 00001011 00000101 00000100 and the address 234.2.3.4 is internally represented as 11101010 00000010 00000011 00000100. The C++ union construct is ideal for representing the two formats, external and internal, of an IP address, as shown. To represent an IP address, we first declare it as a four-byte structure and then we include it in a union declaration composed of this structure and an *unsigned long integer.* Keep in mind that since we do not store the periods, a function is needed to convert the data for output.

```
typedef struct
{
    unsigned char first;
    unsigned char second
    unsigned char third;
    unsigned char fourth;
} ByteType;

typedef union
{
    unsigned  long address;
    ByteType  bytes;
}IP;
```

After the above declaration, you may declare an IP address as follows:

```
IP     IPAddress;
```

Now, you can assign the elements of an IP address as:

```
IPAddress. bytes. first  = 234;
IPAddress. bytes. second =  33;
IPAddress. bytes. third  =   5;
IPAddress. bytes. fourth =   1;
```

The second application of unions is in processing record variants (variable-length records). C++ does not have built-in provisions, as Pascal does, for handling record variants in which there is no fixed contingent of fields. A typical example of this type of record is a payroll system in which there are different records of different sizes. The record size of a person who receives salary at the end of the month is different from the one who receives wages based on the number of hours worked and his or her pay rate. To handle these payroll records, one can easily define two different structures *(struct),* one for each type of employee. However, it might be more convenient to define a single structure with enough fields to record all the necessary information about the two types of employees. In C++, this is possible using the *union* construct. Consider the following example that involves an array of 100 payroll records. The records are of two different sizes for persons who are salary earners and those who earn a wage. The structure for salary earners has only four elements or fields and that of the wage earners has six fields as shown in Figure 5.8.

Figure 5.8 Salary Earners Structure

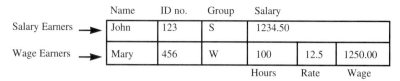

```
/************* Declarations *************/
const int length = 32
typedef  struct
{
   char        name[length];
   long int    id_no;
   char         group;       // salary earner or wage earner
     union  PayType          // union definition
     {
        double     salary;
        struct
        {
           unsigned int   hours;   // hours worked
           double         rate;    // pay rate
           double         wage;
        } earning;                 // end of inner structure
     } member;                     // end of union
} PersonType;                      // end of outer structure
/********* End of declaration *********/

#include <iostream.h>
#include <stdio.h>
#include <ctype.h>
const unsigned int  size = 100;

/********************************************************
* Interface for function GetData                       *
* PURPOSE: To obtain data from the keyboard.           *
* GIVEN:   Reference to structure.                     *
* RETURN:  none                                        *
********************************************************/
void GetData (PersonType&);

/********************************************************
* Interface for function Display                       *
* PURPOSE: To Display the records on the screen.       *
* GIVEN:   Reference to structure.                     *
* RETURN:  None                                        *
********************************************************/
void Display (PersonType&);

void main ()
{
```

```
    PersonType   staff[size];
    int        index = 0;

        // Get data
    for ( ; index < size;  ++index )      // Get data for all.
        GetData( staff[index] );

        //  display information
    for ( index = 0; index < size;  ++index )
        Display( staff[index] );
}

// function  GetData
void GetData (PersonType& p)
{
    int done = 1; // a flag to validate classification
    cout << " Enter name--->";  gets( p.name );  // from <stdlib.h>
    cout << " Enter id_no--->"; cin >> p.id_no;
    cout << "Enter group classification <'S'OR'W'> --->";
    cin >> p.group
    p.group = toupper(p.group);    // Convert to uppercase.
    do
        switch (p.group)
    {
        // salary earner
        case 'S':     cout << "Enter salary-->";
                      cin  >> p.member.salary;
                      break;
        // wage earner
        case 'W':     cout << "Enter Hours worked-->";
                      cin  >>  p. member.earning.hours;
                      cout << "Enter pay rate-->";
                      cin  >> p.member.earning.rate;
                      p.member.earning.wage =
                                      (double)hours * rate;
                      break;

        default:      done = 0;
                      cout >> "\nWrong classification!"
                           << "Enter <'S' or 'W' only>:";
                      break;
    }   // End of switch.
        while (!done);
}

// function Display
void Display (person& p)
{
    cout << p.name  << '\t'
         << p.id_no << '\t';
    p.group = toupper(p.group);
```

```
cout.width( 8 );      // --------
cout.precision( 2 ); // -----.--
cout.fill( '*' );     // e.g., **123.75
cout.setf( ios::fixed, ios::floatfield|ios::showpoint);

switch (p.group)
{
    case 'S':     cout << p.member.salary << '\n';
                  break;

    case 'W':     cout << p.member.earning.wage << '\n';
                  break;
}
}
```

Self-Check Questions 2

1. Suggest an appropriate type for each of the following requirements:

   The information you store about an object will be either one value or another.

   You want to store related information about an object.

2. Declare a suitable structure(s) to control the inventory of the S&T Sounds company, which carries stereos and televisions with the following specifications. (Hint: You should use the *union* type in this question.)

   Name, stock no. (1...30000), supplier, quantity (1...10000), date purchased (yy/mm/dd).

   Stereos with powers ranging from 100 to 1000 watts.

   Televisions with tube sizes of 11...50 and screens of either flat or regular.

3. Can a programmer use the C++ class type in place of *struct?* How?

5.5   FILES

A **file** is a repository of information and consists of records of the same type. Files have two important characteristics. First, they are often very long; that is, the capacity of the file can easily exceed the capacity of the main memory. Second, files typically have a long lifetime. A file often exists before and after the execution of an application program that accesses it.

The major issues in file processing are

- File and program interdependence. This means that an application program must know the logical structure or the format of the records in a file and how they are organized within it.
- The manner in which the records have been stored in order to constitute a file. This is referred to as **file organization.** A file's organization defines the way(s) it may be accessed. Common file organizations used in C++ are:

  Sequential files

  Direct or random files

  Let's look at more information on each type.

Sequential Files

Some files are stored so that access to their records can only be accomplished in the same sequence in which the data have been stored. For example, the data in a teacher's file may be stored in alphabetical order by student names. This type of organization is analogous to an audiocassette that contains various pieces of music. Therefore, a sequential file may be defined as a file in which records are stored either in the order they are entered into the file or in ascending or descending order by a specific key such as an identification number.

To find an individual record in a sequential file, you must perform a sequential (linear) search. This means that each record in the file must be examined until the required one is located. Such a search is time-consuming, especially when the file is large. Also, updating one record requires making a new copy of the file. Therefore, sequential files are impractical for applications that require immediate access to individual records. The best example of this kind of file is magnetic tape files that are used for either backup or archival purposes. Other examples of sequential files are program output on the printer or program I/O with a computer terminal. There are also payroll systems that use sequential organization to produce paychecks every week based on almost every record on the file. By and large, sequential access is a heavily used method of file organization. All programming languages, including C++, support this type of file organization.

Direct Access or Random Files

This type of file organization is analogous to an array's organization. We can access elements either directly or sequentially. As a matter of fact, in some systems a **direct access file** is also called a **virtual array.** C++ also treats a file as an array of bytes and thus supports direct access file processing. Direct access file processing is usually used when there is a high volume of random requests for individual records. For example, when you use your banking card to deposit or withdraw money from an automated transaction machine (ATM), the system goes directly to your record without cycling through each record in the file that precedes yours. Direct access to records is achieved through a unique record key such as an account number, registration number, insurance number, and so on. Finally, the term *random* in this case is synonymous with *direct* and it means that the system cannot anticipate which record will be processed next. For example, after you leave the ATM machine, the computer does not know who the next user might be.

Text Versus Binary Files

A **text file** or **terminal file** is one in which data are stored as a stream of bytes wherein each byte corresponds to a particular character from the host computer's character set. For small- to medium-sized computer systems, the character set is extended ASCII (American Standard Code for Information Interchange) and for IBM mainframes it is EBCDIC (Extended Binary Coded Decimal Interchange Code). It is convenient to think of these files as containing valid printable characters along with certain non-printable characters such end-of-line and end-of-file characters. As a result, text files are human-readable and can be displayed by editors or by printers. Here is an example of data storage on a text file:

The number 123 is stored in three bytes as:

```
00110001  00110010  00110011
ASCII(49) ASCII(50) ASCII(51)
```

In contrast to text files, a binary file is one in which individual bytes may or may not correspond to a particular character set. They use numeric encoding for any control characters, binary values for numbers, and so on. Binary files are suitable for storing information that programs share. Here is an example of data storage in a binary file:

Number 123 is stored in two bytes as:

0000 0000 0111 1011

File Processing in C++

The major I/O operations of C++ are handled through an object-oriented system using a *class* called ios. Remember that a *class* in simple terms is a structure containing a number of data and function members to provide certain services. It is also a new data type that may serve as a basis for a hierarchy of derived classes. For instance, the class *ios*, as illustrated in Figure 5.9, has three derived classes. The header file *iostream.h* includes all four of them.

Since the C++ I/O system is a complex organization, we have only selected and shown the classes that provide major services for standard I/O and file processing. While the class *istream* supports formatted and unformatted input data and the class *ostream* is in charge of formatted and unformatted output information, the class *iostream* provide services for bi-directional I/O operations. We have used the objects (instances) of this class, *cin* and *cout,* extensively, and you are quite familiar with them. Therefore, for the rest of this chapter we will use the other *classes* that provide support for file processing:

- Class *ifstream* derived from class *istream* to support file input operation.
- Class *ofstream* derived from class *ostream* to support file output operation.
- Class *fstream* derived from class *iostream* to support bi-directional file processing.

Opening and Closing Files

Before you use a file for any purpose, you must open it. This is analogous to opening your book before reading. In C++, opening a file means linking it to one of the streams *ifstream,*

Figure 5.9 Class *ios* and Its Derived Classes

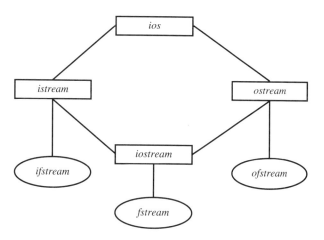

ofstream, and *fstream* for input, output, and bi-directional input and output operations, respectively. The following declaration examples show how to create a file stream for different purposes.

```
ifstream infile;     // Infile is a user file name for input.
ofstream outfile;    // Outfile is a user file name for output.
fstream file;        // File is a user name for both output and output.
```

Upon declaration of a file name, as an internal name, open the file using the *open* function that belongs to all three streams. It has the following prototype:

```
void open (char* filename, int mode, int access);
```

For example,

```
infile. open ("C:\\apps\\recods.txt", ios::in, 0);
```

When you open a file, specify the source of the file, i.e., disk file name and what you want to do with the file. The type of file operation is specified by a desired mode. Files may be accessed in different modes, as shown in Table 5.4. These modes belong to the class *ios* and you have to use the scope resolution character (::) to show their affiliation.

The access mode in the *open* function defines the security level of the file, as shown in Table 5.5. Under Borland C++ environment, these access modes correspond to the file attribute codes.

Table 5.4   Modes of the Class *ios*

Mode	Description
ios::app	Opens for appending a record to an output file, rather than updating an existing record.
ios::ate	Positions file marker at end of file instead of beginning.
ios::in	Opens for input or reading.
ios::out	Opens for output or writing.
ios::binary	Binary mode; default is text.
ios::trunc	Truncates (deletes) file if it exists and recreates it.
ios::nocreate	Open fails if file does not exist (output only).
ios::noreplace	Open fails if file exists unless appending or seeking end of file (output only).

Table 5.5   Security Levels of Files

Attribute	Meaning
0	Normal file: the default parameter value of the open function
1	Read-only file
2	Hidden file
4	System file
8	Archive bit set

If you do not specify an access mode for the opening process, the mode will default to a normal file. Since the access mode is a single value (that is, a power of 2), you may combine several of them by using the bitwise OR operation to create a new value that includes your desired attributes. Examine the following example that makes the access mode of a system file read-only.

```
int access = 0;
int RdOnly = 1;
int SysFile = 4;
access = RdOnly | SysFile;
```

For example, to open a file for reading in normal mode, use the *open* function of *ifstream*. It links the disk file *MyFile.dat* to the stream as a normal file (Access mode 0).

```
ifstream infile;
int access = 0;
infile.open( "d:\\files\\MyFile.dat", ios::in, access );
```

You may also open a file directly, without using the word *open,* at the time of declaration of the file stream:

```
ifstream infile( "d:\\MyFile.dat", ios::in, 0 );
```

The above format is suitable for functions that use a local file name with limited scope. To open a file for read-only, use the open function as:

```
infile.open ("d:\\files\\MyFile.data", ios::in, 1);
```

The following example shows how to create a file of integer values. We have declared an internal name for our file of *outfile,* type *ofstream.* The *open* statement connects the internal name *outfile* to the external (disk) file name and specifies the mode of operation. The mode in this example is *ios::out* to indicate an output operation. Also, when you open a file, check to see whether the opening operation has been successful. This is done by using several member functions of class *ios* as:

- *eof()*   Returns nonzero if the stream encounters an *EOF.*
- *bad()*   Returns nonzero if an error occurs.
- *fail()*   Returns nonzero if an operation fails.
- *good()*   Returns nonzero if no state bits are set.
- *rdstate()*   Returns the current state of the stream.

```
#include <fstream.h>     // for file processing
#include <stdlib.h>      // for exit statement

void main ()
{
   ofstream outfile;// Declares an internal file stream.

      // Open the file for output
   outfile.open( "c:\\files\\my.dat", ios::out);
      // if attempt failed.
   if (!outfile) // similar to if (outfile.fail() )
   {
      cout << "Error opening file.\n";
```

```
        exit (1);      // failure
    }
    else
    {
        for (int index = 1; index < 11; ++index)
            outfile << index << ' '; // Writes to the file.
    }

    outfile.close();      // Close the file.
}
```

The next example shows how to use a file for input operations; that is, to read from an existing disk file into the main memory. We will validate the opening process using all the available status functions of the class *ios.*

```
#include <fstream.h>
#include <stdlib.h>
void main ()
{
    ifstream infile; //Declares an internal file stream.
    int  num;

                      // access mode is input
    infile.open( " c:\\files\\my.dat ", ios::in );

                      // different conditions
    if (!infile)
    {
        cout << "Error opening file.\n";
        exit(1);
    }

    while (infile >> num)      // Read until end-of-file.
        cout << '\n' << num;
    infile.close();

}
```

Previous examples provided a constant name for the disk file such as *"c:\files \my.dat"* to indicate the physical source of the file. This makes the program very file-specific and rigid. In real-life applications, however, you should use a variable name for the source file and prompt the user to provide it. Let us look at the following example:

```
#include <fstream.h>
#include <stdlib.h>
void main ()
{
    const int FilePath = 64;
    ifstream infile;
    char file_name[FilePath]; // the name of the file
    char ch;  // for reading the file character by character
    cout <<"Enter your file name <e.g. c:\\apps\\text.dat-> ";
    cin  >> file_name;
```

```
    infile.open( file_name, ios::in );      // an input operation
    if (!infile)
    {
       cout << "Error! The file does not exist. Case closed!";
    else
    {
       while (infile.get(ch)) // Reads character by character.
             cout << ch;       // Displays the character just read in.
       infile.close();
     } // endif
}
```

Below is a program that compares two text files. The program also shows how to control the *end of file* flags.

```
#include <fstream.h>
#include <stdlib.h>

const int length = 64;  // for file names including their path
void main ()
{
    ifstream first, second;           // to read both files
    char first_file[length],
         second_file[length];         // for the source names
    char ch1, ch2;                    // representing two characters

    cout << "\nEnter the first file's name: ";
    cin  >> first_file;

    cout << "\nEnter the second file's name: ";
    cin  >>  second_file;


            // Attempt to open first file.
    first.open( first_file , ios::in );
    if (!first)
      {
            cout << "\n Attempt to open the"
                 << first file
                 << "failed!";
            exit(1);
      }

// Attempt to open second file
second.open( second_file, ios::in );
if (!second)
{
            cout << "\n Attempt to open the"
                 << second file
                 << "failed!";
exit(1);
}
```

```
                // compare the two files
int index = 0;
for ( ; ;  index++ )  // Terminates by end of file indicators.
{
   if (first.eof()  || second.eof())
       break;

   first >> ch1;       // similar to first.get(ch1);
   second >> ch2;      // similar to second.get(ch2);
   if (ch1 != ch2)
     cout << "\nThe files differ at " << index + 1
          << "th character";
}
   if (first.eof() && second.eof())  // end of both files
       cout << "\nThe files are identical";
   else
       cout << "\nOne file is bigger than the other!";
   first.close();
   second.close();
}
```

The following short program shows how to use the *ios::app* for appending something to a file.

```
#include <fstream.h>
void main ()
{
   ofstream   outfile; // declaration for output file
   outfile.open( "c:\\names.txt", ios::app );   // append mode
   outfile << "Mary  E. Friend\n";   // the text to be appended
   outfile << "Billy June";   // the next piece for appending
   outfile.close();
}
```

Self-Check Questions 3

1. Give an example of an appropriate application for a sequential file.
2. Give an example of an appropriate application for a random-access file.
3. Write the necessary file declaration for opening the disk file *"d:\\cs\\programs\\ fileapp1.cpp"* for updating purposes.
4. Write the necessary code to append the following comment line at the end of the *fileapp1.cpp* program.

```
\\ End of the program
```

Random-Access Files

Random access is simply the ability to go through a file, looking for one or more selected records. It allows you to read from and write to a file as well as update it. As we mentioned before, C++ supports random access (direct access) operations and hence provides programmers with very straightforward facilities. The C++ language views a file as a collection of bytes with indexing beginning at zero. In other words, a file may be viewed as a virtual array. In contrast to an array, in which we use an index to access a particular component, we have to use a special function called *seek* to access a particular element in a file.

```
file-variable-name.seekg(offset number of bytes, from a position); or
file-variable-name.seekp(offset number of bytes, from a position);
```

The letter *g* at the end of *seekg* specifies that the positioning of the file index, also known as **file marker,** is for reading (getting) and, similarly, the letter *p* at the end of *seekp* indicates a writing (putting) operation. The **offset** number of bytes is of type *long integer;* this is the number of bytes you want to move the file marker from a position. This position can be the beginning *(beg)* of the file, a current place in the file *(cur),* or the end of the file *(end).* The offset number of bytes and the position of the file marker are actually used in function *seek* as shown below:

```
file-variable-name.seekg(long int,   ios::beg);   // offset from the beginning
file-variable-name.seekg(long int,   ios::cur);   // from current position
file-variable-name.seekg(long int,   ios::end);   // from the end of the file
```

> **Note:**   The offset number of bytes can be a positive or negative value. It allows you to move the file marker back and forth from any position between the beginning and the end of the file.

In summary, to create and access random access (direct) files, you need to do the following:

- Include the *fstream.h* header file.
- Declare an internal file name of type *fstream* for bi-directional operations.
- Open the file with *ios::in* and *ios::out* modes.
- Use the file name with appropriate extraction or insertion symbols, << and >>, for simple data and *read* and *write* for structured data. The general form for these two functions are:

```
file-variable-name.read(array of bytes, how many bytes); and
file-variable-name.write(array of bytes, how many bytes);
```

The *read* function reads a record, as a block of bytes, with a specified size from a specified position in a file that is given relative to the file's current position. This is a buffered function that allows you to read a large block with a single call.

The *write* function looks like the *read* function but with the word *write* instead of *read*. It transfers data from memory to a specified position in a file. Similar to the *read* function, this function also needs the size of the record in bytes. The *write* function is another buffered function that may be used for transfer of a large block of data from a memory buffer to disk.

Study the sample programs to gain a better understanding of the subject. The first example creates a simple file of lowercase letters and allows you to change one of them from lowercase to uppercase. Since the data are simply single characters, we will use the file name for reading and writing purposes. The example also uses two other functions of the language, called *tellg* or *tellp*, that allow you to mark and remember a particular place in the file for future reference. The general form for these two functions are:

```
long int file-variable-name.tellg(); and
long int file-variable-name.tellp();
```

Figure 5.10   File *alpha.dt*

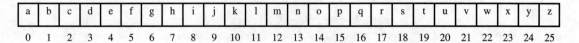

The two functions return the current position of the file pointers in a *long integer* type. Here again, the letters *g* and *p* at the end of the functions stand for *get* and *put*, respectively. Figure 5.10 should help you better understand how function *seek* works.

```cpp
#include <fstream.h>   // file processing facilities
#include <stdlib.h>    // for the library function exit()
#include <ctype.h>     // to process characters
void main ()
{
    fstream  file;      // a single variable for both input and output
    long int marker;    // for holding the status of a desired
                        // position of the file marker char letter;

    // Open the file: Notice the bitwise OR.
    file.open( "d:\\files\\alpha.dat",ios::in | ios::out );
    if (!file)          // Test if open was successful.
    {
        cout << "\n Error opening file";
        exit( 1 );
    }

                                        // Create the file.
    for (letter = 'a';  letter <= 'z';  ++letter)

            file <<letter;              // Write to the file.

            // Now start from the beginning of the file.
    file.seekg( 0L, ios::beg );
            // Advance to the fifth byte from current position.
            // ( 0 1 2 3 4 )


        file.seekg( 4L, ios::cur );     // Advance to letter 'e'.
        marker = file.tellg();          // Remember the current position.
        file.seekg( marker, ios::cur ); // Advance 4 more bytes.
        file >> letter;                 // Read the letter 'i'.
        letter = toupper( letter );     // Change it to uppercase.


    // Move back 1 byte from current position (see the discussion
    // following this program.
        file.seekp( -1L, ios::cur );    // Move back one byte.
        file << letter;                 // write back the letter
        file.seekg( 0L, ios::beg );     // back to the beginning
```

```
file.seekg( 25L, ios::cur );        // advance to the twenty-sixth byte
file >> letter;                     // Read a letter

letter = toupper( letter);          // Change it to uppercase.
cout << letter;                     // Display it on the screen.
file.close();
}
```

Note that upon reading a record, the file marker moves to the next available record in the file. Therefore, to update a record and write it back to its original place, you have to move the file marker backward by the size of the record. This was the reason that we used *file.seekp(-1L, ios::cur)* in the above program.

The last program shows how to create and manipulate a file of structures (*struct*). Again, since you are dealing with structures, you have to use *read* and *write* functions to handle a record as a block of bytes with the following format:

```
filename.read(( char*)& structure, how many); and
filename.write(( char*)& structure, how many);
```

The code (char*)& structure is interpreted as an array of bytes. The program creates a file of ASCII characters with their associated ASCII values (for example, A = 65). Now look at the program:

```
#include<fstream.h>
typedef struct InfoType          // type definition
{
   char ascii;    // ASCII character
   int value;     // ASCII value
};

const int total = 256; // characters of the ASCII system
void main ()
{
   InfoType record;
   fstream file;
   long int marker;

       // create the file
   file.open( "c:\\files\\my.txt", ios::out| ios::in);
   file.seekp( 0L, ios::beg );

   for ( int index = 0; index < total; ++index )
   {
      record.value = index;
      record.ascii = (char)value;

      // Write the information into the file.
      file.write( (char*)&record, sizeof(record) );
   }

       // Now read the file and print out the characters
       // with the ASCII values starting with 65.
```

```
file.seekg( 64L, ios::beg );
for ( index = 0; index < 26; ++ index )   // letters of the alphabet
{
    file.read( (char*)&record, sizeof(record);
    cout << record.value << '\t'
         << record.ascii << '\n';
}

    file.seekg( 0L, ios::beg );             // Starts from the beginning.

        // Advance the file marker to the sixty-fifth  record.
    file.seekg( (64 * sizeof(record)), ios::cur );
    marker = file.tellg();                  // Remember this position.
    file.read( (char*)&record, sizeof(record) );
    cout << "\n\n" << record.value << ' ' << record.ascii;

    file.seekg( 0L, ios::beg );  // from the beginning again
    file.seekg( marker, ios::cur );          // Advance the marker position.
    file.read( (char*)&record, sizeof(record)

    cout << "\n\n" << record.value  << ' ' << record.ascii;

    file.close();
}
```

The *class fstream* also provides you with the *remove(filename)* function that removes a file from the disk. It erases the file specified by *filename* and returns 0 if the file was erased successfully and -1 if an error occurred. Consider the following example:

```
if (remove(file) == -1)
    cout << "\n It could not be removed";
else
    cout << "\nThe file " << file << " is gone!\n";
```

There are also situations in which a file has encountered *end-of-file*. As long as the file remains in this state, input and output operations are not permitted. The solution to this is to clear the state of the file by using the function *clear()* and then writing what you want. The following piece of code demonstrates this situation:

```
char* message  = "Please do not add anything to this file.";

    // Open the file for appending.
    fstream file( "c:\\files\\my.dat", ios::app );
    file.seekg( 0L, ios::beg );

    while (file.get(ch))  // While not eof, read and
                          // do the following
    {
    ...
    ...
    // This loop stops at end of file.
```

```
}

file.clear();        // to clear the eof state.
file.write( (message, strlen(message));
```

> **Note:** The following I/O functions (which were discussed in the first chapter) are applicable to the application files, too.

getline()

gcount()

peek()

putback()

ignore()

Files as Function Parameters

It is common to use files as function parameters. Since files are structured units of information, they should be passed by reference to reduce program overhead. Look at the following prototype example:

```
void GetText(ifstream&, char*);
```

The function reads a string from a file and returns it to its calling function. The code is compatible with the following call:

```
ifstream infile;
char Text [80];
GetText (infile, Text);
```

Self-Check Questions 4

1. How can a file be passed to a function?
2. How is a binary file prepared? Can you print it out using a text editor?
3. Read the following program carefully and show its typical run. To terminate data entry, just press CTRL Z instead of entering data. CTRZ represents end of file in the DOS environment.

```
#include <fstream.h>
   #include <stdlib.h>

   void main()
   {
      const int BuffSize = 128;

      char   buffer[BuffSize];
      ofstream   OutFile;
      OutFile.open("a:\\MyFile.dat", ios::out| ios::in);
      if (!OutFile)
         cerr << "Open failed!" , exit(1); // comma operator
```

```
    cout << "\nEnter a line of text: ";
    while (!cin.getline(buffer, BuffSize).eof())
    {
        OutFile  << buffer;
        cout << "\nNext line: ";
    }
    OutFile.close();
}
```

4. How will you open the file *MyFile.dat* for adding new lines of text? The opening process should also ensure that the file does exist; otherwise, it will fail.

5. Write a code fragment to read the file *MyFile.dat* from the beginning to the end in order to display the lines just written. The output might look like this:

```
LINE #1:  something.........
LINE #2:  something else.....
            .
            .
            .
```

SUMMARY

- While an array is of uniform data type, a structure is a composite data object that may contain similar or different members.
- Structures must be declared before being used.
- To access a member of a structure you should use the member operator (.) or *dot* operator. However, if a pointer has been established to a structure, you should use the (->), a combination of the hyphen and angle bracket, or you may enter *(* pointer). Object.*
- Structures have a wide range of applications in software development, including implementing bitfields. Bitfields are not common in programming, however.
- Structures may have functions as well as pointers to functions as their members. Pointers to functions provide you with more flexibility to develop better code and reuse previously existing functions.
- The C++'s *struct* is a holdover from the C language. However, C++ has a structure of its own, called *class*. The *class* construct is a fundamental tool of data abstraction.
- A *union* construct defines a single memory area that accepts values of different types. It stores a single value at one time and thus provides the capability to overlay variables in memory. It is useful in representing data in alternate ways and in processing record variants.
- C++ supports both sequential and direct access files. It provides programmers with a full range of capabilities through its I/O streams. The header file *fstream.h* contains the classes necessary, such as *ifstream, ofstream,* and *fstream* for input, output, and dual input and output operations.
- Before being accessed, files must be declared and opened properly. The open process tells the system of the file name on the disk, operation mode, and access mode.

- The operation mode of a file may be one or more of the modes defined in *class ios. Class ios* has defined eight modes *(in, out, app, binary, ate, trunc, nocreate, noreplace)* for this purpose. You may combine two or more of them using the bitwise OR operation.
- The access mode is a mode that determines the access level or security of the file. When you open a file, its default access mode is 0 to represent a normal file.
- When you do not need a file any more, close it. Also, do not leave several files open if you are not going to use them.

STYLE TIPS

- Use structures whenever possible to bundle and store closely related data. They allow you to hide the contents of their fields and process them as a whole. It is in a sense a limited approach to information hiding.
- When you are involved in large programs, use the C++ *typedef* to define your structures and unions. *Typedef* provides a safeguard against portability problems. It is also good for maintenance and documentation.
- When you need to declare embedded structures, it is better to declare each structure separately and then put them together.
- Use descriptive names for program structures, unions, and files.
- Use enough indentation to highlight structure members.

SAMPLE PROGRAMS

1. The first program operates on rational numbers. A rational number is denoted as *a/b,* the ratio of two integers, where *b != 0.* Note that the decimal representation of any rational number is either a terminating decimal or a repeating decimal. The program accepts a pair of rational numbers for basic arithmetic operations. The program validates the input data and displays an appropriate message for invalid data. In respect to the output, the program simplifies the answers, if necessary, and displays the result. For simplification purposes, the program uses Euclid's method to find the greatest common divisor of the two numbers in order to divide both of them by the greatest common divisor. For example, if our rational number is 12/14, then the greatest number, also known as the greatest common divisor, that goes into both numbers evenly is 2. Therefore, the simplified version of the rational numbers will be 6/7.

   According to Euclid's algorithm:

   When you divide a positive integer by another positive integer, the greatest common divisor (gcd) of the two numbers is equal to the greatest common divisor of the second integer and the new number produced as a result of their modulus operation. For example, if $m = 12$ and $n = 14$, then $gcd(14,12) = gcd(12, 2) = gcd(2,0)$.

   The *gcd* of a number and 0 is the number itself. This means that the $gcd(2,0) = 2$.

   The program assumes that none of the numerators or denominators will be more than four digits. A terminal session of the program should look like this:

```
This program performs basic arithmetic operations on rational numbers.
Please enter the first number's numerator and press ENTER.          3
Please enter the first number's denominator and press ENTER.        4
Please enter the desired operator <+> <-> <*> </> and press ENTER.  +
Please enter the second number's numerator and press ENTER.         1
Please enter the second number's denominator and press ENTER.       2
The answer to the problem is:                                       5/4
Do you want to continue? Please type <y> or <n> and ENTER.          n
Have a good time!
```

The numerator and denominator of a fraction can be well represented as a structure with two members.

To help you read and understand the code, the general algorithm of the program is presented below. An algorithm shows the broad view of the program and the details of each process are to be hammered out during the refinement steps.

```
Algorithm Rational
      Start
             SET more flag TRUE
             WHILE (continue)
             DO
                    Get first rational number
                    Get second rational number
                    Get operator
                    CASE   operator OF
                           '+':        Process Addition
                           '-':        Process Subtraction
                           '*':        Process Multiplication
                           '/':        Process Division
                    ENDCASE
                    Get response to continue
                    RESET continue
             ENDWHILE
      END Rational.


// ******************* The Program *******************


enum Boolean { false, true };        // Boolean values



// ***** Declaration of the Structure ******************

typedef  struct Rational  // new type
{
             int numer;      // numerator
             int denom;      // denominator
};

// *************** Function prototypes  **************
// This part may be placed in a separate header file.
// ****************************************************
```

```
// ********************************************************
// Interface for function GetData                        *
// PURPOSE: To obtain a single integer value.            *
// GIVEN:   None                                         *
// RETURN:  true if successful; otherwise false          *
// ********************************************************
int GetData();

// ********************************************************
// Interface for function Add                            *
// PURPOSE: To perform addition operation.               *
// GIVEN:   Two reference parameters of rational type.   *
// RETURN:  None. Yields the result through the          *
//          third reference parameter.                   *
// ********************************************************
void Add( Rational&, Rational&, Rational& );
//*********************************************************
// Interface for function Subtract                       *
// PURPOSE: To perform subtraction operation.            *
// GIVEN:   Two reference parameters of rational type.   *
// RETURN:  None. Yields the result through the          *
//          third reference parameter.                   *
//*********************************************************
void Subtract( Rational&, Rational&, Rational& );


//*********************************************************
// Interface for function Multiply                       *
// PURPOSE: To perform multiplication operation.         *
// GIVEN:   Two reference parameters of rational type.   *
// RETURN:  None. Yields the result through the          *
//          third reference parameter.                   *
//*********************************************************
void Multiply( Rational&, Rational&, Rational& );


//*********************************************************
// Interface for function Divide                         *
// PURPOSE: To perform division operation.               *
// GIVEN:   Two reference parameters of rational type.   *
// RETURN:  None. Yields the result through the          *
//          third reference parameter.                   *
//*********************************************************
void Divide( Rational&, Rational&, Rational& );


/*********************************************************
* Interface for function Simplify                       *
* PURPOSE: To simplify the result of the operation      *
*          using the gcd function invoked within        *
*          the function.                                *
* GIVEN:   Two reference parameters of integer type.    *
* RETURN:  None. Simplifies the result in place.        *
*********************************************************/
```

```
void simplify( int&, int& );

/********************************************************
* Interface for function Display                       *
* PURPOSE: To display the result of the operation.     *
* GIVEN:   A reference parameter of rational type.     *
* RETURN:  None.                                        *
********************************************************/
void Display( Rational& );

#include <stdlib.h>
#include <iostream.h>
#include <ctype.h>
/********************************************************
*                    function main()                    *
********************************************************/
void main ()
{
   Rational  first,    second, answer;
   char       operation, keypress;
   Boolean    more, valid;
   more = true; //Allows user to run the program more than once.

   cout <<"This program performs basic arithmetic operations"
        << " on rational numbers.";
   while (more == true)
   {
       valid = true;

              /****************************************
              //           get the first fraction        *
              //****************************************
       cout << "Please enter the first number's numerator"
            << " and press ENTER: ";
       first.numer = GetData();

       do    // get a valid denominator  (nonzero).
       {
           cout << "\nEnter the first number's denominator"
                << " <a non-zero value> and press ENTER: ";
           first.denom = GetData();
       } while (first.denom == 0);       // for validation

              //****************************************
              //          get the second fraction        *
              //****************************************
   cout << "Please enter the second number's numerator"
        << " and press ENTER: ";
   second.numer = GetData();

   do    // get a valid denominator
     {
```

```
        cout << "\nEnter the second number's denominator"
             << " <a non-zero value> and press ENTER: ";
        second.denom = GetData();
     }while (second.denom == 0);     // for validation

            //****************************************
            //           get the operator           *
            //****************************************

cout << "\nPlease enter the desired operator <+> <-> <*> </>"
     << " and press ENTER: ";
cin  >> operation;

            // determine the type of operation
            switch (operation)
            {
                case '+': Add(first, second, answer);
                          break;
                case '-': Subtract(first, second, answer);
                          break;
                case '*': Multiply(first, second, answer);
                          break;
                case '/': Divide(first, second, answer);
                          break;
            default:      valid = false;
            } // end switch

            if (valid == false)
            {
                cout << "\nWrong operator entered.
                     << "\Bye now."
                exit( 0 );     // terminate the program;
            }

            else
            {
                Display(answer);
                cout << "\nDo you want to continue?'
                     << " Enter <y> or <n> and press ENTER: ";
                cin >> keypress;
                keypress = toupper(keypress);
                   if (keypress !='Y')
                   {
                       cout << "\nHave a good time!";
                       more = false;
                   }
            }
        }   // end while
    } // end main
```

```
//*********************************************************
// function GetData to obtain an integer                 *
// The function reads in each integer value as a         *
// string to validate its digits.                        *
//*********************************************************
int GetData()
{
    const int NumSize = 4;
    char number[NumSize];       // program's assumption
    Boolean ok;                 // to validate the digits

    do
    {
       ok = true;
       cin >> number;
                               // validate digits
    for (int index = 0; index < NumSize && ok == true; ++index)
    {
       if ((number[index] < '0') || number[index] > '9')
          {
             ok = false;
             cout << "\nPlease enter a numeric value"
                  << "up to four digits: ";
          }
    } while (ok == false);

       // convert it to integer
       return (atoi(number));  // Uses <stdlib.h>.
}


//*********************************************************
//                  function add                         *
//*********************************************************
void Add( Rational& f, Rational& s, Rational& ans )
{
     int m, n;           // for interim results
     m = f.denom * s.denom;
     n = (m / f.denom * f.numer) + (m / s.denom * s.numer);
     ans.numer = n;
     ans.denom = m;
}


//*********************************************************
//              function subtract                        *
//*********************************************************
void Subtract( Rational& f, Rational& s, Rational& ans )
{
     int m, n;      // for interim results
     m = f.denom * s.denom; // common denominator
     n = (m / f.denom * f.numer) - (m / s.denom * s.numer);
     ans.numer = n;
```

```
        ans.denom = m;
}

/*****************************************************
*                function multiply                  *
*****************************************************/
void Multiply( Rational& f, Rational& s, Rational&  ans )
{
        int m, n;           // for interim results
        m = f.denom * s.denom;
        n = f.numer * s.numer;
        ans.numer = n;
        ans.denom = m;
}

//***************************************************
//                function divide                   *
//***************************************************
void Divide( Rational& f, Rational& s, Rational& ans )
        int m, n;           // for interim results
        m = f.numer * s.denom;
        n = f.denom * s.numer;
        ans.numer = m;
        ans.denom = n;
}

//*****************************************************
// Function Simplify to simplify the answer(if needed).*
// It contains the prototype of the function gcd.      *
//*****************************************************
void Simplify( int& m, int& n )
{
        m = m / gcd(m, n);
        n = n / gcd(m, n);
}

//*****************************************************
// Function gcd to compute the greatest common divisor *
// of two numbers.  Uses Euclid's algorithm            *
//*****************************************************
int gcd( int m, int n )
{
        int  hold;          // for interim values

        while(n != 0)       // while (n)
        {
                hold = m;
                m = n;
                n = hold % n;
        } // end while
        return (m);
}
```

```
//*********************************************************
// function Display to show the answer on the screen.   *
// It contains the prototype of the function gcd.        *
//*********************************************************
void Display( Rational& r )
{
        Simplify( r.numer, r.denom );
        cout <<"\nThe answer to the problem is: "
            << r.numer
            << '/'
            << r.denom;
}
```

2. The second program implements file processing concepts. It gives you an opportunity to examine a piece of code and see how the file processing features of C++ work in a real-life application. The program also shows you how to use the file names as function parameters.

The program is to read a piece of text from a specified disk file and produce a table containing a list, in alphabetical order, of all the distinct words that appear in the text. We have assumed that the maximum number of words in the file is 1000, the size of each word is no more than 16 characters, and the file does not have more than 900 distinct words. Moreover, a word is identified by one or more alphabetical letters. The following general algorithm is presented to help you better understand the code.

```
Algorithm  Distinct Words
START
    Get the file name  ----> Algorithm GetFileName
    Load table         ----> Algorithm Load file (from the file)
    Display file       ----> Algorithm Display file
    Process file       ----> Algorithm Process file
END Distinct Words

//***** The program ********************************
#include <fstream.h>
#include <string.h>
#include <stdlib.h>
#include <assert.h>
#include <conio.h>


//***** Function prototypes *************************
//*********************************************************
// Interface for function GetFileName                     *
// PURPOSE: Obtains the name of the file on the disk.      *
// GIVEN:   The file name as parameter                     *
// RETURN:  A string as the file name through parameter*
//*********************************************************
void GetFileName (char*);


//*********************************************************
// Interface for function DisplayFile                     *
// PURPOSE: Displays the contents of the file.            *
```

```
// GIVEN:   File name on the disk.                    *
// RETURN:  None                                      *
//******************************************************
void DisplayFile( char* );

//******************************************************
// Interface for function ProcessFile                 *
// PURPOSE: Create and display an array of distinct    *
//          words.  Calls two other functions:         *
//          LoadTable and Display.                     *
// GIVEN:   The file's internal name: variable name    *
// RETURN:  None                                       *
//******************************************************
void ProcessFile( char* );

//******************************************************
// Interface for function LoadTable                    *
// PURPOSE: Gets and inserts distinct words.  Calls    *
//          two other functions: GetWord and           *
//          InsertWord.                                *
// GIVEN:   An array of pointers to strings to hold    *
//          distinct words, a reference name for the   *
//          file's identifier, and a reference name of *
//          type int indicating the actual number of   *
//          words.                                     *
// RETURN:  A string as the file name.                 *
//******************************************************
char* LoadTable( char* [], ifstream&, int& );

//******************************************************
// Interface for function ProcessFile                  *
// PURPOSE: Opens the file, generates the table of     *
//          distinct words, displays the words         *
//          and closes the file by calling             *
//          appropriate functions.                     *
// GIVEN:   The file's path name.                      *
// RETURN:  None.                                      *
//******************************************************
void ProcessFile( char* );

//******************************************************
// Interface for function GetWord                      *
// PURPOSE:  Reads a word from the file.               *
// GIVEN:    The name of the  file.                    *
// RETURN:   A string.                                 *
//******************************************************
char* GetWord( ifstream& );

/*****************************************************
* Interface for function InsertWord                  *
* PURPOSE: Inserts a word into the table.            *
```

```
 *   GIVEN:   The string word, name of the array, and      *
 *            the length of the word.                      *
 * RETURN:   None.                                         *
 ********************************************************/
void InsertWord( char*, char* [], int& );


//****************************************************
// Interface for function Locate                    *
// PURPOSE: Looks up a word in the table.            *
// GIVEN:   The string word, name of the array, and*
//          the length of the word.                 *
//  RETURN:  true or false (0 or 1)                 *
//****************************************************
int Locate( char*, char* [], int );


/*****************************************************
//                  main function                    *
//*****************************************************

const int    FileSize = 1000,    // words
             WordLen  = 16,      // maximum size of a word
             distincts = 800,    // up to  800 distinct words
             PathName = 64;      // maximum length of a full path
void main ()
{
   char FileName[PathName];
   GetFileName (FileName);
   DisplayFile( FileName );
   ProcessFile( FileName );
}


//*****************************************************
//          function GetFileName                      *
//*****************************************************
void GetFileName (char * file)
{
   cout << "\nEnter the disk filename and press Enter:",
   cin . getline (file, PathName, '\n');
}


//*****************************************************
//          function DisplayFile                      *
//*****************************************************
void DisplayFile( char* name )
{
   char character;  // to read character by character
   ifstream      ThisFile;
   ThisFile.open( name, ios::in );
   if (!ThisFile)   // Check if open failed.
   {
   cerr << "Cannot open "
```

```
              << name << "\n";
    exit( 1 );
    }

    while (ThisFile.get(ch))  // until reaches end of file
          cout << character;
    cout << "\n";
    ThisFile.close();
    }

//****************************************************
//              function ProcessFile              *
//****************************************************
void ProcessFile( char* name )
{
    ifstream  ThisFile;
    ThisFile.open( name, ios::in );
    if (!ThisFile)
    {
          cerr  << "Cannot open "
                << name  <<  "\n";
          exit( 1 );
    }

    char *table[FileSize];     // Holds distinct words.
    int TblLen;      // Actual number of the words in the table.

          //  Load the table with distinct words of the file.
    LoadTable( table, ThisFile, TblLen );
    cout << "\nThe list of  distinct words in "
        << name << "\n';
     Display( table, TblLen );
     ThisFile.close();
}

//****************************************************
//              function LoadTable                *
//****************************************************
void LoadTable( char* table[], ifstream& file, int& length )
{
    char* word;  // to access a word
    char ch;     // to read character by character
    length = -1;

    while ( ch = file.peek(), (ch != EOF) &&
          (length <= distincts) )
    {
       if ((ch > = 'a' && ch < = 'z') ||
          (ch > 'A' && ch < = 'Z'))
       {
          word = GetWord( file );
```

```
            InsertWord( word, table, length );
        }
        else
            file.get( ch );
    }
}

//*******************************************************
//            function GetWord                        *
//*******************************************************
char* GetWord( ifstream& file )
{
        static char* word;
        char ch;
        int index;

        word = new char[WordLen];
        assert (word != 0);

        while (file.get(ch) && (index < WordSize - 1) &&
                ((ch > = 'a' && ch < = 'z')||
                 (ch > = 'A' && ch < = 'Z'))
        {
                ch = toupper( ch );     // Convert to uppercase.
                *(word + index) = ch;   // Assign to array.
                index++;
        }
        *(word + index) = NULL;
        return word;
}

//*******************************************************
//            function InsertWord                     *
//*******************************************************
void InsertWord( char* word, char* table[], int& len )
{
    int index = Locate(word, table, len); // Locate the word.
    if ( (index > 0) && (len > FileSize) )
        {
            for (int i = len; i > index; —i)
                table[i + 1] = table[i];
            table[index] = word;
            len++;
        }
}

//*******************************************************
//        function Locate using binary search         *
//*******************************************************
int Locate( char* word, char* table[], int len )
{
    int low = 0, high = len;  // two indices for both sides
```

```
int middle;  // middle index
int found = 0;  // a flag to control the loop

middle = (low + high) / 2;  // middle of the table
{
   while ( low < high  && !found )
   {
      if ( strcmp(word, table[middle ] ) == 0 )
         found = 1;  //  terminate the loop
      else if ( strcmp(word, table[middle ] ) > 0 )
             low = middle + 1;
          else
             high = middle + 1;
   }
}


   return found;  // 0 for not found, 1 for found.
}
```

PROGRAMMING ASSIGNMENTS

1. A big integer is an integer that is not supported directly by the primitive data types of
   C++. However, it may be represented as follows:

```
enum Boolean {plus, minus};
unsigned int const base = 10,
digits = 22;     // maximum number of characters
typedef struct
{
   Boolean sign;
   unsigned short number[digits];   // An array of 20 digits
} BigNum;
```

   Write a structured program that reads two big integer numbers up to 20 digits, computes their algebraic sum and prints out the result in a suitable format. Be sure that your
   program takes care of two numbers with the same or different signs and works regardless of the setting of *base*.

2. Given the following declaration, write a structured program to implement a simple library catalog system. The program should be able to handle browsing through the catalog, searching for a particular title, author, or subject, as well as borrowing and returning books, charging late fines of $2.00 per late day, and the acquisition of new
   titles. Limit your functions to no more than ten lines each.

```
typedef struct
{
   int day, month, year;
} date;

typedef struct
{
   char* title;
```

```
        char* author;
        long int CatalogNo;
        int YearPublished;
        int NoOfCopies;
        date BorrowDate;
    } card;
```

3. Write a structured program that reads a file in the form of a stream of words and builds a table containing the distinct words and the number of times each word appears in the file. The program will then:

   Print an alphabetical list with the words encountered together with the frequency of each word. Assume that the file has a maximum of 1000 words and each word has at most ten letters and is recognized by a space before and after it.

   Add the number of words at the end of the file as shown:

   ```
   There are ... words in this file.
   ```

   Hints:

   Examine the sample second program before thinking about this assignment.

   To add a line at the end of a file, first remove the *end-of-file* flag.

   Each cell of the table should look like Figure 5.11.

   The cell indicates that the word *Book* has occurred five times.

4. Remember that C++ supports sequential and random-access file processing. In both file processing methods, when the size of the file increases, the searching time increases too, due to the number of records that must be examined before we can locate a given record position in the file. Therefore, we need to develop another technique that will improve our searching time. One way to achieve this goal is to use an index.

   An index is normally used to reference or search for information. For example, we use an index in the back of a book to find a desired topic. Each element of a book index contains a key topic and a related page number for its location in the book. We can use the same approach to index a file. Similar to a book index, our file index will contain elements composed of a key value for a record from the file and its address in the file. Table 5.6 is a sample index file in which each employee number (as the key) has an associated disk address.

Figure 5.11   Sample Table

frequency	word
5	Book

Table 5.6   Sample Index File

Employee No.	File Address
1234566	896542380
1276567	899765426
1287656	900876544
1288765	986754344
1298765	989862422

In C++ a disk address can be found easily:

```
fstream File;
File.open
   (  "d:\\files\\employee.dat",ios::in|ios::out|ios::binary );
File.seekg( 0L, ios::beg ); // Start from the beginning.
long int address = File.tellg();          // Get the address.
File.seekg( sizeof(record)*5, ios::cur );// Skip six records.
address = File.tellg(); // Remember the new address.
```

Notice that an index file is a separate file of structures, each of which consists of two fields, a record key such as an employee number, student number, etc., and a related disk address. In other words, an indexed sequential system consists of two files, the original file and an extra index file.

An index file has several advantages:

If the size of the index file is relatively small, it can be kept inside the main memory as an array of structures.

It allows you to look up a record key in the index file first before accessing the disk and thus improve searching time significantly.

It allows you to keep more than one record key. For example, a Motor Vehicle Department may keep two keys for each driver, one based on the driver's license number and another from the social insurance number.

Write a program that creates a random-access file for an arbitrary number of students. Each student record contains *student name, student ID, first midterm, second midterm, final exam,* and *average.* The program is required to perform the following:

Create the main files.

Create a sorted index file.

Display a menu for

Showing the entire file.

Showing a record based on student number.

Updating a desired record.

6 Data Abstraction and Object-Oriented Programming

6.1 PREVIEW

In this chapter you will learn:

- The Notion of Abstraction
- Data Abstraction
- C++ and Data Abstraction
- Designing and Implementing Abstract Data Types
- C++ Class
- From Data Abstraction to Object-Oriented Programming

6.2 THE NOTION OF ABSTRACTION

Generally speaking, **abstraction** may be viewed as a model-building concept through which we try to construct perceptive models of real-world entities in order to understand them better, interact with them clearly, and solve problems effectively. It helps us make simple models of complex things, omitting the details that mask our vision. For example, your university's degree plan is an abstraction of what you are required to study in order to achieve a desired degree. The diagrams on the back of televisions, radios, and refrigerators are abstractions of complex electronic systems for maintenance purposes. An atlas actually encompasses **levels of abstraction,** with the whole world on one page, followed by each continent on a separate page, and each country on its own page. Therefore, we may conclude that abstraction is natural to human beings and we have used it in all walks of life, including computer science.

Computer science has used abstraction extensively in hardware architecture and software development. Software development, in particular, has gone through a number of evolutionary phases of abstraction as reactions to technological progress. The first major achievement in abstraction was assembly language code, through which one or more machine-level operations were wrapped into a single English-like instruction. Then came other languages that offered a higher level of abstraction by allowing programmers to write instructions to represent many low-level activities. As you may have noticed, in both phases programmers were given a chance to write programs without worrying about the details of the machine on which the program would run. Then came the most revolutionary method of software design, when procedural languages such as ALGOL, Pascal, Modula-2, and PL/I allowed programmers to abstract out the basic operations of complex software and define their specifications. As we have said earlier, procedural abstraction worked for a period in which technology was not as advanced as it is today and the ambitions for application development had not reached their current level.

6.3   DATA ABSTRACTION

One of the major problems of structured programming is that it often leads to situations in which the original specification of an application pervades every individual component of the code. As a consequence, the software becomes very rigid, brittle, and unchangeable. That is, the code and specifications are so tied up with each other that a simple change in specifications may cause serious problems across the system. This leads to a critical issue, **software extensibility.** Extending software, using procedural abstraction, is a very risky and difficult task. In the past most software applications that needed a major global change have either been abandoned or have been dealt with through local fixes. Furthermore, the code under these circumstances becomes program-specific and cannot be reused. Therefore, procedural abstraction is not sufficient for modern programming environments where large applications have to go through frequent extensions and modifications.

Today the focus of programming has shifted to data abstraction, which is not conceptually all that different from the procedural abstraction that has been used for many years. The two paradigms are similar in that both use the abstraction notion; that is, programmers abstract some concepts from a mass of programming details and unify them to create either new procedures—in the case of procedural abstraction—or invent new data types in data abstraction. Both forms of abstraction focus on the application requirements without being tied to the underpinning details of any particular hardware implementation or methods of data representation and manipulation. However, while the emphasis of procedural abstraction is on the application's goal (how the task is to be done), the focus of data abstraction is primarily on the data (what is to be done) being used by the application. In other words, one is a goal-driven approach and the other is a data-driven paradigm.

Data abstraction has strong roots in mathematics and is now being extensively used in computer science. Actually, the concept of data abstraction in programming dates back to the late 1960s when languages such as Simula and Smalltalk were developed. In general, we describe an **abstract data type (ADT)** by its functionality (rather than its implementation) as an entity with the following properties:

- Name
- Domain (consisting of a set of values whose representation is not openly specified)
- A set of primitive or basic operations on the elements of the domain
- A set of rules to govern the primitives and their semantics (the meaning)

For example, one can think of the integers in mathematics as an ADT integer with the following properties:

ADT name:	Integer
Domain:	−infinity to +infinity
Operations:	Addition, subtraction, multiplication, division, and modulus operations
Rule(s):	A set of rules to define the ordinality of the numbers as well as the legality of operations

Note that in the context of data abstraction, an operation is a function designed to process a set of values based on a well-defined set of specifications that define the state of values before and after the operation. The second example shows an **ADT rational number** as an ADT in mathematics:

ADT name:	Rational
Domain:	a/b (where *a* and *b* belong to the ADT integer)
Operations:	Addition, subtraction, multiplication, and division
Rule(s):	b != 0 (Thou shall not divide by 0.)

Let us look at another example that does not belong to the field of mathematics. This time we define an **ADT thermostat** to set and monitor the temperature of some place:

ADT name:	Thermostat
Domain:	−50 to +50 (two arbitrary values)
Operations:	Turn on, turn off, initialize, change, display
Rule(s):	Some electrical or electronic circuit specifications

The ADT **stack** is a familiar computer science example with the following properties:

ADT name:	Stack
Domain:	A number of elements
Operations:	Initialize, push, pop, check empty status, check full status, get number of items in the stack
Rule(s):	The elements are inserted, inspected, and removed from one end only; in addition, the status of an empty stack is *True* if stack does not contain elements, and *False* otherwise; similarly, the status of a full stack is *True* if the stack size has been reached, and *False* otherwise

Notice that the above examples illustrate a single level of abstraction. In practice the data abstraction process, as well as procedural abstraction, normally leads to a hierarchy or collection of abstract data types, each with their own properties. In other words, an ADT should be viewed as a collection of interrelated abstractions. An example of such an ADT would be geometrical shapes, such as point, line, square, rectangle, triangle, parallelogram, circle, diamond, and so on. Therefore, a hierarchy of data abstractions for a geometrical shape, such as a square, may be created as the following:

First:	**ADT name:**	Point
	Domain:	*x* and *y* coordinates of type ADT integer
	Operations:	Initialize point, display point
	Rules:	*x* and *y* are on the same plane

Second:	**ADT name:**	Line
	Domain:	Two values of type ADT point
	Operations:	Initialize line, determine length, display length
	Rules:	Two points are on the same plane
Third:	**ADT name:**	Square
	Domain:	Four values of type ADT line
	Operations:	Initialize, move, rotate, compute area, compute perimeter
	Rules:	The lines are connected to each other with 90° angles

As we have seen, in data abstraction the data are considered an important and integral part of application development. We bind both the data and basic operations on the data together as a single abstract data type. Therefore, the entire system is viewed as a group of abstract data types interacting together. Data abstraction such as this has the following advantages:

- There is little or no global data in the application. Data and operations are united in such a way that the logical building blocks of the system are no longer algorithms, but abstract data types.
- Each abstract data type can be easily modified without having to disturb the original code. This allows you to reuse and incorporate many of your types in different projects.
- Code becomes free from the original program specifications and hence you can adapt, change, refine, and improve the code more readily.

There are several languages such as Pascal, Ada, Smalltalk, and C++ that support the notion of abstraction. The advantage of C++ over the others is that it is widely used in industry and has been recognized as a suitable language for managing today's complex applications.

6.4   C++ AND DATA ABSTRACTION

Remember that data abstraction is a technique to invent a new data type based on its functionality. A new data type is normally defined in terms of either the intrinsic (built-in) data types of a language or the abstract data types created by the programmer. For example, we declared our ADT stack as *integer* type, which is an intrinsic or standard type; we declared the ADT line and ADT square based on the user-defined *point* type and *line* type, respectively. Since the eventual phase of data abstractions is implementation, we need a language that provides some of the basic ingredients needed to construct an ADT. These ingredients include the standard data types and some facilities to extend the language's capabilities.

C++ is a powerful language that provides a rich set of built-in data types, including *char, short, int, long, float,* and *double,* as well as its *class* facility for implementing abstract data types. A C++ class, as we will see later in this chapter, contains a number of features and concepts that allow programmers to abstract new data types as if they were an integral part of the language. Listed below are other features of C++ that make it suitable for designing and implementing abstract data types. They will be covered extensively in this chapter.

- Versatile functions:
  Overloaded functions
  Inline functions
  Default-parameter functions
  Variable parameter functions
- Templates for dealing with generic data:
  Function templates
  Class templates
- The *this* pointer
- Overloaded operators

Self-Check Questions 1

1. Briefly explain the purpose of data abstraction.
2. Explain the following terms in your own words:
   domain
   primitives
   rules
3. Define an ADT time, as an entity, and define its properties as presented in this chapter.

6.5   DESIGNING AND IMPLEMENTING ABSTRACT DATA TYPES

After defining an abstract data type, the programmer's next step is tying it to reality. This means that its domain must be represented and its primitive operations must be implemented on a computing system. Something that previously was system-independent must be re-worked in order to be executed in an implementation platform. Note that this process can still lead to platform independent code; that is, processing logic that uses an ADT (client code) can be developed without regard to how the type is represented or how the operations are implemented. This process, which is a part of the application's design, includes two steps:

- Representation
- Specification

    Representation involves encapsulating the domain of an abstract data type. In C++ it is achieved using basic scalar *arrays, structures (struct),* and/or *class.* As we will soon see, the C++ class with all its built-in features and concepts is well suited for representation purposes. Specifications, on the other hand, describe the allowable operations of an abstract data type and can be realized through C++ functions.

6.6   C++ CLASS

A class describes the common characteristics of a domain of objects. It allows program-mers to create their own program-specific data types and unify their **representation** and **operations** under one umbrella. A C++ class has the following attributes:

- Tag name
- Data members
- Member functions
- Access levels for selected regions
- Self-referencing pointer *(this)*

As far as the first three attributes are concerned, there is no difference between a *struct* and a simple, single-level *class* construct. The distinction between the two starts with the access levels in class definitions. As we have said earlier, class members are by default private to their class. This means that the class variables that are private can be accessed only by the member functions of the same class and no other part of the program. Member functions are usually declared public to provide interfaces, whereas data members are typically declared private or protected. Examine the following program carefully. It defines a class called *Part* as a new data type and creates an object of that type using the class name *(Part)*. In addition, note that the class uses two new keywords, *private* and *public,* to specify the access level of its data members and member functions. These keywords are called *access specifiers.*

```
const int length = 32; // for part names
class Part
{
    private:  // Specifies the following data members as private.
        long int  _PartNo;
        char      _name[length];
        double    _price;

    public:   // Specifies the following member functions as public.
        void Init();     //function prototype to initialize data members
        double GetPrice() {return _price;}
        void DisplayInfo()
    {
        cout  <<'\n' << _name
              <<'\t' << _PartNo <<'\t'<< _price;
    }
};   //End of class Part
```

Note: We will use the underscore character (_) with the names of class data members as a style matter throughout this chapter to mark them off clearly and separate them from the corresponding parameters used in class interfaces.

```
// Definition of function Init()
// Notice the use of the scope resolution operator (::)
// between the class name and function name to indicate
// ownership of the function.  Class Part is the owner of
// function Init().

void Part::Init()
{
    cout << "\nEnter Part number -->:      ";
    cin  >> _PartNo;
    cout << "\nEnter Part name -->:        ";
```

Figure 6.1   The Class *AutoPart*

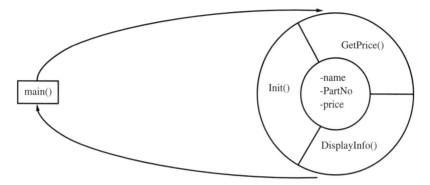

```
cin.getline(_name, length, '\n');  // Read the name.
cout << "\nEnter price -->:      ";
cin  >> _price;
}   //end of function Init
```

Figure 6.1 illustrates the concept of the class, its member data, and interface functions.

```
              // A driver program (client) to implement class Part

#include <iostream.h>
void main()
{
    Part AutoPart; //AutoPart is an object.
    AutoPart.Init();
    cout<<AutoPart.GetPrice();
    AutoPart.DisplayInfo();
```

As the client of class *Part,* the main function has access to the public section of the class only. A class has data and functions (interfaces). The public interfaces—those declared as *public*—is what the world knows; the private, mostly data, is a matter of implementation and needs to remain accessible to class interfaces and nothing else.

Exercise

---

1. Use the following code after class *AutoPart* and see what happens. (Can you guess?)

```
#include <iostream.h>
void main()
{
    Part  AutoPart;
    AutoPart.Init();
    cout  << '\n'  << AutoPart._price
                    << '\t'  << AutoPart._name
              << '\t'  << AutoPart._PartNo;
}
```

2. Given the following class declaration for an ADT integer, as we discussed earlier in this chapter, write the necessary code (implementation) for the class interfaces and test your code by writing a short client (driver) program.

```
#include <iostream.h>
//**************************************************
//                                                 *
//   class           Integer                       *
//   Purpose:        To implement an ADT integer.  *
//                                                 *
//**************************************************
class Integer
{
  private: //representation of the ADT integer
           int  _data;

  public:  // specifications for ADT integer:
                  // operations
           void Add( int );
           void Subtract( int );
           void Multiply( int );
           void Divide( int );
           void Modulus( int );

                  // initialization
           void Init();

                      // output
           void Print();
};  // end of class Integer
```

Self-Check Questions 2

1. Compare and contrast a class and a structure.
2. What is meant by the term *access specifiers?* Why does a class need them?
3. Explain the following terms:

   Specification for the operations

   Representation of the ADT

   Implementation of the operations
4. Devise the ADT book and provide as many operations as seem appropriate for selling books in bookstores.

In the following sections, you will examine the powerful features of C++ constructors and destructors. They play a critical role in initialization, cleanup, and other operations associated with resource allocation and de-allocation.

The Constructor Function

We used function *Init()* to initialize the data members of our class Part in the previous example. Although this method of initialization works well, C++ provides its own facility, called a **constructor** function. A constructor function is a member function that is used to create, initialize, and copy the objects of a class automatically. In other words, a constructor removes responsibility of initialization from the user, thus preventing human error. Let us now rewrite the previous program, using class *Part,* by removing the function *Init()* and

adding a C++ constructor function instead. Note that it will be defined like any other function, except that it has the same name as the class it belongs to and no return type.

```cpp
#include <iostream.h>
#include <string.h>

const int length = 32;   // for part names

class Part
{
  private:   // Defines private members of the class.
             long int   _PartNo;
             char       _name[length];
             double     _price;

  public:    // public interfaces of the class
             // class constructor
             Part( long int, char*, double ); // constructor prototype
             double  GetPrice(); // Returns an object's price.
             void DisplayInfo(); // Displays an object's information.

             ~Part() {}; // class destructor (discussed later)
};

/////////////////////////////////////////////////

// Implementation code (definition of functions)
// class constructor
Part::Part( long int PartNo,  char* name,  double price)
{
  _PartNo = PartNo;
  strcpy( _name, name);
  _price = price;
}

// function GetPrice
double Part::GetPrice()
{
  return _price;
}

// function DisplayInfo
void Part::DisplayInfo()
{
  cout << endl << _name
       << '\t' << _PartNo
       << '\t' << _price;
}

/////////////////////////////////////////////////

void main()
```

```
{
  // Create an object by invoking the class constructor.
  Part  AutoPart( 1234567L, "vanity mirror",  25.25 );

  cout << AutoPart.GetPrice(); // Displays price.
  cout << endl;

  AutoPart.DisplayInfo();// Displays all the information.
}

~Part(){}; //destructor (discussed later)
};          //end of class Part
```

Another advantage of constructor functions is localization. That is, if you see an object produces undesired contents, you should first check the constructor of the object and be sure of proper initialization.

When a programmer creates an object as an instance of a class, the constructor function is invoked automatically. As a consequence, the run-time system provides the memory required for initializing its members of the object and the constructor does the required initialization. Constructors have certain characteristics. They

- use the same name as the class they belong to.
- do not return any values (not even *void*)—they are *void by default.*
- may be included more than once in a class, each with a different parameter list; that is, a class may have **overloaded constructor functions.**
- may have an empty parameter list, known as a *null* or default constructor; as a consequence, the declaration of its object(s) does not require parentheses.
- may have any number of default parameters.
- cannot be a member of a *union.*
- cannot be inherited (though a derived class can call the base class's. constructors)
- cannot be declared *static, const,* or *volatile.*
- cannot be called explicitly by client code.

Remember also that if you do not provide a constructor function, the compiler will generate a default constructor. The compiler-generated constructors may cause severe errors when dynamically allocated data members are involved.

A constructor may have default parameters. Note that having a default-parameter constructor and a default constructor together in a program causes ambiguity error, as shown in the example. The class ambiguous has two constructors, one without parameters (default constructor) and one with a default parameter list. Both constructors are invoked in the same way to create an object of the class as shown. As a consequence, the compiler will generate a fatal error.

```
class  ambiguous
{
private:
          float    _radius;              ...
          float    _height;
public:
```

```
          //default constructor
          ambiguous() { _radius = _height = 0; }

          // constructor with default parameters
          ambiguous( float = 0.0,    float = 0.0 );
                            . . .
                            . . .
                            . . .
};

ambiguous::ambiguous( float radius, float height)
{
     _radius = radius;
     _height = height;
}



//a driver program to demonstrate the reason for ambiguity error
void main()
{
     //  The compiler does not know which constructor to invoke in the
     //  following declaration.
     ambiguous   object;  // Causes error: compiler's confusion.
                            . . .
                            . . .
                            . . .
};
```

The Destructor Function

As discussed earlier, each time you create an object of the class, the program automatically executes a constructor function to enable you to initialize the object members. In a similar way, C++ allows you to define a *destructor* function for cleanup purposes that automatically executes when an object goes out of scope. The key points about the class destructor are that it

- uses the same name as its class with the symbolic tilde (~) before it.
- does not return any values.
- may not occur more than once in its class; in other words, a destructor cannot be overloaded.
- has an empty parameter list.
- cannot be a member of a union.
- cannot be inherited; it can be called if it is used with a fully qualified name, such as *ClassName::~ClassName.*

Consider the following program that uses an ADT called *Rectangle* with two constructors and one destructor. Notice that one of the constructors has parameters and the other one does not use any initializers.

```
Class Rectangle
{
 private:
```

```
            Int    _length, int _width;
      public:

                // inline code for class interfaces
                Rectangle(int  length, int width)
                {
                  _length = length;
                  _width  = width;
                }

                Rectangle()
                {
                   _length = _width = 0;
                }

                int area()
                {
                   return _length * _width;
                }

                ~Rectangle() {};
      };
```

> **Remember:**   You may omit a destructor that does not use code (e.g., statements using the
> *delete* operator) and get the same result. An example of such a destructor is *~Rectangle() {}* in
> the above class.

```
class Rectangle
{
 private:
         int    _length;
         int _width;
 public:

         // inline code for class interfaces
         Rectangle(int  length, int width)
         {
           _length = length;
           _width  = width;
         }

         Rectangle()
         {
           _length = _width = 0;
         }

         int area()
         {
           return _length * _width;
         }
```

```
        ~Rectangle() {};
};


// driver program for testing the ADT Rectangle

#include <iostream.h>
void main()
{
  Rectangle  MyRoom( 10, 20 ); // Uses the parameterized constructor.
  Rectangle  YourRoom;  // Uses the default constructor.
  YourRoom = MyRoom; // compiler assignment
  cout  <<  MyRoom.area() <<  '\t'
        <<  YourRoom.area(); // Displays 200        200
}
```

A class destructor automatically removes the instances (objects) of the class. If the class does not contain dynamically allocated storage, it does not require code between its braces ({}). However, if it has used the *new* operator to dynamically allocate memory, it requires the *delete* operator to free the space. For example, if a data member of a class is defined as

```
double*    SalesData;
```

we may create an array by using the following statement in the class constructor:

```
SalesData = new int[ 12 ]; // for 12 months
assert( SalesData  != 0.0 );
```

The destructor of the class will free the allocated memory as shown:

```
delete    []SalesData;
```

> **Note:** If the *new* operator has used square brackets ([ ]), the *delete* operator needs square brackets, too. The square brackets used with the *delete* operator, as shown in the example, should be left empty, preceded by the data member to be deleted. The square bracket also indicates that you need to delete more than one cell. As a result of the delete operation, the storage will be removed but the pointer variable will stay until the termination of the program.

Self-Check Questions 3

1. What are the rules for writing a destructor function?
2. When is a destructor called?

Overloaded Constructors (Default, Parameterized, Copy)

As we have seen before, a class may have more than one constructor function. Consider the following example, using a class called *Address Book,* to demonstrate this concept.

```
const  int NameLength  = 32,
           AddressLength = 128;


class AddressBook
```

```
{
  private:
          char    _name[NameLength];
          char    _address[AddressLength];

  public:
          //default constructor
          AddressBook();

          //constructor with parameters
          AddressBook(char*, char*);

          //copy constructor
          AddressBook( AddressBook& );

          void show();

          // destructor
          ~AddressBook();
}; //end of class AddressBook
```

The class *AddressBook* has three constructors, as follows:

1. Default constructor   `AddressBook();`

   A default constructor allows you to create objects without initializers. This means that declaration of the object does not require parentheses, as shown:

   Function Prototype

   ```
   AddressBook();
   ```

   Function Call

   ```
   AddressBook book;
   ```

   This type of constructor is used by the compiler to create objects without details.

2. Constructors with parameters, **parameterized constructors**, as shown below:

   Function Prototype

   ```
   AddressBook( char* name, char* address);
   ```

   Function Call

   ```
   AddressBook MyBook("James Dean", "120 Burk St.");
   AddressBook YourBook("Edward Brown Jr.", "100 W.49th Ave.");
   ```

3. Copy constructors, which copies one object into another member:

   Function Prototype

   ```
   AddressBook(const AddressBook& Info);// using reference
   parameters
   ```

   Function Call

   ```
   AddressBook YourBook(MyBook);
   ```

A copy constructor creates a new object from an existing object. The basic syntax of the prototype for copy constructors is

```
ClassName (const ClassName& object);
```

Notice that copy constructors *must* take a single parameter, which is a *const* reference to the class. If you pass the argument by value, it will cause an infinite recursion. The reason for this undesired phenomena is that the compiler would call the copy constructor when making a copy of the argument on the stack. This would again call the copy constructor when making a copy of the argument on the stack, and so on.

A common usage for this kind of constructor is

```
AddressBook    MyBook("Kaytlyn",   "100 49th W. Avenue");
AddressBook    YourBook(MyBook); // Uses copy constructor.
```

Both *MyBook* and *YourBook* now have identical contents.

There is a legitimate reason for including a copy constructor as a part of the class design. However, in the absence of such an explicit copy constructor, the compiler will provide the default copy constructor of its own for copying semantics. What the compiler does is known as **memberwise** copying or **shallow** copying. Memberwise copying is bitwise copying for built-in types and involves calling the custom assignment function, using the *assignment* operator (if available), or the default copy constructor /assignment functions.

A question may arise as to why we need a user-defined copy constructor when the compiler can provide one. To answer this question, let us see how the compiler handles the copying process through its default copy constructor. The compiler performs a type of copying known as *shallow* copying; that is,

- All the values stored in data members are copied from the old object to the new one;
- If the member is a pointer, this means that only the value of the pointer (the memory address) is copied. The object pointed to is not copied. As a consequence, the object pointed to will be *shared* among two or more objects.

The shallow copying of the default copy constructor of the compiler may lead to undefined results due to the fact that the destructor of both objects, the old one and the new one, will try to deallocate the same memory space.

In order to circumvent the compiler's shallow copying, programmers should define a copy constructor to perform a deep copy. That is, all the members, whether or not of type *pointer,* are copied from one object to another. Thus, memory spaces are specifically allocated to each member of the new object.

> **Note:** The shallow copying problem occurs when classes allocate data dynamically.

We are going to demonstrate this problem by writing a short program using a class called *string*. The class *string* uses a *pointer* variable as well as a copy constructor.

```
#include <string.h>
#include <iostream.h>
          class  string
          {                              |
             private:
```

```
            int    _length;
            char   *_text; // a pointer to character(s)

        public:
            string() { _length = 0; _text = NULL; } // default constructor
            string( const char* text); // constructor
            string( const string& objstr); //copy constructor
            void display() const { cout << _text; }
            ~string();// destructor to free the allocated memory
};


        //   Constructor, with a value parameter of type
        //   pointer to char, i.e., a line of text
        string::string(const char*  text)
{

            _length = strlen(text);   // from string.h
            if ( _length == 0 )
                _text = NULL;
            else
                {
                  _text = new char[_length+1];
                  strcpy(_text, text);   // from string.h
                }
        }


        //   Copy constructor identified by a reference parameter of
        //   type class object
        string::string(const string& objstr )
{

            _length = objstr._length;
            if (objstr._text == 0 )
            _text = NULL;
            else
                {
                  _text = new char[_length+1];
                  strcpy(_text, objstr._text);
                }
}


        // class destructor (to be discussed later)
        string::~string()
        {
        if (_text != 0)   // or if (*_text != NULL)
        delete []_text;
        }
```

The following driver program demonstrates the application of the class *string*.

```
void main ()
{
   char* HeSaid = "...there is no new thing under the sun!";
    string  first(HeSaid); //  Creates an object from a text.
```

```
    string  next(first);    //  Uses copy constructor.
    first.display();        //  Displays the statement.
    cout << endl;           //  Starts a new line.
    next.display();         //  Displays the same statement.
}
```

You should note that the statement

```
string next = first;
```

also involves copy constructor.

Figure 6.2 shows what happens when we use our user-defined copy constructor. The copy constructor creates an identical copy of an object.

We said earlier that if we do not provide a user-defined copy constructor, the compiler will provide the default copy constructor of its own. However, the compiler will not allocate separate memory to the member that is of type *pointer to object*. Instead, it will copy the value of its pointer, *memory address 12CA,* as shown in Figure 6.3.

Figure 6.2   Use of the Copy Constructor

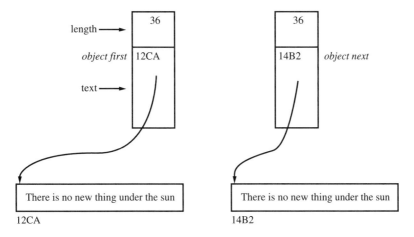

Figure 6.3   Use of the Compiler's Default Copy Constructor

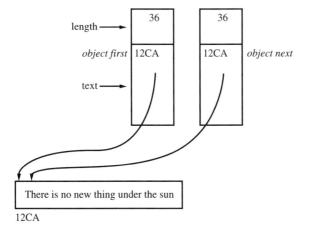

The problem with this copying method is that when the program goes out of scope, the destructor of the class will twice try to destroy the address of the same data member, which is not acceptable. Run the program and see the results for yourself. Test the program once with the copy constructor and once without.

You learned to call the copy constructor when you want to initialize an object to be a copy of another one. This is quite obvious. For example,

```
AddressBook    Mine( yours ); or    Mine = yours;
```

Copy constructors are also called whenever an object is passed by value to a function due to the need for storage. For example, in the following class declaration, the interface *rebate* uses an object of type *Date,* through pass by value, to check whether or not a particular purchasing date is entitled to rebate. Notice that pass by value involves overhead (extra time and space) and should be avoided whenever possible.

```
class  Date
{
  private:
        . . .
        . . .
        . . .
  public:
        Date( int = 0; int = 0; int = 0;) // constructor with default parameters
        Date( Date& ); // copy constructor
            . . .
            . . .
            . . .
        int rebate( Date );  // a pass by value example
        Date NextDate();  // returns an object of type Date

            . . .
            . . .
            . . .
};
```

Finally, the copy constructor is called when a function returns an object. For example, function *NextDate* returns an object of type *Date* and as a consequence, the copy constructor will be invoked.

Self-Check Questions 4

1. What is a constructor function?
2. In what sense is the constructor function unique?
3. What is meant by the default constructor?
4. Implement the functions of the following class definition and then write a driver function, *main(),* to show its application.

```
class student
{
    long    _StudentNo;  // private by default
  public:
        student();
        student(long int);
```

```
        ~student() {};
        long GetStNo() const
        {
            return _StudentNo;
        }
    };
```

5. Write a user-defined copy constructor for the *class Student*. Show how would you use it.

Constructor Conversion Functions

You may initialize the data members of a class using selected data members of other classes. This capability offers you the possibility of writing useful interfaces in both application and systems software. To understand this concept, let us write a simple program. The program defines an ADT called *date,* whose data members are initialized through the members of the time structure *tm* found in the *time.h* header file. You should know several things about the *time.h* header file before considering the next example.

- The structure *tm* holds the components of a calendar time, called the **broken-down time** as follows:

```
struct   tm
{
  int   tm_sec;      // seconds after the minutes
  int   tm_min;      // minutes after the hour
  int   tm_hour;     // hours since midnight
  int   tm_mday;     // day of the month
  int   tm_mon;      // month since January
  int   tm_year;     // years since 1900
  int   tm_wday;     // days since Sunday (0...6)
  int   tm_yday;     // days since January
  int   tm_isdst;    // Daylight Savings Time flag
};
```

- The *time.h* header file provides, among other functions, two functions called *localtime()* and *time()* as shown below, which return a *pointer* to the time structure of type *tm.*

```
        // Function localtime converts calendar time pointed to
        // by timer into broken-down time, expressed as local
        // time.

        // pre:  pointer to current time at address timer
        // post: pointer to structure time of type tm

            tm*    today = localtime(&timer);



        // Function time determines the current calendar time,
        // typically measured in seconds elapsed since midnight,
        // January 1, 1970.  If timer is not equal to Null, time
        // stores the current time at address timer.

        // pre:  pointer to current time at address Time
```

```
                             // post: pointer to time structure of type tm
                        tm* today = time(&timer);


        #include<iostream.h>
        #include<time.h>

                    class date
                    {
                        int _day, _month, _year;

                    public:
                        date() {}      //default constructor

                            //constructor conversion function
                        date(time_t);   // uses the system's time
                                void display()
                                {
                                    cout << "\nThe date is: "
                                        << _day << '/' << _month
                                        << '/' << _year;
                                }
                        };    // end of class

                        date::date(time_t timer)
                        {
                            // Obtain the current time and store it at
                            // address today.

                            tm* today = localtime(&timer);
                            _day   = today->tm_mday;
                            _month = today->tm_mon + 1;
                            _year  = today->tm_year;
                        }

                            void main()
                    {
                    // Read the time and date into
                    // variable calendar.
                    time_t calendar = time(NULL);
                    date  ThisDay(calendar); //Calls the constructor.
                    ThisDay.display();         //Shows today's date.
                    }
```

6.7   FROM DATA ABSTRACTION TO OBJECT-ORIENTED PROGRAMMING

According to Webster's dictionary, an object "denotes a person or a thing to which action or feeling is directed." You are an object, a car is an object, an airplane is an object, and a piece of paper is an object. Associated with an object are certain characteristics. For example, a person, as an object, has weight, a collar size, a waist size, height, blood pressure, and so forth. A car is an object that has weight, capacity, length, and so on. In addition, an object has certain behaviors and actions. For example, a car starts, moves, speeds up, slows down, and changes direction. Furthermore, an object may be tangible or intangible. Examples of intangible objects are mathematical domains such as integer number, real number, complex number, vector, matrix, and so on.

Regardless of its type, an object has certain values that determine its **state** and certain **behaviors** that are used to manipulate that state. Therefore, we may say that an object is something that exists, as a physical thing or a conceptual entity, and manifests some behavior when acted upon. Moreover, in contrast to a passive variable of given type, an object is an active entity. It can show reactions to other objects and manipulators in the program.

> **Note:**   State and behaviors indicate the existence of an object.

In programming, an object is an abstract data type that embodies certain attributes (data) and behaviors (functions). Similar to an ADT, an object is defined by its functionality, and we develop hierarchies of objects with their appropriate components and their conceptual boundaries via an abstraction process.

Objects exhibit three important characteristics:

* Encapsulation
* Inheritance
* Polymorphism

Let's take a closer look at each.

Encapsulation

Encapsulation places the data and implementation in a "capsule" and allows the outside world to get at it only by its interfaces. Encapsulation:

* Provides a mechanism to prevent clients from accessing data and operations that are to be hidden (information hiding).
* Provides a window to the object components through its open interfaces only.
* Defines an appropriate level of knowledge (data) and number of activities (functions) each object of the hierarchy should possess.

One example of encapsulation with which you are familiar is the C++ *iostream.h* file. The file has several levels of classes with appropriate provisions for each operating system. The details of these classes are hidden from the users. What you use are the objects, such as the *cin* and *cout* streams.

Encapsulation also provides a tool for managing the complexity of an application by breaking that complexity into small, manageable pieces and distributing them among individual objects.

Encapsulation controls the permission to access data members and member functions of a class through the keywords *public, protected,* and *private.* These keywords are also known as **access specifiers** with the following meanings:

- *Public* data members and member functions of a class are visible across the application; that is, other functions and classes can use them without any restrictions.
- *Private* data members and member functions of a class are not accessible outside the class.
- *Protected* data members and member functions of a class are accessible to its *derived* class(es) and to the class itself. It creates a wider scope of accessibility and facilitates inheritance among classes. Therefore, this mode is used when you anticipate that new classes may be derived from a particular class.

Finally, Object-Oriented Languages (OOLs) allow you to enforce encapsulation through mechanisms embedded in them.

The data members of a class, by default, are private. However, you may explicitly specify them as private, protected, or public. Furthermore, a class may have all three specifiers. Consider the following example, which demonstrates the use of access specifiers. The class *Book* shows the representation and specifications of the ADT *Book*. Notice that class *Book* has been planned to be used as a base class from which other classes can be derived. (Deriving a class from another class(es) is known as *inheritance,* which we will discuss later in this chapter.)

```
class  Book
{
  private:   // No outside access allowed.
      char* _title;
      char  _isbn[10]; // International Standard Book Number

  protected: // Access is limited to derived classes.
      double _price;
      void   ShowPrice() { cout << _price << "\n"; }

  public:    // public interface
      Book(char* title,  char* isbn, price);
      void   ShowData() { cout << _title << "\t" << _isbn
                               << "\n";
      ~Book() {};       // destructor function
};
```

Exercise

Write the necessary definition for the constructor of class *Book* and test it with a driver program.

Inheritance

The term **class inheritance** refers to the capacity of a class to inherit behavior and/or implementation from another class. Class inheritance allows an object to behave as an instance of one or more different classes. Through inheritance, you may create new classes from existing ones and build class **hierarchies** and **networks.** The class from which you derive is called the **base** class, and the new class is called the **derived** class. A class hierarchy is formed when the several layers of derived and base classes emanate from each other. On the other hand, a network is built around a class, which has several base classes. The latter is also called **multiple inheritance.** When you derive a class, the new class inherits all or some of the characteristics of its base class, depending on the class access provisions. In addition, the derived class typically adds new members to what it has inherited from the base class.

There are several design reasons to derive a class. One is to save development time. For example, if you need to create a class for an application and there is already another class available that is close to what you need, you could derive a new class from it simply by changing a few parts of the old class. Moreover, if you make some changes to the base class for performance improvement, the derived classes would benefit from those changes through inheritance. Another reason to derive classes is to build a class hierarchy and increase the functionality of the class. Class hierarchy allows true representation of data abstraction. (Derived classes also allow *polymorphism,* an important property of objects that is discussed later in this chapter.)

A derived class is defined by using its base class name with **colon (:) syntax** as shown. The colon syntax means *from;* that is, class *RectangleType* is derived from class *BaseType.*

```
Class RectangleType: public BaseType {...}
```

The decision to build derived classes is a design issue. Therefore, you should know exactly what you need from a base class—how its derived class suits the design of the application without disturbing any parts, and finally, what level of access is to be provided for inherited members as well as those of the new class. Also, always bear in mind that a derived class must be homogeneous with its base class(es). That is, a derived class must always be *a kind of* base class(es) plus more members. For example, permanent employees and temporary employees are a kind of employees, as shown in Figure 6.4. Therefore, you may design two separate classes, *permanent* and *temporary,* derived from class *employee.*

The derived class normally specifies the access level to its inherited members on the heading line of the class as *public, protected,* and *private:*

- *Public*: Specifies that the access permissions of the inherited members of the derived class will be exactly the same as they were in the base class
- *Protected*: This means that the public members of the base class will become protected and the protected members of the base class will become private
- *Private*: Restricts the access permission of all inherited members to private level

Table 6.1 summarizes the effects of access specifiers on inherited members of derived classes.

Figure 6.4   Example of Class

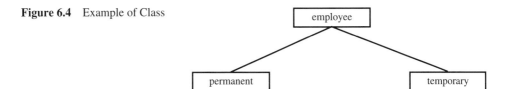

Table 6.1   Effects of Access Specifiers

Base Class Access Specifier	Privately Derived Access	Publicly Derived Access	Protectedly Derived Class
private	inaccessible	inaccessible	inaccessible
protected	private	protected	private
public	private	public	protected

The following simple program demonstrates the use of the inheritance concept. The program uses a base class for a geometric shape. Two other classes, *Rectangle* and *Circle,* are derived from the base class.

```
#ifndef __SHAPES_H    // protection against multi-inclusion
#define __SHAPES_H

#include<iostream.h>

const float pi = 3.14;

        //declaration of the base class
class SquareType    // a base-type class
{
 protected:    //Allows inheritance.
        int _Line;

    public:
    // constructor with default parameter
    SquareType(int length = 5){_Line = length;}
    int CalcArea()   {return _Line * _Line; }
    ~SquareType()   {}    // destructor

};      //End of class SquareType

//   class RectangleType, derived from SquareType
//   Note that the access mode of inherited members
//   will remain unchanged.



class RectangleType: public SquareType // derived class
{
    int _AnotherLine;   // private by default

 public:  // See the note after this class.
    RectangleType( int first, int second):
    // colon syntax using constructor call plus extra code
    SquareType(first) {_AnotherLine = second;}
    int CalcArea()   {return _Line * _AnotherLine; }
        ~RectangleType()   {};
};   //End of class RectangleType
```

The constructor of *RectangleType* may be written differently, as follows:

```
RectangleType::RectangleType( int first, int second)
{
    SquareType(first);  // constructor call
    _AnotherLine = second;
}


//declaration and definition of class CircleType
```

```
class CircleType: public SquareType
{
public:
   CircleType(int first): SquareType(first){}  // constructor call
   int CalcArea(){return _Line * _Line * int(pi);}
   ~CircleType()  {};

};       //end of class CircleType declaration and definition

#endif
```

The following program illustrates the application of derived classes: square, rectangle, and circle.

```
void main ()
{
//-----------Declaration of objects-----------
   SquareType          square(5);
   RectangleType       rectangle(10,20);
   CircleType          circle (100);

   cout<<square.CalcArea()     << endl;
   cout<<rectangle.CalcArea()  << endl;
   cout<<circle.CalcArea();
}
```

> **Note:** Derived classes do not inherit the constructors and destructors of the base class. They can call them to build the members of their own objects.

Self-Check Questions 5

1. Why do we use inheritance?
2. Explain the effects of different access specifiers in base and derived classes.
3. It is a good practice to leave the data member of the class *Private* and allow the derived classes to access the data through protected member functions. For example,

```
#include <iostream.h>

class  SquareType
{
  private:
        int    _Line;

  public: // using inline functions
        SquareType( int length = 5 ) { _Line = length; }
        int CalcArea()  { return _Line * _Line; }
        ~SquareType() {}

  protected:  // accessible to classes derived from SquareType
        int  GetLine() { return _Line; }  // returns the value of _Line
}; //end of class SquareType
```

```
class RectangleType : public SquareType
{
  private:
        int  _AnotherLine;
  public:
        RectangleType( int, int ); // constructor

        // Calculates area using inherited protected function.
        int CalcArea();
        ~RectangleType() {}  // destructor
}; //end of class RectangleType
```

Complete the interfaces of the derived class RectangleType by writing the necessary code and then write a driver program to test the class *RectangleType*.

Polymorphism

The term **polymorphism** refers to the ability to take on many shapes. In the context of object-oriented programming, it refers to the abilities of different objects in a hierarchy to respond differently to the same message. For example, we may develop a hierarchy of classes to manipulate different geometrical shapes such as a square, rectangle, triangle, and circle, with functions for computing the area, computing the perimeter, drawing, coloring, rotating, and displaying each. Across the hierarchy, we use the same names for functions that perform the same task, but for different shapes, for example, we will have a function called *rotate* in each class to rotate the respective shape in that class. Now through the *rotate* function, the user can send a message to any desired shape in order to manipulate that particular shape. Therefore, we can also say that *polymorphism* refers to the situation in which the methods in a class hierarchy respond in *different ways* to the *same message,* depending on the type of object for which the method is invoked. The following discussion is of virtual functions, which makes it possible to have true inheritance and polymorphism.

Virtual Functions

We use the modifier *virtual* with several things in the computer field. We have *virtual* memory, *virtue* terminals, *virtual* windows, *virtual* arrays, *virtual* functions, and *virtual* reality. What does *virtual* mean? In computing, it means that something "acts like it is there when it really is not."

When we say something is *virtual,* we mean "it is and it isn't." In the context of object-oriented programming, however, the name *virtual* does little to describe how virtual functions work. The C++ keyword *virtual* before a function name guarantees the proper execution of the functions with identical names in the class hierarchy by keeping track of where the function call originated. When you use nonvirtual functions in a normal situation, the compiler resolves the calls to functions at compile time, which is termed **early binding**. Early binding sometimes causes problems when referencing function members with identical names in different classes. To avoid early binding problems, C++ allows you to declare the function name as *virtual.* The keyword *virtual* in front of the function makes the compiler postpone the binding decision until run time. In other words, the path of execution is determined at run time, not at compile time. The late binding process is accomplished through a special table that C++ sets up for every object type that contains or inherits a *virtual* function member. The mechanics of what happens inside the compiler is quite complicated and involves some overhead. To simplify the process, virtual functions are implemented by way of a table of function pointers or addresses that point to virtual functions of the class. By maintaining this table, C++ can determine a path of execution that would not be possible to determine at compile time. When a virtual function is called, the language looks up the function address in the table to implement the correct one.

To better understand the concept of **virtual functions,** let us examine an example. It has a hierarchy composed of two classes, one is called *Dog* and the other is called *Puppy.* The class *Dog* has three functions: a constructor, an *OrderScript()* function, and an *Order()* function. The derived class *Puppy* has a constructor and an *OrderScript()* function. There are two functions with the same name *(OrderScript()),* but with different tasks in these classes. We expect a dog called Tana to do one thing and another one called Smokey to do something else. However, when you run the code, you will see that both Tana and Smokey do the same thing. The reason is that when you issue the order, the function *Order()* is executed within the scope of class *Dog,* the base class. In other words, the function *OrderScript()* of the class *Dog* will be run instead of the *OrderScript()* function of the class *Puppy.* To resolve this undesired phenomenon, simply declare the function *OrderScript()* as a *virtual* function. Try to run this program with and without the keyword *virtual.*

```
#ifndef __DOGS_H
#define __DOGS_H

class dog
{
protected: // for inheritance purpose
    char* _name;

public:
    dog(char* name);  //constructor with a parameter
    ~dog() {delete []_name; } // Free up the array.
    virtual void OrderScript() // inline function
    {cout << _name << ", "
        << "Go and fetch the ball\n"; }
    void Order () {  OrderScript(); }
};       //end of class dog

dog::dog( char* name)  // definition for constructor dog
{
    _name = new char[strlen(name) + 1];
    strcpy(_name, name);
}


        //a derived class puppy
class puppy : public dog  // puppy derived from dog
{
public:
```

```
    puppy( char* name) :dog(name){} // Calls class dog.
    void OrderScript()
    {
        cout << _name
             << ", "
             << "Go and chase the dog.\n";
    }
}; //end of class puppy

#endif
```

Following is a program to demonstrate the binding issues between classes.

```
void main ()
{
    dog    MyDog("Tana");
    puppy YourDog("Smokey");
    MyDog.Order();
    YourDog.Order();
}
```

You should have noticed that the problem with class functions arises when different objects in a hierarchy of classes share the same function name. One possible solution is obviously to use different names. However, this is neither practical nor useful from a design viewpoint. Additionally, it creates a program that is difficult to read and interpret. Another solution is to overload the function member name and use the *scope resolution* operator (::) to refer to the base class member. Although this solution is not that bad, in a large project with many classes, the details of referencing would become confusing. C++ has resolved these problems by providing the *virtual* functions as an intrinsic facility of the language. Using *virtual* functions with their power and flexibility is another major step toward true object-oriented programming. In summary, when there are several functions in a class hierarchy, with the same name and argument types, and you want to localize the effects of these functions within their own class scopes, declare the function in the highest level class as *virtual*. Finally, the *virtual* declaration is for member functions only. It does not apply to data members of base and derived classes.

Pure Virtual Functions and Abstract Classes

In C++ you may assign a value to a function for various reasons. One such reason is declaration of a **pure virtual function** in which the function is set to zero as shown:

```
void display( ) = 0;
```

A *pure virtual* function is a class member function that is declared but not defined. In other words, it does not have an implementation of its own. The derived classes must provide the necessary implementation for pure virtual functions.

When a function is declared as pure virtual, the class in which the class is present is called an **abstract class.** Note that an **abstract** class cannot be used for declaring any objects as instances of that class. It is defined, as a design requirement, to serve a base for other classes. Finally, any class derived from an abstract class may either define a matching function to override the *pure virtual* function or leave it pure. In the sample program following this discussion, the class *Date* is an abstract class, containing a *pure virtual* function, and as a consequence the following declaration is not permissible.

```
Date LaborDay(3,9,1996);
```

Consider the program to see how a *pure virtual* function works. The example is an implementation of ADT Date, as an abstract class, which accepts numeric values and prints out the same date either in numeric format (25/9/1998) or in alphanumeric notation (25 September, 1998).

```
#include<iostream.h>

class Date    // an abstract class with a pure function
{
        protected: // for inheritance purposes
                int _day, _month, _year;
        public:
          Date(int day, int month, int year)
                { _day = day; _month = month; _year = year;}

                // pure virtual function
          virtual void display()= 0;  // do nothing
};  // end of class Date

// class Numeric derived from class Date


    class Numeric: public Date
    {
    public:
        Numeric(int day,int month, int year):Date (day, month, year)
        {}; // Calls constructor Date.

void display()
    {
        cout << endl  <<  _day  << '/' << _month
            << '/'   <<  _year;  // inherited data
    }
    // end of class Numeric
    };
            // class AlphaNumeric derived from class Date
class AlphaNumeric: public Date
{
    public:
AlphaNumeric(int day, int month, int year)
    : Date(day, month, year){} // Calls constructor Date.
      void display();
};  // end of class AlphaNumeric

// definition for function display of class AlphaNumeric
```

```
void AlphaNumeric::display()
{
    static char* MONTHS[]={   "Wrong Month", "January",
                              "February", "March", "April",
                              "May", "June", "July", "August",
                              "September", "October",
                              "November", "December"
                         };

        (_day < 1   || _day   > 31)? cout << "wrong day!" :
         cout << _day << ' ';
               (_month < 1 || _month > 12)? cout << MONTHS[0]:
               cout << MONTHS[_month];
               cout << ", " << _year;
        };

    void main ()
    {
            Numeric       *Today =  new Numeric(15,2,1998);
            AlphaNumeric  *Another =  new AlphaNumeric(15,2,1998);
            Today->display();
            cout << endl;
            Another->display();
            delete Today, delete Another;  // required statements
    }
```

Polymorphism Revisited

Now that you understand how virtual functions work, take a look at an example that uses polymorphism to see how the same object takes on different forms. We are going to use the previous program that used the class *dog* and class *puppy*. This time we will use a pointer variable rather than an ordinary data type. Note that when you use a pointer to the base class, you may use the same pointer for its derived classes too, since a derived class is considered as *a kind of* a base class. As a consequence, depending on the instance object pointed to by the pointer, the result of the operation will differ.

In the following program, the same interface name, *order,* causes different behaviors for different objects.

```
#include <iostream.h>
void main ()
{
    dog *subject = new dog("Tana");
    subject->Order();
    delete subject;
    subject = new puppy("Smokey")
    subject->Order();
    delete subject;

}
```

Exercise

Review the following program and see how it implements polymorphism by using *virtual* functions, in the class declaration and pointers in the application. The program can be expanded into a more useful application.

As we said earlier, *polymorphism* refers to a situation in which objects belonging to different classes respond to the same message, usually in different ways. Since objects of different classes have different sizes and different configurations, we cannot use ordinary variables for addressing different objects of dissimilar classes. Instead, we should use pointer variables because pointer types are addresses and they require the same amount of memory regardless of the size of their related objects.

```cpp
#include <iostream.h>
class Accounts        //  banking accounts
  {
        public:
            virtual void AcctType()
            { cout << "\nAccount unknown";}
};

        //  first level of derived classes from class Accounts

        //  first derived account from class Accounts
        //  Registered Retired Savings Plan (RRSP)

class RRSP : public Accounts
{
        public:
            void AcctType ()
            { cout <<"\nRegistered Retired Saving Plan"; }  };

        // second derived account from class Accounts
// Guaranteed Investment Certificate
class GIC : public Accounts
{
        public:
            void AcctType () { cout << "\nGuaranteed"
                                    << "Investment"
                                    << "Certificate"; }
};

        // third derived account from class Accounts
        // Mortgage Account
class Mortgage :public Accounts
{
        public:
            void AcctType () { cout << "\nMortgage account"; }
};

        //  fourth derived account from class Accounts
        //  All-In-One Account (combination account)
class AllInOne : public Accounts
{
        public:
```

```
                void AcctType ()
                {
                        cout << "\nAll in one account";
                }
};


//   second level of derived classes

//   first derived account from class AllInOne
class Saving : public AllInOne
{
        public:
                void AcctType ()
                { cout << "\nsaving account"; }
};


//   second derived account from class AllInOne
class Checquing : public AllInOne
{
        public:
                void AcctType ()
                { cout << "\nChecking account"; }
};


//   third derived account from class AllInOne
class CreditLine : public AllInOne
{
        public:
                void AcctType ()
                {   cout << "\nPersonal line of credit"; }
};


    // a driver program to test the classes and demonstrate
    // how objects with different internal structures share
    // the same external interface: true polymorphism
void main ()
{
    Accounts accts;
    RRSP     rrsp;
    GIC      gic;
    Mortgage mortgage;
    Saving   saving;
    Checquing check;
    AllInOne all;

//   using pointers to call virtual functions
    Accounts     *AnAccount;
    AnAccount = &rrsp;
    AnAccount->AcctType( );  cout << endl;

    AnAccount = &all;        cout << endl;
    AnAccount->AcctType();

    AnAccount = &saving;
    AnAccount->AcctType();
```

```
// using references to call virtual functions

        Accounts&    RetireAcct = rrsp;
        RetireAcct.AcctType();   cout << endl;

        Accounts&    SaveAcct   = saving;
        SaveAcct.AcctType();
}
```

Virtual Base Classes

A hierarchy of derived classes in a project may lead to a major ambiguity problem. Consider a situation in which a base class AB is the immediate parent of the derived classes A and B, and both in turn are the parent classes of class C. Then, suppose that class AB defines a data member x (see Figure 6.5). This member will be inherited by A and B from their immediate parent AB. Since class C is derived from both A and B, it inherits x from both parent classes. This phenomenon in which one class inherits two sets of one data x is not acceptable and causes a resolution problem for the compiler.

To avoid the duplication of inherited members, the intermediate base class(es) (i.e., class A and class B) must specify their parent class as a **virtual base class.** As a result of this declaration, only one set of members will be inherited from a *virtual base* class regardless of how many inheritance paths exist between the base and derived classes.

The following example using a *virtual base* class demonstrates the application of this concept. The ADT **utility** defines four pieces of data to be used by its immediate children, *Electricity* and *Gas* classes, and its grandchild *UtilityBill.* Since class *UtilityBill* inherits two identical copies of the same data through classes *Electricity* and *Gas,* we declared these two classes as virtual to prevent ambiguity problems for the compiler.

```
#include<iostream.h>
#include<string.h>

const int Length = 128;   // for the title of the company
class Utility
{
public:
    short        _Watt;
```

Figure 6.5   Duplication of Inherited Members

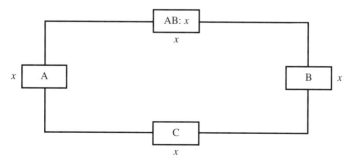

```
    short     _CubicFeet;
    double    _WattRate;
    double    _GasRate;
}; // end of class utility

// class Electricity derived from class utility
class Electricity: public virtual Utility
{
public:
    Electricity(short Watt, double WattRate)  // inline
        { _Watt = Watt;  _WattRate = WattRate;}

    void display()
    {
        cout.width(8);
        cout.setf(ios::floatfield|ios::showpoint);
        cout.precision(2);
        cout << "$ " <<  _Watt * _WattRate;
    }

    ~Electricity()  {};
    }; // end of class Electricity
    // class  Gas derived from class Utility
    class Gas: public virtual Utility
    {
    public:
        Gas(short CubicFeet,  double   GasRate)
        { _CubicFeet = CubicFeet; _GasRate= GasRate; }
        void display()
    {
        cout << "  $" << _CubicFeet * _GasRate;
    }
        ~Gas()   {};
};// end of class Gas

    // class UtilityBill derived from
    // class Electricity and class Gas
class UtilityBill: public Electricity, public Gas
{
        char _title[Length];

public:
    UtilityBill(char* title, short Watt, short CubicFeet,
        double WattRate, short GasRate) :
    Electricity(_Watt, WattRate), Gas(_CubicFeet,
                                       GasRate)
            {strcpy(_title, title);}


void display();      // prototype
~UtilityBill()  {}   // class destructor

};  // end of class UtilityBill
```

```
        // definition for function display
void UtilityBill::display()
{
   cout << "                        " << _title;
   cout << endl << "Total consumption for this month: "
        << endl << "Electricity: " << _Watt << " kilowatts";
   Electricity::display();
   cout << endl << "Gas: "<< _CubicFeet << " cubic feet";
   Gas::display();
}

// a driver program to test the classes
void main ()
{
   UtilityBill  Bill("B.C. Utilities Corp.", 200, 30, 4.0,
                     5.0);
   Bill.display();
}
```

Self-Check Questions 6

1. What is to be achieved by the following class using virtual functions? What is the output of the program?

```
Class message
{
 public:
        virtual  announce()
     {  cout << "\nThis is a test."; }
};

class next : public message
{
 public:
        virtual  announce()
     {  cout << "End of test."; }
};

void main()
{
        message  *ptr = new message;
        ptr ->announce();
        delete ptr;

        ptr = new next;
        ptr ->announce();
        delete ptr;
}
```

2. What would happen if you removed the keyword *virtual* from the *announce* function in the derived class *next?*

The *This* Pointer

The *this* pointer is a C++ facility that provides member functions with access to the current object, the object in active state, or an object that is in action or is being executed. Each time a member function is invoked, the *this* pointer comes into existence pointing to the current object as an implicit parameter of the function.

Consider the following program as a partial code for basic operations on fractions. It uses the *this* pointer in three functions. Also, note that when a function returns an object pointed to by the *this* pointer, the returning object is of type reference. That is, the *this* pointer allows an object instance to refer to itself.

```cpp
#include <iostream.h>

const int BadDenominator = -9999;

class FractionType
{
 private:
        int    _numerator;
        int    _denominator;
 public:
        FractionType(int = 0, int = 1);   // constructor
        FractionType (const FractionType& );   // copy constructor
        FractionType& SetNumerator( int ); // set numerator
        FractionType& SetDenominator( int );// set denominator

        void display();
        ~FractionType() {}
};   //end of class

//definition of interfaces
//class constructor
FractionType::FractionType( int numer, int denomer )
{
 _numerator   = numer;
 _denominator = (denomer == 0 )? BadDenominator: denomer;
}

//copy constructor
FractionType::FractionType(const FractionType&  fraction)
{
 if( &fraction != this)// guard against self assignment
   {
     _numerator   = fraction._numerator;
     _denominator = fraction._denominator;
   }
}

// set the numerator of the fraction
FractionType&   FractionType::SetNumerator( int numer )
{
```

```
 _numerator = numer;
 return *this; // return the object in process
}


// set the denominator of the fraction
FractionType& FractionType::SetDenominator( int denomer)
{
 _denominator = (denomer == 0 )? BadDenominator: denomer;
 return *this;
}

// function display
void FractionType::display()
{
 (_denominator == BadDenominator)? cout << "\illegal fraction!" :
 cout << _numerator << '/' << _denominator;
}

void main()
{
 FractionType    first(2,0);
 FractionType    second;

 second.SetNumerator(1);
 second.SetDenominator(2);

 first.display();
 cout << endl;
 second.display();
}
```

A function that returns an object pointed to by the *this* pointer should return a reference to the object. For example,

```
FractionType&  SetNumerator( int ); // set numerator
```

returns a reference to the class object through the *this* pointer. This attribute of the *this* pointer allows you to concatenate several function calls into a single one. For example

```
second.SetNumerator( 2 );
second.SetDenominator( 3 );
```

can be written as:

```
second.SetNumerator( 2 ).second.SetDenominator( 3 );
```

What happens in the above statement is that the dot operator (.) associates from left to right; thus the concatenation evaluates to the leftmost component and returns a reference to its right component, reducing the statement to

```
second.SetDenominator( 3 );
```

Finally, you can use the *this* pointer to prevent self-assignment operations. Self assignment means assigning an object to itself, which may cause severe errors when the objects contain dynamically allocated data members. We used this feature in our copy constructor as a guard against self assignment.

Self-Check Questions 7

1. Explain the meaning of the *this* pointer in your own words.
2. Is there a place(s) that we could remove the *this* pointer statement in the following program and achieve the same results?

```
#include <iostream.h>
class ThisExample
{
  private:
          int  _number;

  public:
          ThisExample() { _number = 0; }
          ThisExample( int );

          // to increment data member by d value

          ThisExample& Inc( int );
          void show();
          ~ThisExample() {}
}; // end of class

//  definition of class interfaces

// class constructor
ThisExample::ThisExample(int number)
{

  this->_number = number;  // equivalent to (*this). _number
}

// function Inc to increment data member by a given value
ThisExample&  ThisExample::Inc( int IncValue)
{
  this-> _number = this-> _number + IncValue;
  return *this;// return the object in process
}

void ThisExample::show()
{
  cout << _number;
}

void main()
{
  ThisExample   first;  // Uses null constructor.
  ThisExample   second( 125 );// another initialized object
```

```
    first = second.Inc(10);
    first.Inc(15);
    first.show();// displays 150
  }
```

Static Data Members and Static Member Functions

Remember that a static variable retains its value between successive function entries. It is also allocated and initialized to zero, by default, at compile time and its memory will remain allocated for the duration of the program. You may also initialize a *static* data member explicitly. C++ allows you to declare data members of a class to be *static* too. A *static* data member also remains in existence for the duration of the program. As a consequence, the value of a static data member is shared by each instance object of the class in which it is declared. You should also note that a static data member in order to exist must be defined outside of the class at file scope. In other words, the declaration of a static member inside the class does not automatically define the variable. The following example shows how a *static* data member is declared. The class has a regular piece of data and a *static* one.

```
#include <iostream.h>
class share
{
    // The following static data keeps track of the
    // number of objects created in the application.
    static int _tally;        // static data
    int        _value;        // normal data
public:
    // The class constructor increments the
    // static data each time an object is
    // created.
        share(int number = 10) // constructor
          {_tally++; _value = number; };
        void display() {cout << "\n" << _value
          << '\t' << _tally;
};

// The following destructor shows how to
// decrement the static data each time its object goes out of
// scope.
~share()  {_tally--; };
};

// The following file scope declaration is
// a syntax requirement for static data members.

int share::_tally;
```

In the above class, the *static* data member has been initialized to zero by default. Therefore, each time an instance of the class is constructed, its value will be incremented by 1, thus keeping track of how many objects have been created. Now run the following program and see the result.

```
void  main()
{
   share first(100);
   first.display();            //displays      100      1

   // another object
   share second(200);
   second.display();           //displays:     200      2
}
```

You may initialize a *static* data member explicitly by the declaration outside the class as shown here:

```
int share::_tally = 0;
```

Another method for initialization of a *static* member is through a separate, overloaded constructor. Consider the following example:

```
#include <iostream.h>
class share
{
   static int _tally;
   int        _value;
 public:
   // a constructor to increment the static member
   // each time an object is created
   share(int number = 10) {_tally++; _value = number;}
   share(int num, int StaticData) { _value = num;
   _tally = StaticData;}


   void display()
   {cout << endl  << _value
        << '\t' << _tally; }

   ~share()  {_tally--; };// decrements static data.
};

int share::_tally; //syntax requirement

void main()
{
   share first(100,100);    //constructor with static data
   first.display();         //displays:     100      100

//another object
  share  second(200);       //constructor without static data
  second.display();         //Displays:     200      101
}
```

Static data members are normally manipulated through specific member functions, which in turn are declared as *static*. In other words, to manipulate *static* data members you may use static functions. Now look at the following example.

```
#include<iostream.h>
class share
{
    static int _tally;
    int _value;
public:
    share(int num = 10){_tally++; _value = num;};

         // static function to manipulate static data
    static void  InitStatic(int StaticData)
         {_tally = StaticData; }

    void display()
{cout << endl << _value <<'\t'<< _tally;}
~share()  {_tally--; }
};

int share::_tally;       //syntax requirement

void main ()
{
    share     first(100);

    first.InitStatic(50); // Uses the static function.
    first.display();      //Displays:    100     50

//another object
    share       second(200);// Does not use static function.
    second.display();      //Displays:         200     51
}
```

Note that static member functions have two properties:

- They are fully accessible throughout the program even if you have not created an object for their classes:

```
void main ()
{
    // A statement to show how to reference a static data member
       when no objects exist
    share::InitStatic(50);
    share     object(100); // Includes static data member with a
                                  value of 50.
    object.display();       // Displays 100    50.
}
```

- They have no access to nonstatic data members, and as such they cannot use *this* pointers to point to an object.

Self-Check Questions 8

1. What does a *static* data member do?
2. What are rules for using *static* data members?

3. Write the necessary implementation of the following class declaration:

```
class  UserFee  // This class charges you 25.50 for each object.
{
        static  float  _fee;

    public:
        UserFee();
        void DisplayFee();
};

float  UserFee::_fee = 25.50;
```

4. Write a driver program, *main()*, to test the class.

Constructors in the Base and Derived Classes

The execution of constructors in the hierarchy of base and derived classes is done in a top-down fashion, starting from the base class followed by its derived class(es). This order of constructor calls guarantees that all the members of the base class object are built first to enable the derived class object(s) to access its public and protected members. Respecting the arguments of the constructor function of a derived class, the declaration of the constructor will specify the argument(s) to be used from the base class as well as its own arguments. For example, in the derived class *RectangleType* (unsigned *int* first, unsigned *int* second):BaseType(first), the colon (:) syntax specifies that an argument from the base class constructor, *first,* in addition to its own argument, *second,* is used in the class constructor.

In cases where there are multiple constructors in a base class, the compiler will call the appropriate constructor based on the types of arguments in the base constructor argument list, as specified by the derived class constructor.

Destructors in the Base and Derived Classes

Class destructors execute under two conditions:

1. The program goes out of scope or
2. You use the *delete* operator anywhere to free up the memory allocated to the objects of the base and derived classes.

Under the first condition, the execution of destructor functions follow a bottom-up process. That is, when an object of a derived class goes out of scope, the destructor for the derived class executes first, and then the destructor of the base class executes. This order of destructor calls is important because of dependencies. Notice that if a destructor executes as the result of the *delete* operator, only the base destructor will execute and the process will skip the destructor of the derived class. As a consequence, the memory allocated to the derived class will never be deleted and will cause serious problems. To solve this problem, declare the destructor for the base class to be a virtual function.

Note that objects that are built by the *new* operator require the *delete* operator for their removal if the object contains data members. The following example illustrates these concepts:

```
#include<iostream.h>
#include<string.h>
class furniture
{
   private:
   char* _model;

   public:
   furniture(char* model)
       { _model = new char[strlen(model)+1];
          strcpy(_model, model);
       }
       virtual ~furniture()  // virtual destructor
       {
          cout <<"\nfurniture's destructor is "
              << "running!";
          delete []_model;
       }
};

// class desk derived from class furniture
class desk : public furniture     // derived from furniture
{
   private:
       int _length, _width, _height;

   public:
       desk(char* model, int length, int width, int height)
          : furniture(model)    // base constructor call

       { _length = length;
         _width = width;
         _height = height;
       }

   ~desk()   {  cout <<"\ndesk's destructor is "
                   << "running!";
              }
};
```

The following program allocates memory for an array of objects of *base* type using the *new* operator.

```
void main ()
{
   furniture item[2];//pointers to base class
   item[0] = new desk("MDR123P-OFFDEP",2,3,6); // object desk
   item[1] = new furniture("PPR779-OFFDEP");   // object furniture
   // The following statement calls the base class constructor.
   // The following statement calls the desired class constructor.
   delete item[0];//Points to derived class desk.
   delete item[1];//Points to base class furniture.
}
```

In the function *main( )*, the pointers in the array are of type *furniture*, and the *delete* operator calls the destructor function for the class even when the pointer points to a *desk* class object unless the destructor of class *furniture* is declared as virtual. It is also advisable to declare the destructors as *virtual* when you have *virtual* function members in your class declaration.

In summary:

- A constructor function cannot be declared *virtual,* because it is called to create an object of a specified class and is explicitly called.
- Destructor functions may be declared *virtual.* In this case, the destructors of derived classes override the base class destructor, even if they have different names.

Exercise

1. Study, run, and observe the behavior of the following program.
2. Suggest *virtual* declarations, where appropriate, to produce the desired results.

```
//   The following program demonstrates the concept of virtual
//   functions in a derived class.

#include<conio.h>
#include<string.h>
#include<iostream.h>

//******************   class location ******************
class location
{
protected:  // for inheritance purposes

     int _x, _y;  // coordinates
public:
location()  {_x = 1; _y = 1;  }  // default constructor
     location(int x, int y){_x = x; _y = y;}  // constructor
     ~location() {};
};//End of class location

//************** class character **************
class character: public location
{
protected:
     char _symbol;  // a character
public:
     character() : location()  {_symbol = '*'; }
     void show()    {cout << _symbol;  }
     void setc(char ch)  { _symbol = ch; }  // initialize
     void MoveTo(int x, int y)
          { _x = x; _y = y;
               gotoxy(x,y); show();
}
     ~character() {} };
```

```
//end of class character

//*************** class string **************
class string : public character
{
    private:
    char* _text;  // string
public:
    string(char* text) // constructor
{ _text =   new char[strlen(text)+1];
          strcpy(_text, text);
    }
    void show()  {cout << _text; }
    void sets(char* another) // Initialize _text.
    { _text = new char[strlen(another)+1];
          strcpy(_text, another);
}
    ~string()  {delete []_text;  }
};  //end of class string

//a driver program to use the class hierarchy
void main()
{
    string      TheString("");  // null string
    TheString.sets("This is a string");
    TheString.MoveTo(40,25);
    TheString.show();

}
```

The Keyword Friend

One of the basic concepts of data abstraction is information hiding, through which the data members and member functions of a class are protected by staying under the full control of their class. C++ implements this concept by using different access permissions or specifiers, including *public, private,* and *protected.* While this is an important concept, there are times that the design of the application requires more freedom of access between certain components of the software in order to avoid using an unnecessary number of global data and functions. To accommodate this requirement, C++ offers *friend* functions to create a bridge between non-related classes, objects, and methods (functions). One may argue that other object-oriented languages do not use such a facility and still do the job admirably. While that is true and although we should try to do our tasks without using friend functions as much as we can, there is a counter argument that the use of the keyword *friend* in C++ makes programs cleaner, easier, and, to some extent, more efficient. The use of *friend* eliminates the need for calling member functions and thus reduces overhead. To make a function or a class *friend,* we use the keyword *friend* before the identifier.

The common uses of the keyword *friend* are

- to grant a nonmember function access to private and protected members of a class.
- to bridge two unrelated classes.
- to operate on a pair of objects when one of them is external.

Note that when function is declared as friend, this function is *not* considered a class member. As a consequence, *friend* functions are not privileged to have *this* pointer. Also, the keyword *friend* is only used with the function prototype and not with the function definition. Now that the concept is clear, let us write some examples to understand it better.

The first example shows how a nonmember function, function *format,* can have access to the private members of a class by declaring it as a friend of the class. Note that since the function *format* in class *date* is not a member function, we did not use the *scope resolution* operator (::) for the definition of the function. Also, look at the main program and see that we called function *format* directly, like any other function without any restrictions.

Function *format* in the *date* determines the name of the day specified by a date using the *dd/mm/yyyy* notation. For example, if you specify a date as 28/10/1982, the program will display "Wednesday." The function uses the formula known as **Zeller's congruence** to find a code in the range of 0 to 6 representing seven days of the week starting with Sunday.

Code = (int (2.6m - 0.19) + d + y + y / 4 + c / 4 - 2c) % 7 where

m is the month number with March = 1, April = 2, May = 3, ..., December = 10, and January and February are 11 and 12 of the previous year.

y is the year in century; for example, in 1996, the value of *y* is 96.

c is the century number in year; for example, in 1996, the value of *c* is 19

For example, if the date is 27/10/1982, the program will display:

```
Wednesday - 27/10/1982

#include<iostream.h>
#include<stdlib.h>
#include<string.h>

class date
{
    int _day,  _month, _year;

public:
    date()  {};
    date (int day, int month, int year)
        {_day = day; _month = month; _year = year; }
friend void format(date);     // nonmember
void display()
{
    cout << endl;
    date dte = *this;
    format(dte);
```

```cpp
    cout << " - " <<  _day << '/'
         << _month << '/'  << _year;
}
~date()  {}
};

//****   definition for function format ****
void format(date dte)// nonmember function
{
   if (dte._month < 3)  //(before March)?
   {
      dte._month += 10;  // Adds 10 to month
      dte._year—;        // decrement year
   }
   else
      dte._month -= 2;            // subtract

   // find century
   int Century = dte._year / 100;

   // find year
   int Year = dte._year % 100;

   // Finds day's code
   int DayCode =
      ((int)( 2.6 * dte._month - 0.19 ) +
      dte._day + year + year/4 + century/
      4 - 2 * Century )  % 7;

   switch(DayCode)
   {
      case 0:    cout << "Sunday";      break;
      case 1:    cout << "Monday";      break;
      case 2:    cout << "Tuesday";     break;
      case 3:    cout << "Wednesday";   break;
      case 4:    cout << "Thursday";    break;
      case 5:    cout << "Friday";      break;
      case 6:    cout << "Saturday";    break;
      default:   cout << "Wrong date!";break;
   }
}

void main ()
{
   date   birthday(27,10,1982);
   birthday.display();//Wednesday 27/10/1982
   cout<<endl;

   // Calls function format as a public interface.
   format(birthday);
}
```

The second example demonstrates the use of the keyword *friend* to bridge two classes. There are two classes called *Brother* and *Sister*. Class *Sister* has declared class *Brother* as *friend* to grant it permission to access its members.

```cpp
#include<iostream.h>
#include<string.h>
const int size = 32;   // size of full names

class Sister
{
private:
      char _name[size];
public:
      Sister(char* name)  { strcpy(_name, name); }
      void ShowSister()  {cout << _name;   }
      friend class Brother; // grants access
}; // end of class Sister

class Brother
{
   char _name[size];
public:
      Brother(char* name)  {strcpy(_name, name);   }
      void ShowSister(Sister she)  // Friendships grants access.
          {
                cout<< she._name;    // through friendship
                cout << " is " <<  _name  << "'s "
                    << "sister";
          }
};  // end of class Brother

void main ()
{
   Brother   brother("Cyrus");
   Sister    sister("Suzanne");
     // display Suzanne is Cyrus's sister
   brother.ShowSister(sister);
}
```

Finally, the third example uses the keyword *friend* to bridge two classes, this time for a different purpose. We write a function to convert one class into another and call it a **converter function.** Class converter functions are in fact operator functions that give different meanings to classes and create different classes based on available ones. Note that class converter functions have the following characteristics:

- They use the keyword *operator* as a function name
- They do not require type of returned value on the function headings
- They have a return statement

It has been assumed that you are familiar with binary, octal, and hexadecimal numbers. The brief explanation is just to help you understand the following examples.

Although computers operate on binary numbers (0s and 1s), it is more convenient for us to view this data in a more understandable format such as octal (base-8) and hexadecimal (base-16). Both systems are being used to represent computer memory and instructions because:

- Binary numbers are usually long and cumbersome to read.
- There is a direct correspondence between binary and octal or hexadecimal numbers. Each digit in an octal number represents 3 binary bits (0 or 1) and each digit in a hexadecimal number represents 4 binary bits.
- The storage elements of computers are multiples of 8 or 16. Thus it is convenient to show their contents as octal or hexadecimal.

Table 6.2 shows how each sequence of 3 bits translates into a decimal (base-10) or octal value.

Each octal digit position represents a power of 8. This is helpful in calculating the value of an octal number. The process is called place-value summation.

$$1234_8 = 1 \times 8^3 + 2 \times 8^2 + 3 \times 8^1 + 4 \times 8^0 = 512 + 128 + 24 + 4 = 668_{10}$$

Figure 6.6 converts a decimal number to octal. The conversion algorithm divides the decimal number successively by 8: remainders in reverse order of occurrence produce the octal result. For example, number $668_{10} = 1234_8$. Consider the successive divisions:

Table 6.2 Conversion Table

Binary	Decimal	Octal	Binary	Decimal	Octal
000	0	0	1001	9	11
001	1	1	1010	10 (base)	12
010	2	2	1011	11	13
011	3	3	1100	12	14
100	4	4	1101	13	15
101	5	5	1110	14	16
110	6	6	1111	15	17
111	7	7	10000	16	20
1000	8	10 (base)			

Figure 6.6 Conversion Algorithm

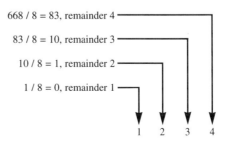

```
#include<iostream.h>
#include<string.h>
#include<stdlib.h>

class Decimal;      //forward reference for the compiler: optional
class Octal         // for base 8 numbers
{
private:
     int* _OctValue;
public:
     Octal(int number  { _OctValue = new(int);
                         *_OctValue = number;
                       }
     void show()  { cout <<*_OctValue; }
     friend class Decimal;      // Grants access.
};   // end of class Octal

class Decimal
{
private:
     int *_DeciValue;
public:
     Decimal(int num = 0)  { _DeciValue = new(int);
                             *_DeciValue = num;
                           }
     operator Octal();  // class converter
};

// definition for function operator Octal: converter



Decimal::operator Octal()      //no return type declaration
{
    const int base   = 8;      //octal base
    Octal      value = 0;
    int        answer = 0;

      // using successive divisions
      while (*_DeciValue != 0)
      {
         int remainder =*_DeciValue % base;
         answer = answer * 10 + remainder;
         *_DeciValue /= base;
      }
      return answer;
  }

void main ()
{
```

```
Decimal      Decival = 27; // decimal value
Octal        OctalVal = 0; // octal value

        //converts from decimal to octal
    OctalVal = DeciVal;
    OctalVal.show();
}
```

Self-Check Questions 9

1. Why do we need to use *friend* functions in C++?
2. Compare and contrast *friend* functions with member functions of their befriended class.

Type Conversion Using Type Cast Operators

In the previous example, we used a C++ operator function to convert our class *Octal* to class *Decimal.* The operator function that we used for class conversion is also known as the **type cast operator function.** *Type cast operator* function can also be used for changing a user-defined class into a standard data type such as *integer* and *float.* To understand this concept better, we will write a program using the *type cast operator* function to change our class of octal type to integer type. Notice that the *cast operator* function does not have a return type declaration in its function header; however, it is a member of the class for which it serves a purpose. As said earlier, to convert an octal value to decimal, write the octal number in its place-value summation form and then evaluate. For example, $1234_{(8)} = 1 \times 8^3 + 2 \times 8^2 + 3 \times 8^1 + 4 \times 8^0 = 512 + 128 + 24 + 4 = 668_{(10)}$.

```
#include<iostream.h>
#include <math.h> // for power function

class Octal
{
private:
        int*       _OctVal;
public:
        Octal( int number = 0 ) // constructor function
        { _OctVal = new int; *_OctVal = number; }

        operator int(); // type cast operator
        void display()
        { cout << endl << *_OctVal; }
};   // end of class Octal

//definition for the type cast function
Octal::operator int()   // no return type declaration
{
   const int base = 8; // octal base

   int decimal = 0; // for the answer
   int length  = 0; // for the length of the octal value
   int hold    = *_OctVal; // Keeps a copy of the data member.
```

```
      // Find the length of the octal number.
      while(hold != 0)
      {
         length++;
         hold /= 10;
      }

      // Find the decimal value: place-value summation.
      hold = *_OctVal;          // Get a copy of the octal val.
      int index = 0;
      while( index < length )
      {
         int digit = hold % 10; // get a digit
         decimal   = decimal + pow(base, index) * digit;
         hold /= 10; // shed the digit
         index++;
      }

      return decimal;
}

void main()
{
   Octal      OctalNumber = 1234;
   int        DecimalValue;

// OctalNumber.display();// Displays 1234.

   DecimalValue = (int)OctalNumber;  // type cast conversion
   cout << endl << DecimalValue; // Displays 668.
}
```

Operator Overloading

C++ allows you to redefine the operators of the language in order to meet specific needs of an application. This ability is called **operator overloading.** One of the overloaded operators that you are familiar with is the (>>) operator that you already use for both input and shift operations. You can further overload the same operator for other reasons.

Overloading operators is designed to extend the capabilities of the language for implementing the real-life needs of abstract data types. For example, if you have an ADT of type class *date,* you can create instances of this class and apply the operator (-) on them to find out the time difference between two dates. Consider the following piece of code:

```
date  BirthDay(15,9,1965);
date  Today(1,1,1998);
date  age;
age = Today - BirthDay;
Today.ShowAge();
```

In the above code, the operator (-) is applied to two objects, *Today* and *BirthDay* to find the age of the person on January 1, 1998. In other words, the operator (-) can now be used for both numeric values, as originally intended, and for the objects of class *Date*. This is what is meant by operator overloading. Note that while operator overloading is an attractive feature of the language, many programmers prefer to use it infrequently. They write member functions such as *add(), subtract(), remove(),* and so on, instead. However, if you decide to overload an operator, try not to change the original meaning of the operator. For example, do not change the meaning of the operator (+) to mean subtraction. You should also consider the following restrictive points in operator overloading:

- You cannot overload the following operators
    - ::   (member-access operator)
    - .   (member-access operator)
    - .*   (member-access operator)
    - ?:   (conditional expression or operator)
    - sizeof (size operator)

  because they have a predefined meaning when applied to a class object.
- You cannot create new operators other than those specified in the language.
- You cannot change the existing meaning of operators for standard types. For example, the operator (+) has a meaning for numerical values; you cannot change it to (-).
- You cannot change the number of operands an operator takes.

    To overload an operator, you have to create a function operator, similar to that used for the type case operator function, with the following general format:

```
type  operator symbol(argument list)  // argument list
{
      function body
}
```

    Examine the following program using the class *Date* and the *friend* operator function to overload the (-) operator in order to apply it to the objects of type class *Date*.

```
#include <iostream.h>
#include<stdlib.h>
#include<string.h>

class Date
{
  private:
          int _day, _month, _year;
  public:
          Date(int day = 0, int month = 0, int year = 0 )
          { _day = day; _month = month; _year = year; }

          //overloading (-) sign
          Date operator-( Date& ); // prototype

          void ShowAge()
          {
            cout << _year  << " years, "
                 << _month << " month(s) and "
```

```
                            << _day    << " day(s)";
                      }
}; // end of class Date

//definition of overloaded operator function
Date   Date::operator-( Date& second)
{
    Date   diff; // Difference: uses constructor with default
                 // parameters.

    //The this pointer points to the implicit parameter.
    Date   first = *this; // for computing Diff = first - second

    if ( first._day < second._day ) // Adjust days for subtraction.
        first._day += 30, --first._month;

    if ( first._month < second._month ) // Adjust months.
        first._month += 12, --first._year;

    //calculate the difference
    diff._day   = first._day   - second._day;
    diff._month = first._month - second._month;
    diff._year  = first._year  - second._year;

    return diff;
}

void main()
{
    Date   BirthDay(4,1,1940);
    Date   Today(1,1,1998);

    Date   age = Today - BirthDay;
    age.ShowAge(); // displays 57 year(s)  11 month(s) 27 day(s)
}
```

The operator functions may be defined as either ordinary functions or as *friend* functions. If you define them as ordinary functions, they should have at most a single argument. For example, in class *Date,* we overloaded the *minus* operator (-) using a single argument called *second.* When there is a single argument, there is an implied, invisible, left-side object in the argument list, too. That left-side argument can be accessed through the *this* pointer. Let us have a closer look at the statement used in the main function:

```
Date age = Today - BirthDay;
```

The object *Today* is the left-side object that we used in our subtraction operation. Although we did not declare it directly as a function argument, we were able to reference it without any problems.

When you want to use two instances of a class or two instances of two different classes as arguments for operator overloading, you must use a *friend* operator function. Let us now overload the *minus* operator (-) using two instances of class *Date.* Note that the code for both is the same; the only difference is the function declared as *friend*. As a consequence, it is not a member of class *Date* anymore and we do not use the *scope resolution* (::) operator to show its affiliation. Also, remember that the keyword *friend* is used with the function prototype and not with the function definition (implementation).

```
#include <iostream.h>
#include<stdlib.h>
#include<string.h>

class Date
{
  private:
          int _day, _month, _year;
  public:
          Date(int day = 0, int month = 0, int year = 0 )
          { _day = day; _month = month; _year = year; }

          //overloading (-) sign
          friend Date operator-( Date&, Date& ); // prototype

          void ShowAge()
          {
            cout << _year  << " years, "
                 << _month << " month(s) and "
                 << _day   << " day(s)";
          }
}; // end of class Date

//definition of overloaded operator function
Date  operator-( Date& first, Date& second)
{
   Date  diff; // Difference: uses constructor with default
parameters.

   if ( first._day < second._day ) // Adjust days for subtraction.
     first._day += 30, --first._month;

   if ( first._month < second._month ) // Adjust months.
     first._month += 12, --first._year;

   //calculate the difference
   diff._day   = first._day   - second._day;
   diff._month = first._month - second._month;
   diff._year  = first._year  - second._year;

   return diff;
}

void main()
```

```
{
    Date  BirthDay(4,1,1940);
    Date  Today(1,1,1998);

    Date  age = Today - BirthDay;
    age.ShowAge(); // displays 57 year(s)  11 month(s)  27 day(s)
}
```

Note that an overloaded operator may or may not be a class member. The question is: When should an operator be declared as a member or a nonmember *(friend)?* There are simple rules that govern the declaration of member and nonmember operator functions in C++. We classify the operations of the operator functions as *binary* and *unary*. **Binary operators** such as addition, subtraction, multiplication, and division have two operands, whereas **unary operators** require only one operand. In binary operations, consider the following:

- An overloaded operator function to be declared as a member requires a single explicit argument. Its second argument, as an implicit one, is accessed through the *this* pointer. The implicit operand provides access to the left-side operand of the binary operations.
- An overloaded operator function to be declared as a *friend* requires two explicit arguments because it does not have access to the *this* pointer. The rule also applies to other *friend* functions. That is, when there are two arguments, as objects of similar or dissimilar classes the function should be declared as *friend*.

For unary operators (e.g., -5, +5), consider similar rules. An overloaded operator function, as a class member, needs no arguments. On the other hand, a *friend* function in the same role needs one explicit argument. For example, examine the following program in which the *unary* operator minus sign (-) has been overloaded using overloaded operator function. It does not have any arguments and is a member of the class *(SignedVal)* in which it has been declared. Also, notice how the main function calls the operator function in order to change a data member, but with a different sign.

```
#include<iostream.h>
class SignedVal
{
    int _value;
public:
        SignedVal(int num)  {_value = num; }
        void display()      {cout << _value; }
        int operator-() {return -_value; }
};

void main()
{
    SignedVal first(50), second(-50);
    int         number;
    number =   -first;
    first.display(),    cout << '\t' << number;
    number = -second;
    cout << endl;
    second.display(),    cout << '\t' << number;
}
```

Self-Check Questions 10

1. Does overloading functions and operators give you more power to write abstract statements and expressions? Can you accomplish this by doing something else?
2. Can you overload all C++ operators?
3. Given the following class declaration,

```
class date
{
private
    int _day, _month, _year;
public:
    date( int day = 0,  int month = 0, int year = 0 );
    friend date operator+(date&  first, date& next);
    void print();
};
```

can you think of an application that can use the overloaded plus operator (+)?

The programs that you have seen in this chapter, so far, contained overloaded minus (-) and plus (+) operators. Let us take a look at an example using as many overloaded operators as possible. The familiar class *Integer,* representing integer numbers, is a suitable vehicle to discuss the concepts involved. You can trace the implementation of the class interfaces to see how they work. The class *Integer* is given below:

```
class Integer
{
  private:
        int    _IntegerValue;
  public :
      Integer(int IntegerVal = 0 );  // constructor function
      Integer operator+(int);   // allows object + n
      friend Integer&  operator+(int,  Integer&); // allows n + object
      Integer operator++();     // allows prefix operation: ++object
      Integer operator++(int);  // allows postfix operation: object++
      Integer operator--(); // allows prefix operation: --object
      Integer operator--(int);  // allows postfix operation: object--
      Integer  operator= ( const Integer&  );    // overloaded assignment
      friend Integer& operator+=(Integer&, int); // allows  object1  += number
      friend Integer operator-(const Integer&, const Integer&); // object = obj1-obj2
      friend  istream& operator>>( istream&,  Integer& ); // for input operations
      friend ostream& operator<<( ostream&, Integer& );  // for output operations
      void display( ) { cout << endl << _IntegerValue; }  // to display information

      ~Integer() {}; // destructor function
}; // end of class Integer
```

Overloading the Plus (+) Operator

The first overloaded operator function, *operator+*(int), allows you to increment an integer number by a certain value. This function also has access to the *this* pointer because it is a member function. Now consider the implementation of the function.

```
// overloaded operator to increment the data member by a certain value
Integer    Integer::operator+(int value)
{
    Integer  number; // a temporary value
    number = *this;  // Assigns the current object.
    number._integerValue += value; // increments
    return number;
}
```

We may also use the *this* pointer in a different way and achieve the same results. Notice that the new version returns a reference type through the *this* pointer. Compare the two versions and see how the same results may be achieved using different statements.

```
Integer&  Integer::operator+(int value)
    {
        _IntegerValue += value;
        return *this;
    }
```

Let us write the class constructor and examine the following code to see the result:

```
// class constructor
Integer::Integer( int IntegerValue )
{
    _IntegerValue = IntegerValue;
}

#include <iostream.h>
void main()
{
    Integer    data(100);   // Constructs the object.
    data = data + 10;       // Increments the object by 10.
    data.display();         // Displays 110.
}
```

Notice that the function *operator+*(int value) uses an object of class *Integer* type through its *this* pointer. This object, as we said earlier, is an implicit left-side argument of the function. As a consequence, when the function accepts the notation *object + value* and not *value + object*. For example, *data + 10* is correct, but *10 + data* is incorrect. There are two alternatives for solving the problem.

- Write another function as shown below. Notice that the new function simply invokes the previous one. Furthermore, the function is declared as *friend* because it has two explicit arguments.

```
friend    Integer&   operator+( int,    Integer& );  // prototype

Integer&  operator+(int   value,   Integer&  number) // implementation
{
    return number + value;   // A reference type returns reference too.
}
```

Now, the following code is valid.

```
#include <iostream.h>
void main()
{
  Integer    data(100);   // Constructs the object.
  data = data + 10;       // Increments the object by 10.
  data.display();         // Displays 110.
  cout << end;

  data = -10 + data;      // Increments the object by -10.
  data.display();         // Displays 100.
}
```

- There is another way to overload the plus (+) operator using a single *friend* function to handle both expressions such as *data = data + 10* and *data = 10 + data.* You may replace the two existing overloaded operator (+) functions with this one.

```
friend Integer operator+( Integer&,   Integer& );  // function prototype

Integer operator+( Integer&  left,   Integer&  right) // function definition
{
  Integer   temp;
  temp._IntegerValue = left._IntegerValue + right._IntegerValue;
  return temp;
 }
```

In the above example, the *friend* function *operator* uses explicit arguments as the left and right operands. The result of this is an implicit conversion. That is, if one of the operands is a simple integer, the compiler will apply an implicit conversion provided by the constructor function to the integer operand, creating a temporary object of correct class type for the addition operation.

An object, similar to C++ variables, can also be incremented or decremented using specially developed operator functions for these purposes. The next section addresses this topic.

Overloading the (++) and (--) Operators

The class uses the following prototypes for auto-increment (++) operator. Note the similarity between the two functions. The prefix function does not require any parameters while the postfix function uses just an *int* type without an identifier.

```
// prefix auto-increment (++) operator function
Integer Integer::operator++( )
{
  _IntegerValue += 1;
  return *this;
}

// postfix auto-increment (++) operator function
Integer Integer::operator++(int) // uses dummy int
{
  _IntegerValue += 1;
  return *this;
}
```

Why do you need two functions for the same operation? You may want to use the operator (++) in both prefix and postfix as shown in the program below. The function with parameter signifies a postfix operation to the compiler.

```
void main()
{
   Integer     data(100);
   ++data;   // prefix increment
   data++;   // postfix increment
   data.display(); // Displays 112.
}
```

Note that the same concept applies to the auto-decrement operator too. Now let us see how other overloaded operators are developed and used. The next overloaded operators are for assignment operators (=, + =).

Overloading Assignment Operators (=, + =)

Overloading assignment operators, also known as custom assignment member functions, allows you to perform memberwise assignments. They are used primarily when an object has data member(s) of *pointer* type and you want to be sure that data members receive memory spaces, rather than pointer assignments, as a result of default assignments by the compiler. Notice that if the class does not provide an overloaded assignment operator function, the compiler provides, by default, shallow copying. Therefore, since the class *Integer* does not involve data members of pointer type, it is safe to conclude that it does not need any overloaded assignment operators. After completing the interfaces of this class, you will see another example that requires both deep copying and an overloaded assignment operator. However, remember that the overloaded assignment operator function allows assignment chaining, such as:

```
Integer            first(100);
Integer            second,  third;

third = second = first;  // chaining assignment
third.display(); // Displays 100.
```

Now let us write the custom assignment operator function.

```
// overloaded assignment operator
Integer  Integer::operator= ( const Integer&  integer )
{
   if (&integer != this) // protects against self assignment
   _IntegerValue = integer._IntegerValue;
   return *this;
}
```

In the above example, we used the simple assignment operator. You may also overload the compound assignment operators, i.e., (+ =) for using in the program. As a result of an overloaded compound assignment operator, you will be able to write such statements as:

```
Integer            data(120);
data += 30;
data.display(); // Displays 150.
```

Now let us write the custom assignment operator function for the compound assignment operator (+ =).

```
Integer& operator+=(Integer&  integer, int  number)
{
  integer = integer + number;  // Uses the overloaded plus operator.
  return integer;
}
```

Another overloaded operator of the class *Integer* is the overloaded minus (-) operator, which allows you to subtract one object from another. The code for this is given below:

```
//  definition of the overloaded operator minus (-)
Integer operator-(const Integer&  left, const Integer& right)
{
  Integer      integer;
  Integer._IntegerValue = left._IntegerValue - right._IntegerValue;
  return integer;
}
```

As a result of the above function, you may now write the following statements in your program.

```
Integer      first(100),  second(102);
Integer      third;

third = first - second;
third.display();  // Displays -2.
```

There are two other operators, the insertion (<<) and extraction (>>) operators, that if overloaded allow you to input and output objects of a class similar to standard data types.

Overloading the << (Insertion) and >> (Extraction) Operators

The true spirit of object-oriented programming is the ability to overload the (<<) and (>>) operators and perform input and output operations on abstract types similar to those of standard types. To do this, we can create an alias, reference, for *cin* object (class istream) and another one for *cout* object (class ostream) and use them for reading and writing data members of the desired object. Examine the following overloaded *friend* function. Note that the user-defined identifier *input* is an alias or reference for the keyword *cin* of the class istream.

```
istream& operator>>( istream& , Integer& );  // function prototype
```

```
// function definition
istream& operator>>( istream& input, Integer& number)
{
  input >> number._IntegerValue;
  return input;
}
```

Now, the following code is valid.

```
void main()
{
   Integer    AnObject;

   cout << "\nEnter an integer value: ";   // e.g. 125
   cin >> AnObject; // application of the (<<) operator
   AnObject.display();   // displays 125
}
```

Why is there a need for returning *istream* and *ostream* objects in overloaded functions? Notice that both *cin* and *cout* objects allow chaining input and output operations, such as:

```
cin   >>  x  >> y  >> z;
cout  <<  x  << y  << z;
```

What each of the above statements does is perform a desired I/O and returns another *cin* or *cout* object for further operations. For example, the statement *cin >> x >> y >> z* reads in the value of the variable *x* from the standard I/O and returns another *cin* statement:

```
cin >> y >> z;
```

In turn, the new statement reads in the value of the variable *y* and returns a new *cin* statement *(cin >> z)*. The process continues until there is no more data left for input operation.

In the above function, the user-defined data type input is a reference type similar to object *cin* of the class *istream*. The keyword *friend* has established a bridge between two classes *istream* and *Integer*. The declaration and use of reference variable input in the overloaded function allows you to use its counterpart, *cin*, in the client program such as *main()*.

Similar to (>>), you may overload (<<) for output operations as shown. Use the class *ostream* and a user-defined object with a descriptive name such as output for writing operations.

```
ostream& operator<<( ostream& , Integer& ); // function prototype


// function definition
ostream& operator<<( ostream& output, Integer& number)
{
   output >> number._IntegerValue;
   return input;
}
```

Now, the following code is valid.

```
void main()
{
   Integer    AnObject;

   cout << "\nEnter an integer value: ";   // e.g. 125
   cin  >> AnObject;   // application of the (<<) operator
   cout << AnObject;   // displays 125
}
```

There are several other overloaded operators. In another example, the class *Date* involves dynamically allocated data and is an excellent chance to revisit the concepts of the copy constructor and custom assignment member functions. Both are necessary to prevent shallow copying. Moreover, it gives you a chance to see how other overloaded operators, including the subscript operator ([ ]) and the function call operator, are written and used.

Study and run the following program and see how the copy constructor and custom assignment members function work. Notice that the function display() of class *Date* is declared as a constant function. A constant function indicates that it does not change the state of any objects. To declare a function as *constant,* write the keyword *const* after the function heading in both the declaration and the definition.

```cpp
#include <stdlib.h>
#include <string.h>
#include <iostream.h>

class Date
{
private:
        int _day, _month, _year;
        char *_note;

public:
        Date();
        Date ( int day, int month, int year,  const char *note );

        Date ( const Date& date );
        Date& operator = ( const Date& date );
        void display() const;
        ~Date();
private:
        void init (int day, int month, int year,  const char * note);

}; // end of class Date

// Implementation of interfaces
// function Init
void Date :: init (int day, int month, int year,  const char *note)
{
  _day = day;
  _month = month;
  _year = year;

  int length = strlen(note);
  _note  = new char [ length + 1 ];
  strcpy( _note, note );
}

// default constructor
Date :: Date()
{
```

```cpp
    _day = _month = _year = 0;
    _note = 0;
}

// class constructor
Date :: Date (int day, int month, int year, const char *note)
{
  init ( day, month, year, note );
}

// copy constructor
Date :: Date ( const Date& date )
{

  init ( date._day, date._month, date._year,   date._note );
}

// overloaded assignment operator: custom assignment
Date& Date :: operator = ( const Date& date )
{
  if ( this != &date )  // Guard against self assignment.
 {
   delete _note;
   init ( date._day, date._month, date._year,   date._note );
 }
 return *this;
}

// function display: output
void Date :: display() const
{

  cout << "On the day of "
       << _day << "/" << _month << "/" << _year
       << ", remember:\n\t";

  cout << _note;
  cout << "\n";
}

//class destructor
Date::~Date()
{
  if (_note != NULL )
    delete [] _note;
}
////////////////////////////////////////////////////////////////

void main()
{
```

```
Date    Birthday(5,9,1995, "Kaytlyn was born.");
Date    Schoolday(3,9,2001, "Kaytlyn goes to school.");

Date    first;     // Uses default constructor.
first = Birthday; // Uses overloaded assignment operator.

Date    second = Date(Schoolday); // Makes a copy of  Schoolday.
first.display();    // Displays the message of the object Birthday.
second.display(); // Displays the message of the object Schoolday.
}
```

Now that you are familiar with the class *Date,* let us introduce two other overloaded operators, the subscript and function call or substring operators.

Overloading the Subscript Operator ([ ])

Overloading the subscript operator allows you to perform subscripted access to the elements of an array that is a member of an object. The reference to the returned value allows you to use it both as a right value and a left value. Consider the following code:

```
// function prototype
char&  Date::operator[]( int index );


// function definition
char& Date::operator[](int  index)
{
   return _note[index]; // or *(_note + index)
}
```

Now that you can use the overloaded subscript in your programs:

```
void main()
{

   Date Birthday ( 5, 9, 95, "Kaytlyn was born." );
   Birthday.display();

   cout << Birthday[5] << endl;  // Display the fifth letter ('y').
   Birthday[5] = 'i';   // Change the fifth letter from 'y' to 'i'.

   Birthday.display()   // Displays Kaytlyn.
   cout << endl;
}
```

We can now proceed to the next overloaded operator, the *function call ()* operator.

Overloading the *Function Call ()* Operator

The function call operator allows you to create function-like notations to send different messages to the objects by accepting different arguments. For example, the following function captures the text component of an object:

```
    // function prototype: to copy the text component of the object
    void  operator()(char*  );

    // function definition
    void  Date::operator()(char*  string)
    {
      strcpy(string, _note);
    }
```

Now you can use the overloaded *function call* operator in your programs, as shown below:

```
void main()
{

  Date Birthday ( 5, 9, 95, "Kaytlyn was born." );
  char      text[80];  // a container array to hold the text
  Birthday(text);      // Copies the text component of the object Birthday.
  cout << text;        // Displays Kaytlyn was born.
}
```

Exercise

Given the following function prototype, write a member function for an overloaded substring operator, using parentheses, to produce a desired portion of the text component of an object. The function selects and returns a number of characters, starting at a given subscript.

```
char* operator( )( int from, int HowMany );
```

Overloading the New and Delete Operators

The *new* operator may be overloaded for different purposes. One common reason is using either function *malloc()* or function *calloc()* of the C language. Consider the following example. It also overloads the *new* and *delete* operators. The overloaded *new* operator allocates space for an array of specialized size and fills the space with a desired character. Notice that the overloaded function for the *new* operator needs a declaration of *size_t size* [e.g., *void* new* operator *(size_t size);*] as a part of its syntax. The built-in *size_t* refers to the size of the allocated generic memory.

The following overloaded function attempts to first create a block of memory and store a desired character in the elements of the block. This is accomplished by the following facilities:

- The built-in type *size_t*, which is the unsigned integer type *ui_type* of a data object declared to hold the result of the *sizeof* operator. It is based on:

  ```
  typedef ui_type size_t;
  ```

- Function *malloc()* from the *<stdlib.h>* library is used to perform dynamic storage allocation during run time. The number of bytes required is passed to *malloc,* which returns a pointer to the block of new bytes if they are available; otherwise, it returns a *null* pointer.

- Function *memset( )* from the *<string.h>* library stores *(unsigned char) ch* in each of the elements of the array of *unsigned char* with size *n* as shown below:

```
void *memset(void *s, int ch, size_t n);
```

- Function *free( )* de-allocates the data object whose address, as a pointer, has been passed to it:

```
void* free( void *ptr);
```

```
#include <iostream.h>
#include <stdlib.h>

// ****** overloaded new operator  ******
void *operator new(size_t size,  int    filler)
{
    void        *ptr;  // a generic pointer

    if ((ptr = malloc(size)) != NULL)
    memset(ptr, filler, size);
    return ptr;
}


// ----------- overloaded delete operator
void operator delete(void *type)
{
    free(type);
}
```

Note the syntax of the new operator in the following client code. The character between the *new* operator and the type specifies that the allocated block should be initialized with that character.

```
const int max = 100;
void main()
{
    // ------ allocate a  block filled with zeros
    char     *block  =  new ('0') char[max];

    // ------ display the array
    for (int i = 0; i < 100; i++)
     cout << " " << block[i];

    // ------ release the memory
    delete block;
}
```

Another reason for overloading the *new* operator is forcing the *new* to use a desired area of the memory for a class object, such as a desired buffer or stack area. The next

Figure 6.7 Stack Size

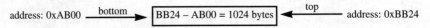

address: 0xAB00 —— bottom ——→ | BB24 – AB00 = 1024 bytes | ←—— top —— address: 0xBB24

example implements this concept using the abstract data type (ADT) stack. The ADT stack is a structure into which data are inserted and from which data are removed from one end only, called the **top of stack.** A stack is also known as a **LIFO** (Last In First Out) organization.

The following program creates and manipulates a generic stack capable of storing any data types, such as integers, floating-point numbers, characters, or classes. Moreover, it also overloads the new operator to allocate memory space only from the stack area. The stack size, by default, is 1024 bytes, as shown in Figure 6.7. Notice the arbitrary addresses of both ends of the stack.

The following top-level algorithm describes the overall operation of the program. Furthermore, each function has also been explained in detail to help you understand the processes involved.

```
Algorithm GenericStack:
START
CREATE       stack
CREATE       the object to be stored on the stack
GET          stack address for the object
CALL         the stack constructor to store the object on the stack
DISPLAY      the contents of the stack
POP          the object
FREE UP      the object's memory
END GenericStack.
```

The objects of the following class are to be pushed onto the stack for the purpose of testing.

```
Const  int  size = 127;  // an arbitrary size
class test
{
  private:
    char _text[size];

  public:
    test()
    { strcpy (_text, "This is a test!");}
    test(char* str ) { strcpy (_text, str); }
    void display()    {cout << _text;}
    ~test() {};
};
```

The following class, *class GenericStack,* creates a stack suitable for any type of data. Figure 6.7 shows the shape of the stack in the main memory. Note that the stack top is initialized to the desired size, representing an empty stack, and reaches zero, through decrementing, when the stack is full.

```
#include <iostream.h>
#include <stdlib.h>
#include <string.h>

const int size = 1024; // 1k bytes
class GenericStack
{
  private:
    char*  _top;        //  pointer to stack top
    char*  _bottom;     //  pointer to bottom of stack
    char*  _current;    //  pointer to current position
  public:
    GenericStack(unsigned  sze = size); // default  size

    // Push a block of unsigned bytes (generic)
    // addressed by the pointer of type void.
    int push(unsigned block,  void*  item);

    // Pass the address of a desired block
    // to the calling function.
    void* pop(unsigned block);

    // Reserve a block and pass its address
    // to the calling function.
    void* GetBlock(unsigned block);

    ~GenericStack() { delete _top;  }
};  // end of class

//  constructor of class GenericStack
GenericStack::GenericStack (int sze)
{
    _top = new char[sze];
    if (_top == NULL )
        cout << "Out of memory!" , exit(1);
    else
        _bottom = _current = _top + sze;
}

//  definition of interface push
int GenericStack::push(unsigned block,
                          void  *item)
{
    if (_top > (_current - block) )
        return 0;
    _current -= block;

    //  memmove copies source (block of data)
    //   from source (item) to destination (current).
    memmove( _current, item, block);
    return 1;
}
```

```
// definition for interface pop
void*  GenericStack::pop(unsigned block)
{
    if (_bottom < (_current + block) )
    return NULL;

    char*  temp = _current;
    _current += block;
    return temp;
}


//   definition for interface GetBlock
//   The interface reserves a block, but
//   does not assign any values to it.

void* GenericStack::GetBlock(unsigned block)
{
    if ( _top >  _current - block )  // if not ok?
    return NULL;
    _current = _current - block;      // Adjust current.
    return _current;                  // Return current.
}


//   Overloads the new operator.
void*  operator new(size_t size,  void* ptr)
{
    _size = size;    // a dummy statement: required
    return ptr;
}


//   the client program to test the stack

void main()
{
    GenericStack     stack;      // Create object stack.

    test   string;               // Create object string.
    test*  obj = &string;        // Get object's address.

    char*  pointer;              // Make a pointer to byte.

// Call GetBlock to reserve a block on stack.
pointer =(char*)stack.GetBlock(sizeof(test));

    // Construct the object on the stack.
    obj = new(pointer) test;
    obj->display();         // show it

    // Delete the object's contents.
    obj->test::~test();
```

```
                    // Adjust the current pointer.
            stack.pop( sizeof(test));
}
```

The Rules for Overloading an Operator

C++ has the following rules regarding overloading operators:

- You may overload all C++ operators except

  . *direct member*

  * *direct pointer to member*

  :: *scope resolution*

  ?: *conditional operator*

  sizeof

- The predefined precedence and associativity rules of the operators cannot be changed.
- You must use the operators in their standard format. That is, if you overload the *plus* operator (+), the overload must still use it in the form *operand + operand*. Moreover, you cannot change precedence or associativity.
- You may not define your own operators by choosing a character, such as #, and attempt to overload it.
- The overloading function is similar to any other C++ function, but for the function name use the keyword *operator* followed by the desired operator symbol. It can be either a member function, *non-static,* or a *friend* function. However, the operators =, (), [], and -> must be overloaded as member functions.
- At least one of the arguments of the overloaded function must be an instance of the class to which it belongs.
- The overloaded operator *new* takes an argument of type *size_t* and returns *void** (a pointer to void).
- The overloaded operator *delete* takes an argument of type *void** and returns *void*.*
- The created overload only applies to the instances of the class to which it belongs.

Self-Check Questions 11

1. Why do we need to overload the operation >> (insertion) and the operator >> (extraction)?
2. Given the following class declaration, write the necessary implementation and use a driver program to show its application.

```
class string
{
        char _text[512];
        int _length;
    public:
        string(char* str);
        char* operator+(char* another);
        void display();
};
```

3. Can you write a regular function to accomplish the same result as an overloaded operator function?

Embedded Objects

An object of one class may be declared as a data member of another class normally as a part of the design requirements. The object used as the data member is called an **embedded or enclosed object** and the class that uses the guest object is referred to as the **host or enclosing class.** When you decide to use embedded objects, know that:

- The object must have been defined previously. It is necessary for the compiler to know the size of the object for memory allocation reasons. The exception to this rule is when you use a pointer or a reference to an object of one class within another class.
- When necessary, the enclosing class calls the constructor of the enclosed object with appropriate argument(s) using colon (:) syntax. Consider the following example of using an embedded object. It uses the class *Date,* which was presented earlier. Below is the declaration of class *Date* to refresh your memory.

```
#ifndef _DATE_H
#define _DATE_H
class Date
{
  // private by default
  int _day, _month, _year;
  char*      _text;

  public:
     Date();
     Date( int day, int month, int year, const
           char* text);

     Date( const Date&);
     Date& operator=(const Date&);
     void display() const;
     ~Date();   // destructor

  private:
void init(int day, int month, int year
          const char* text);
};
#endif



#include <iostream.h>
#include "date.h"

class Employee
{
        Date  _employed;  // embedded object

  public:
        // The colon syntax invokes the constructor of the embedded object.
        Employee(const Date&  empl ) : _employed(empl)
```

```
        void show()
                {_employed.display(); }
                ~Employee() {};
 };   // end of class Employee

 char*    FirstReason =
                "Extensive teaching background";
char* NextReason    =
                "Extensive industry experience";

void main ()
{
        Date        EmployDate(1,9,1993, FirstReason);
        Employee    Michael(EmployDate);
        Michael.show();
}
```

Nested Data Types

A class can contain any legal C++ types including structures, other classes, and enumeration. This concept helps you meet the design requirements of the application and also simplify and clarify class declarations by using structures as data members instead of several loose variables. Consider the following example in which the class stack contains a data member named *employee,* which in turn is an array of structures. The structure *employee* may have many fields in real-life applications. Its separate declaration helps code clarity and the class becomes more meaningful. In addition to structure *employee,* the class uses an enumeration of type *boolean* as its nested member. When you read the code, pay attention to the way the elements of *employee* and *boolean* types are being used.

As we said earlier, the stack is a structure into which data are inserted and from which data are removed from the top of stack. Notice that the class has four member functions:

- Adding an item to the stack, also known as **push onto the stack**
- Removing and displaying an item from the stack, also known as **pop from the stack**
- Testing the stack to see whether or not it is empty
- Testing the stack to see whether or not it is full

```
#include <string.h>
#include <iostream.h>
#include <stdio.h>

const int length = 32;
typedef struct  EmployeeType
{
    long int _ID;
    char     _name[length];
}// end of structure

const int StackSize = 100;  // initial size of the stack
class stack
{
```

```
        EmployeeType *_table      // array of objects
        int        _size;
        int        _top;

public:
    // type definition: BOOLEAN
        enum boolean  {false, true};
        stack()  {}      //default constructor
        stack (int size = StackSize)// default parameter
        {
         _size  = size;    _top = 0;
         _table = new EmployeeType[_size];
        }
// Return true if push is successful;
// otherwise, return false.
boolean push();

// Return true if pop is successful;
// otherwise, return false.
boolean Pop();

// Return true if stack is full;
// otherwise, return false.
boolean full();


// Return true if stack is empty;
// otherwise, return false.

boolean empty();
~stack();
};  // end of class stack
/////////////////////////////////////////////////

// Watch the way that boolean type is used below.
stack::boolean  stack::push()
{
    if(full() == false) // or if ( !full () )
    {
        cout << "Enter ID:";
        cin  >> _table[_top]._ID;
        char name[length];   // Names up to 32 bytes.
        cout << "\nEnter name:  ";
        gets(name);    // from <stdio.h>
        strcpy(_table[_top++]._name, name);
        return true;
    }
    else
    {
        cout<<"full stack!";
        return false;
```

```
    }
}  // end of function

//  Pop an item and display it.
stack::boolean  stack::Pop()
{
   if (empty() == false) // or if ( ! empty () )
   {
       --_top;
       cout << _table[_top]._ID << '\t'
            << _table[_top]._name << '\n';
       return true;
   }
   cout << "empty stack!";
   return false;
}

stack::boolean  stack::full()
{
   return (_top == _size - 1)? true : false;
}

stack::boolean stack::empty()
{
   return (_top == 0)? true : false;
}


   // destructor function
stack::~stack()
{
   while (empty() == false)
       delete _table[_top]._name, --_top;
   delete []_table[;
}


// The following program sets up an array of ten
// objects of type stack and uses three of them for
// test purposes.
```

Notice the declaration of the variable flag of boolean type in the program. Since the type definition of the user-defined boolean has happened within the class stack, we use the scope resolution (::) operator to show where it comes from. By doing this, we limit the scope of our boolean type to the class level.

```
void main ()
{
   stack::boolean flag;    // Watch the way that we declared
                           // boolean type

   stack      table(10);   // an arbitrary size

   for (int index = 1; index <3; ++index)
```

```
            flag = table.push();

        flag = table.Pop();
        while (flag)

        flag = table.Pop();
} // end of program
```

Generic Classes Using Templates

Earlier, we discussed function templates that let us create generic functions for processing different types of data without any need to create different types of functions. Class templates have conceptually the same purpose. They allow you to create generic classes without specifying the type of one or more data members, thus eliminating the need for writing similar classes. Declarations of class templates are prefixed by a *template* specification:

```
template  <class type>
class classname
{
    .
    .
    .
};
```

The declarations *template <class type>* and class *classname* are actually one declaration. We put them in two lines for clarity purposes. To declare an object of a desired type, use a notation similar to the following:

```
classname <int>      object1;   // Makes the object to be of integer type.
classname <floa>     object2;   // Makes the object to be of float type.
classname <char>     object3;   // Makes the object to be of character type.
classname <char*>    object4;   // Makes the object to be of string type.
```

Consider the following example that demonstrates the use of class templates. The class defines another generic stack, based on the *class template* declaration, to be used for different data types. The ADT stack is a good choice for this topic since you are now familiar with the operations of this data structure.

```
#include<iostream.h>
#define MaxSize   100
template <class AnyType>      //generic type AnyType
class GenStack                //generic stack
{
        int       _stacktop;
        AnyType   _stack[MaxSize];

public:
        GenStack()   {_stacktop = -1;  }  // initialization
        int push(AnyType);//Returns 1:success 0:failure.
        int pop(AnyType&);//Returns 1:success 0:failure.
```

```
            int full()  { return _stacktop == MaxSize;  }
            int empty() {return _stacktop == -1;}
    };   //end class
```

Note when you write the definition (code) of the interfaces:

- The keyword *template* followed by angle brackets are used as a part of the function heading;
- The class name, such as *GenStack,* is to be followed by angle brackets showing the defined type.

```
template <class AnyType>  // syntax requirement
int GenStack < AnyType>::push(AnyType data)
{
   if(!full())
   {
     _stack[ ++_stacktop ] = data;
     return 1;
   }
   else
   {
     cout<<"stack is full";
     return 0;
   }
}

template <class AnyType>
int GenStack< AnyType>::pop(AnyType& data)
{
   if (!empty())
   {
     data = _stack[ _stacktop-- ];
     return 1;
   }
   else
   {
     cout<<"stack is empty!";
     return 0;
   }
}
```

Now, let us see how our generic class works.

```
void main ()
{
   // declaration of two stacks of different types
   GenStack<int>   numbers;//an object of type integer
   GenStack<char*> names;//an object of type string
   int   age = 100;
   char* name;
   int   pushflag, popflag;

   pushflag = names.push("Years old!"); // Puts the text on the string stack.
```

```
    pushflag = numbers.push(age); // Pushes age onto the numeric stack.

    if(pushflag)
        pushflag = names.push("She is");
    popflag = names.pop(name);

    if (popflag)
    cout << name;

    popflag = numbers.pop(age);

if (popflag)
    cout << age;

popflag = names.pop(name);

if (popflag)
cout << name;
}
```

Finally, class templates have two properties that are worth remembering:

- A template class definition cannot be nested within another class.
- A template class can be derived from another template or non-template class.

Exercise

An ADT queue is a structure from which data may be removed from one end, called the **front of the queue,** and into which data may be inserted at the other end, called the **rear of the queue.** Given the following specifications and representation for an ADT queue, write the necessary implementation for the specified operations; and write a driver program to create different instances of queue (objects) and test them with different data types.

Specifications:

Creates an instance of the ADT queue

Pre: none
Post: an ADT instance

```
void Init (int = 100);
```

Appends an item to the queue

Pre: queue
Post: queue with the new item; returns 1 if successful; otherwise returns 0

```
int insert (int);
```

Receives an item from the queue

Pre: queue
Post: a queue item (if available)

```
int remove ();
```

Peeks to see the first available item

Pre: queue

Post: the same queue

```
int Peek();
```

Checks to see if queue is empty

Pre: queue
Post: 0 or 1 flag

```
int IsEmpty();
```

Checks to see if queue is full

Pre: queue
Post: 0 or 1 flag

```
int IsFull();
```

Returns the array's memory to the operating system

Pre: the queue's array
Post: nothing

```
void destroy();
```

Representation and specifications:

```
const int size = 100; // Queue size
class Queue
{       // representation
    int *_quese;
    int _Qsize;
    int _head;
    int _tail;
    int _count;
public:  // specifications
        Queue (int Qsize = size);
        int   Insert(int);
        int   remove();
        int   Peek();
        int   IsFull();
        int   IsEmpty();
        void Destroy();
        ~Queue ();
};
```

Self-Check Questions 12

1. What is accomplished by using class templates?
2. Given the following class declaration, write the necessary implementation and write a driver program to show how it works.

```
template <class T>
class   something
{
        T   _data;
    public:
            something () {}
            something ( T );
```

```
                    something(const  something <T>& );  // copy constructor
                    friend  ostream& operator<<(ostream&, something<T>&);
          };
```

SUMMARY

- Recent advances in computing architecture and data communications have opened new frontiers in software development. The demand for new applications, with more functionality and capabilities, has risen dramatically. As a consequence, new applications have become complex and voluminous. To achieve the goals of the new frontier, the traditional paradigm of procedural abstraction is no longer adequate.
- Data abstraction, a means for defining a data type in terms of its functionality, has become a useful approach to solve today's complex problems of software design and development. The focus of data abstraction is on the data used by the application. The end result of data abstraction is an abstract data type (ADT) with the following attributes:

  Name

  Domain

  A set of primitive operations

  A set of rules

- C++ class, a means for describing the common characteristics of a domain of objects, allows you to define specific, but reusable, data types and unify their representation and implementation under one umbrella. A *class* type, in contrast to a traditional *struct* type, provides conceptual capabilities such as constructors and destructors for object-oriented programming.
- Constructor functions are used to create and initialize the data members of an object automatically. They are also used to copy the elements of one object into another. There are three types of constructors:

  Constructors with initializers or parameters

  Default constructors

  Copy constructors

- Constructor conversion functions allow you to convert one class into another.
- An object is an instance of a class that has *state* and *behavior*. We can change the *state* of a class through its *behaviors*.
- Object-oriented programming involves:

  Encapsulation

  Inheritance

  Polymorphism

- Encapsulation places the data and functions of the class in a "capsule" and allows the outside world to get to it through their open interfaces.
- Inheritance allows you to create new classes from existing ones and build hierarchies and networks. The class from which you derive is called the *base* class and the new class is called the *derived* class.
- *Polymorphism* is the capacity for an object to respond differently to the same message.

- *Virtual* functions cause the path of execution to be determined at run-time instead of compile-time. The process involved is called *late binding.*
- Constructor functions cannot be declared as *virtual.* However, you may define destructors as *virtual. Virtual* destructors guarantee the proper release of the allocated memory of both base and derived classes when classes allocate data dynamically.
- A *pure virtual* function is one that is declared and not defined. The name of the function is preceded with the keyword *virtual.* A *pure virtual* function makes its related class an *abstract* class.
- *Abstract* classes do not have implementations of their own. The derived classes provide the necessary implementation.
- A base class may be declared as *virtual.* A *virtual base* class prevents inheritance of multiple copies of data by a derived class.
- The C++ *this* pointer points to the current object that is executing. It is a useful tool for accessing active objects.
- Data members and member functions of a class may be declared as *static.* A *static* data member remains in existence for the duration of the program. A function may also be declared as *static.* The role of such functions is to manipulate *static* data members.
- The keyword *friend* is used for:

    Granting nonmember functions access to private and protected members of a class

    Bridging two classes

    Operating on two objects when one of them is external

- The operator function of C++ is a built-in feature of the language. It is used for type conversion as well as operator overloading. This capability extends the power of the language for implementing the real-life need of abstract data types.
- An object of a class may be declared as a data member of another class.
- A user-defined data type, similar to standard types, can be used as a member of a class.
- Class templates of C++ allow you to create generic classes.

STYLE TIPS

- All style tips, including indentation decisions, naming identifiers and their semantic meanings, and documenting methods apply to object-oriented programming, too. Moreover, in object-oriented programming, object-oriented analysis (OOA), and object-oriented design (OOD) play important roles in creating meaningful classes and objects.
- Modular programming is emphasized. A module is a compilation unit containing specifications and implementation of abstractions. Therefore, a module should contain a specification file, such as *spec.h,* and an implementation file, such as *imp.h* or *imp.cpp* (in the case of project files). The specification file contains all declarations and prototypes related to the abstraction and the implementation file contains the actual code for the prototypes and, possibly, some private data. Both files will be used by the client program, i.e., *main( ),* using the *#include...* directive.
- Understanding object-oriented design includes identifying the objects, their functionality and their relationships. When you see the objects, you can build and implement

classes, hierarchies, and networks for them. (One possible method for developing classes is using the CRC Cards (Class, Responsibility, Collaboration) concepts by Wirfs-Brock, et al. (1989).

- Remember that an application, as an end product, must be reliable. Reliable software is always correct and robust. It does what it is supposed to do and never terminates abnormally. One way to achieve this goal is to incorporate assertions, testing, and debugging in the program as early as possible.

- Use access specifiers correctly and consistently. Declare member functions as *public* unless they perform something that is solely internal. Declare data members as *private* or *protected* depending on the design requirements. Provide appropriate access to member functions for the client programs. You may always declare data members as *private* and specify their access rules through public and protected interfaces.

- There are different styles that programmers consider and use in their programs. The whole idea behind using a style is adhering to some consistent rules in order to develop a clear, legible, and understandable program. There is no single correct style. Therefore, no matter what style you follow, consistency is emphasized throughout.

Use the following style guide for object-oriented programs:

Order the class sections as *private*, *protected*, and *public*.

Data members are to be *private* or rarely *protected*. Try not to use *public* data members. An exception to this rule is when you use an *enumeration* type, as an embedded type, in which you want the type to be accessible to the client programs. (See the example earlier in this chapter.)

It is a good practice to begin the names of data members of the class with the underscore (_) character to make them distinct.

Constructors come first, then other member functions, then a destructor at the end.

Member functions are declared inside the class, but not defined there unless the code is a single line. A single-line function is a good candidate for an *inline* function. However, in a large project, the rule is: No *inline* functions.

Normal indentation rules apply to class identifiers, access specifiers, and braces.

Declare member functions and reference arguments *const* when applicable. The keyword *const* is a guarantee that the function does not change any members. It is a good guard against accidentally modifying data members. Constant functions are known as **accessor** functions. That is, they do not change anything. In contrast, functions that change data members are called **mutators.**

In a class with many different features, order them as:
enum declaration(s)
local classes and structures
constructors: default constructors, active constructors, and copy constructors
mutators
accessors
static functions
memory management
data (could also be at the beginning as we have used in this book)

In respect to *friend* functions, the *friend* declarations are normally placed at the end of the public section of the class.

Document the class itself by a header comment, as shown:

```
//***********************************************************
//    CLASS NAME:      ...
//    PURPOSE:    Write what an object of the class
//                does.
//
//    STATES: List the situations that change the
//    behavior of member functions.  For example, in our
//    stack, the two situations "empty" and "full" change
//    the behavior of the "push" and "pop" functions.
//***********************************************************
```

> **Note:** The following sample programs include the style suggestions.

SAMPLE PROGRAMS

1. Write a menu-driven program to implement a telephone directory (Figure 6.8) based on the following specifications:

   Insert a new entry.

   Find an entry.

   Remove an entry.

   Print a desired record.

In addition, the instances of the directory should accept virtually any number of entries. That is, it should not terminate the program as a result of a "full status" situation. When the directory reaches a full status, it should increase in size as required, such as by 25 percent for this program, to accommodate new entries.

The following program is a possible solution for creating a telephone directory with the given specifications. It has been fully documented to help you understand the program and learn programming style as well.

Figure 6.8 Telephone Directory

Nahid Kashani	555-8324
Suzanne Tasalloti	555-4765
Kevin Carlisle	555-9876
Kaytlyn Tasalloti	555-7654
Karie Nelson	555-9876
Mathew Tasalloti	555-5432
Cyrus Kashani	555-6087

```
#include <iostream.h>
#include <stdlib.h>
#include <stdio.h>
#include <assert.h>
#include <string.h>
#include <ctype.h>

const int staff = 20; // the original size of the directory
//************************************************************
//   CLASS NAME:      PhoneEntry
//   PURPOSE:         To create a record composed of name and
//                    phone number
//************************************************************
class   Directory;  // forward reference

class   PhoneEntry
{
   char*  _name;
   char*  _phone;
   friend class  Directory;
};


//************************************************************
//   CLASS NAME:      Directory
//   PURPOSE:         To create a simple directory
//   STATE:           No special behavior in class objects
//
//************************************************************
class Directory
{
   PhoneEntry*     _table;  // table of names and phones
   int             _count;  // number of elements in the directory
   int             _size;   // size of table
  public:
     Directory( int size = staff); // initial size
     void insert(char*, char* );   // insert name and phone
     char* find(char*)  const;     // find and return phone number
     int remove(char* );           // remove an entry
     ~Directory();                 // destructor
  private:
     void expand();                // Expands the directory if needed.
     int lookup(char*)  const;     // Look up a name.
};   // end of class

//***************** THE CLASS CONSTRUCTOR ******************
//
//   PURPOSE:     To create an object
//
//************************************************************
Directory::Directory(int size)
{
```

```
   _table = new PhoneEntry[size];
   _count = 0;
   _size = size;
}

//************INTERFACE FOR function insert********************
//
//    PURPOSE:      To insert an entry into the directory
//                  (if does not exist)
//
//    PRE:          An active directory
//
//    POST:         Directory with the new entry (if successful)
//    REMARKS:      1. The function will call function lookup for
//                     duplicate entry.
//                  2. The function will call function expand (if
//                     necessary).
//
//***************************************************************
void Directory::insert(char* name,  char* phone)
{
   int index = lookup(name);
   if (index == _size)
     expand();  // Increase the size of the directory.

   if (index == _count)
   {
     _count++;
     _table[index]._name = new char[strlen(name) + 1];
     strcpy( _table[index]._name, name);
   }
   else
       delete [] _table[index]._phone;  // overwrite phone number

   _table[index]._phone = new char[strlen(phone) + 1];
   strcpy(_table[index]._phone, phone);
}

//************INTERFACE FOR function find: (accessor)*****************
//
//    PURPOSE:      To find a phone number related to a given name
//
//    PRE:          An active directory
//

//    POST:         Returns phone number, if successful; otherwise, null
//
//    REMARKS:      Since the function is an accessor, it is
//                  declared as const.
//
//*******************************************************************
```

```
char*  Directory::find(char* name)   const
{
   int index = lookup(name);
   if(index < _count)
     return _table[index]._phone;
   else
     return NULL;
}


//***************INTERFACE FOR function remove***************
//
//  PURPOSE:       To find an entry related to a given name

//  PRE:           An active directory

//  POST:          Same directory less than an entry (if done)

//  REMARKS:       It calls function lookup for possible
//                 existence of the entry in the directory.
//************************************************************
int Directory::remove(char* name)
{
   int index = lookup(name);
   if (index == _count)
     return 0; // Item was not deleted (did not exist).

   delete  [] _table[index]._name;
   _table[index]._name = NULL;
   delete  [] _table[index]._phone;
   _table[index]._phone = NULL;
   _count--;    // adjust counter

            // Check if the item was last entry.
   if (index == _count) // last entry deleted
         return 1;      // item successfully deleted
// Bring the last entry to the empty cell and close the gap.
_table[index]._name  = new char [strlen( _table[_count]._name ) + 1 ];
_table[index]._phone = new char [strlen( _table[_count]._phone ) + 1 ];
strcpy( _table[index]._name,  _table[_count]._name );
strcpy( _table[index]._phone, _table[_count]._phone );

// remove the last entry
delete _table[_count]._name,  _table[_count]._name = NULL;
delete _table[_count]._phone, _table[_count]._name = NULL;

return 1;   // Item was successfully deleted and the directory was adjusted.
}


//***********INTERFACE FOR function lookup (accessor)***********
//
//  PURPOSE:       To check if an entry exists in the directory
```

```
//   PRE:           An active directory
//
//   POST:          Returns the index, if found; otherwise count
//                  value.
//   REMARKS:       None
//*********************************************************
int Directory::lookup(char* name) const
{
   for (int index = 0; index < _count; ++index)
     if (strcmp(_table[index]._name, name) == 0 )
       break;
   return index;
}

//*************INTERFACE FOR function expand*************
//
//   PURPOSE:       To increase the size of directory
//   PRE:           An active directory
//
//   POST:          Same directory with a larger capacity
//
//   REMARKS:       It also updates the size of directory.
//*****************************************************
void Directory::expand()
{
   int  NewSize = 2 * _size;  // Make its size double.
   PhoneEntry*  NewTable = new PhoneEntry[NewSize];
   assert(NewTable != 0);   // if memory is allocated

   for (int index = 0; index < _count;  ++index)
     NewTable[index] = _table[index]; // copy old entries

   delete []_table;   // Remove old directory.
   _table = NewTable; // Create new directory.
   _size = NewSize;   // Update size.
}

//********************The Class Destructor************
//   PURPOSE:       To free up the memory
//*************************************************
Directory::~Directory()
{
   for (int index = 0; index <_count; ++index)
      {
     delete  []  _table[index]._name;
     delete  []  _table[index]._phone;
      }
   delete [] _table;
}

//***** A client application to test the class*****
```

```
//************ PROTOTYPE FOR  InsertEntry************************
//
//  PURPOSE:        To get data from standard device and insert into
//                  the directory using its counterpart interface
//
//  PRE:            An active directory
//  POST:           None
//  REMARKS:        None
//******************************************************************
void InsertEntry(Directory& );


//***********PROTOTYPE FOR RemoveEntry)**********************
//
//  PURPOSE:        To remove an entry if it exists, from the
//                  directory
//  PRE:            An active directory using its counterpart
//                  interface
//  POST:           None
//
//  REMARKS:        None
//**************************************************************
void RemoveEntry(Directory&);


//****************PROTOTYPE FOR  GetPhone****************
//
//  PURPOSE:        To find a phone number based on a name
//
//  PRE:            Directory using its counterpart interface
/
//  POST:           Phone number
//
//  REMARKS:        None
//
//*********************************************************
void GetPhone(Directory& );

enum  BOOLEAN{false, true};
const int length = 80;

void main()
{
   Directory      list;
   char           instruction;
   BOOLEAN        Finish = false;

   do
    {
      cout << "\nEnter instruction:   Insert an entry<i>,"
           << " Find a name<F>, "
           << " Remove an entry<R>,  Get a phone No. <G>,"
           << " and Quit <Q>: ";
```

```
        cin  >> instruction;
        instruction = toupper(instruction);  //  Make it upper-case.

        switch(instruction)
        {
        case 'I':  InsertEntry(list);  break;
        case 'G':  GetPhone(list);     break;
        case 'R':  RemoveEntry(list);  break;
        case 'Q':  Finish = true;      break;
        default :  cout << "\nInvalid  instruction! try again ";
                                       break;

        }
      }while ( Finish == false);
}

//*******Definition for function InsertEntry*******
void InsertEntry (Directory& dir)
{
   char  NameBuff[length];   // maximum size for name
   char  PhBuff  [length];   // maximum size for phone number

   cout << "\nName:  ";
   cin.getline(NameBuff, length, '\n');  // You may also use
                                  // gets(NameBuff)

   cout <<"\nPhone No.:  ";
   cin >>PhBuff;

   dir.insert(NameBuff, PhBuff);
}

/*******Definition for function GetPhone*******/
void  GetPhone(Directory& dir)
{
   char  NameBuff[length];  // maximum name

   cout << "\nName:";
   cin.getline(NameBuff,length, '\n'); // You may also use
                                  // gets(NameBuff)
   char*   PhoneNo = dir.find(NameBuff);

   if (!PhoneNo)
     cout << NameBuff << " not found in directory!";
   else
     cout << PhoneNo << "\n";
}

//************PROTOTYPE FOR  RemoveEntry***************
//
//  PURPOSE:      To remove an entry for directory
//
```

```
//  PRE:          Directory using its counterpart.
//
//  POST:         None
//
//  REMARKS:      None
//
//**********************************************************
void RemoveEntry(Directory& dir)
{
    char  NameBuff[length];  // maximum size
    int   success;

    cout << "\nEnter Name:   ";
    cin.getline(NameBuff, length, '\n'); //  You may also use
                                         //  gets(NameBuff)
    success = dir.remove(NameBuff);
    if (success)
    cout << "\n\nSelection removed. ";
    else
    cout << "Sorry, entry not found. ";
}
//***********************The END***********************
```

2. French verbs are similar to English verbs in that they have both regular and irregular forms. To conjugate the regular verbs, you should remove the last two letters of the verb *(ir, er, re)* and, depending on the desired operation, append a string as shown in Table 6.3.

   The conjugation of irregular verbs differs from that of regular verbs. They are handled case by case and do not follow any particular patterns. Therefore, to conjugate a particular irregular verb, follow the specific rules of that verb. For example, for the verb *aller,* the conjugation involves the infinitive form *aller* and one of the following end strings: ALLEZ, ALLON, VA, VAIS, VAS, VONT. Write a program to conjugate French verbs according to the stated rules of the French language.

   The following program is a possible solution to conjugation of French verbs. As you will see, the *Display()* function member does different tasks under different conditions. The program consists of three units or modules. A definition module for class hierarchy

Table 6.3   French Verbs

Operation	–ir	–er	–re
First	–is	–e	–s
Second	–is	–es	–s
Third	–is	–e	" "
First	–issons	–ons	–ons
Second	–issez	–ez	–ez
Third	–issent	–ent	–ent

representing the ADT regular verb, its derived classes, and supporting declarations. Another module contains implementation of the function members. The client program *main()* demonstrates the implementation of the ADT. Notice that class *RegVerb* is an *abstract* class because function *Display()* has been declared as *pure virtual.*

```
#include <iostream.h>
#include <string.h>
#ifndef  VERBSPEC_H
#define  VERBSPEC_H
//****************************************************************
//    FILE:          verbspec.h
//    SPECIFICATIONS This file exports nominatives and the class
//                   hierarchy as RegVerb and IrregVerb
// //*************************************************************

// an enumerated type definition for conjugation purposes
// the enumeration type from first person singular (fps) to
// third person plural (tpp)
enum  persons  { fps,  sps, tps, fpp, spp, tpp };

// Type definition for the verb nominatives (end strings)
typedef char nominatives[8]; // an arbitrary size


// initialization of nominatives

nominatives  er_nom[] = {   "e     ", "es     ", "e     ", "ons    ",
                            "ez     ", "ent    "                    };


nominatives  ir_nom[] = { "is     ", "is     ", "it     ", "issons",
                          "issez ", "issent"                   };


nominatives  re_nom[] = { "s      ", "s      ", "      ", "ons    ",
                          "ez     ", "ent    "                    };



const  int size = 16;   // maximum size of words
//****************************************************************
//    CLASS NAME:  RegVerb (Regular Verbs) : Abstract class
//    PURPOSE:     To serve as a base class for derived classes
//
//    STATES:      Stable:  It is not implemented
//****************************************************************


class RegVerb
{
```

```
 protected:    // Allow inheritance.
     char      infinitive[size], root[size];
     persons  person;
     int       length;

 public:
     RegVerb( char[]);   // parameterized constructor
     virtual void display() = 0; // pure virtual function
     void conjugate();
      ~RegVerb() {};
};      //     ****    end of class verb   ****

// **********    declaration of derived classes   **********
//*********************************************************
//    CLASS NAME:    reType: for verbs ending with -re
//    PURPOSE:       To form verbs ending with -re
//    STATES:        The behavior of functions is consistent.
// *********************************************************
class reType : public RegVerb
{
 public:
   reType(char *Verb ) : RegVerb( Verb ) {}
   void display();
   ~reType() {}
 };   // end of class


//*********************************************************
//    CLASS NAME:    irType: for verbs ending with -ir
//    PURPOSE:       To form verbs ending with -ir
//    STATES:        The behavior of functions is consistent.
//*********************************************************
class irType : public RegVerb
{
public:
     irType( char  *Verb) : RegVerb(Verb) {}
     void display ();
};    // end of class


//*********************************************************
//    CLASS NAME:    erType: for verbs ending with -er
//    PURPOSE:       To form verbs ending with -er
//
//    STATES:        The behavior of  functions is consistent.
////*********************************************************

class erType : public RegVerb
{
 public:
     erType ( char  *Verb) : RegVerb(Verb) {}
     void display();
};    //end of class
```

```
//********   declaration of irregular verbs    ********

//*****************************************************
//    CLASS NAME:    IrregVerb: derived from regular verb
//    PURPOSE:       To form irregular verbs
//    STATES:        The behavior of functions is
//                   consistent.
//*****************************************************
class IrregVerb : public RegVerb
{
   nominatives present[size];
   public:
   IrregVerb(nominatives, nominatives, nominatives,
             nominatives,  nominatives, nominatives,
             nominatives);
     void display();
     ~IrregVerb (){}
};   // end of class

#endif
```

The next file contains the definition of interfaces, implementation code, of the classes. The file may be called *verbsdef.cpp* or *verbsdef.h* depending on whether you use a project or a regular file.

```
#ifndef VERBSDEF_H
#define VERBSDEF_H
//*********************************************************
// INTERFACE FOR RegVerb
// PURPOSE: To initialize the infinitive and the root
//*********************************************************
RegVerb::RegVerb( char *TheVerb )
{
length = strlen ( TheVerb );
strcpy ( infinitive, TheVerb );

for ( int index = 0; index <= length - 1; index++)
   root[index] = infinitive[index];
person = fps;
}


/************************************************************
 *       INTERFACE FOR conjugate function (regular verbs)   *
 *       PURPOSE:  To initialize the infinitive and the root *
 ************************************************************/

void RegVerb::conjugate()
{
  cout <<  "Conjugation of the verb  ";
  cout <<  infinitive;
  cout <<  " :"  << endl;
  cout <<  "---------------------------------"  << endl;
```

```
  person = fps;
  do
   {
     display();
     person++;
   }
  while ( person <= tpp );
 } // end of function

/*****************************************************************
 *                                                               *
 *      INTERFACE FOR irregular verb constructor                 *
 *      PURPOSE:  To make a complete verb                        *
 *****************************************************************/
IrregVerb::IrregVerb( nominatives  infini, nominatives  fpsing,
                      nominatives  spsing, nominatives  tpsing,
                      nominatives  fpplur, nominatives  spplur,
                      nominatives  tpplur ): RegVerb (infini)

{
   strcpy(present[(int)fps], fpsing);
   strcpy(present[(int)sps], spsing);
   strcpy(present[(int)tps], tpsing);
   strcpy(present[(int)fpp], fpplur);
   strcpy(present[(int)spp], spplur);
   strcpy(present[(int)tpp], tpplur);
}


/*********************************************************
 *      INTERFACE FOR display (irregular verbs)          *
 *      PURPOSE:  To print out the verb                  *
 *                                                       *
 *********************************************************/
void IrregVerb::display()
{
  cout  << present[(int)person]  << endl;

}

/*****************************************************************
 *      INTERFACE FOR display verbs    (erType, irType, reType)  *
 *      PURPOSE:  To print out the verb                          *
 *                                                               *
 *****************************************************************/

void erType::display()
{
  cout << root << er_nom[(int)person] << endl;
}
```

```
void irType::display()
{
  cout << root << ir_nom[(int)person] << endl;
}

void reType::display()
{
  cout << root << re_nom[(int)person] << endl;
}
        ///////////////////////////////////////////////////////////

#endif
```

Now let us run the following program and test the class. Although it is not a true polymorphic, the program demonstrates the polymorphism attribute of the classes well.

```
#include "verbspec.h."
#include "verbsdef.h"
void main()
{

    reType  Vendor ( "Repondre" );
    Vendor.conjugate();

    cout << endl << endl;
    IrregVerb irregular ( "Aller","Vais","Vas","Va","Allons",
                                "Allez","Vont" );
    irregular.conjugate();

    cout << endl  << endl;

    irType    Finish ( "Finir" );
    Finish.conjugate();

    cout << endl  << endl;

    erType Climb( "Manquer" );
    Climb.conjugate();

    cout << endl;
}
```

PROGRAMMING ASSIGNMENTS

1. A political party has asked a pollster to determine the popularity of a particular piece of legislation. Using object-oriented programming paradigms, write a program for polling a number of people whether or not they support the party's plan and determine the number of those who do and those who do not like it.

2. Date, composed of day, month, and year, is an ADT with a lot of programming applications. Almost every business record has a field with one or more date attributes such as birthday, employment date, admission date, promotion date, and so forth. Therefore, if you develop an ADT date, it will be a useful class to be included in other applications.

   Given the following declarations and specifications for the said ADT date, write the necessary implementation for each member function and then test them all by writing a short but useful program. The ADT date will use the system's clock for the correct date.

```
static int DAYS[2][12]={ {31,28,31,30,31,30,31,31,30,31,30,31},
                         {31,29,31,30,31,30,31,31,30,31,30,31
                       };

static char* MONTHS[]={"January", "February", "March", "April",
"May", "June", "July", "August", "September", "October",
"November", "December"
};

class Date
{
    int day, month, year;
    char* Month;
public:
     Date(); // default constructor
     Date(time_t);  // Constructs Date.  from time.h file
void display();
void operator = (Date&);  // assignment overloading
Date operator+(int);       // Adds an integer to date
friend Date operator+(int, Date&);   // for n + date.
friend Date& operator+=(Date&, int); // for date + n
friend Date& operator++(Date&);
Date& GMT();// Returns Greenwich mean time.
friend  int operator <(const Date&, const Date&); // less than
friend intoperator ==(const Date&, const Date&);  // equal
friend istream& operator >>(istream&, Date&);
friend ostream& operator<<(ostream&, Date&);
~Date();
};      //class end
```

3. The ADT set is an unordered collection of objects of a desired type. A set can be represented using an array as shown in Figure 6.9.

   Design an ADT generic set based on the following specifications. Then write a driver program to test the validity of your application.

   Create an empty set.

Figure 6.9   Array Representing an ADT Set

5	7	0	9	4	6	3	1	2	8

Create a set from an array.

Create a set through initialization.

Insert a member into the set.

Remove a member, if it exists, from the set.

Determine whether or not a value is a set member.

Determine if two sets are equal.

Determine if two sets are not equal.

Find the intersection of two sets (those elements that belong to both sets).

Find the difference of two sets (those elements that belong to the first set but not the second).

Find the union of two sets (those elements that belong to first set or to the second).

Determine if a set is a subset of another set.

Use C++ standard IO facilities for input and output of set objects.

If set s1 contains 4,7,9,8,5, and set s2 contains 4,8,10,15, then the following examples will show how these specifications work.

Number 5 is in s1 and not in s2 (Set Membership).

The intersection of s1 and s2, shown as s1 * s2, is a set of 4 and 8 (Set Intersection).

The union of s1 and s2, shown as s1 + s2, is a set of 4,5,7,8,9,10,15 (Set Union).

The difference between s1 and s2 shown as s1 - s2, is a set of 5,7,9 (Set Difference).

Finally, s1 is not equal to s2 (Set Inequality).

4. In preceding chapters we have frequently used singly dimensioned arrays for different purposes, such as stacks and queues. However, there are many applications in which it is necessary to consider arrays of dimensions higher than one. Of particular importance is the two-dimensional array or matrix in which the position of elements must be specified by giving two coordinates, which are typically called row and column coordinates or indices. In addition, some concepts regarding the implementation of matrices are addressed. Note that within the main memory, storage locations are not arranged in the grid-like pattern. Instead, they are arranged in linear sequence beginning with location 0, and then moving on to 1, 2, and 3. Because of this pointers can be used to easily manipulate the elements of a matrix. The focus of this problem is design and implementation of matrices using object-oriented programming techniques.

Study the following sample program to learn the representation, implementation, and application of a generic matrix. The class *Matrix* illustrates how to declare a matrix and its associated interfaces. In addition, it shows you how to use the *new* and *delete* operators for allocating dynamic memory for matrices. Note that the matrix in the main program can be constructed from singly dimensional arrays of different types.

After learning the program, write the necessary interfaces and definitions for the following specifications:

Multiply two matrices to create a new matrix by multiplying the corresponding elements of two matrices.

Transpose a matrix into a new matrix by interchanging its rows with the corresponding columns.

Assign one matrix to the other.

Create a matrix based on the *minor* of an element *x* in a matrix. The new matrix is the submatrix formed by deleting the row and column containing *x*. For example, the minor of the element **5** in the following matrix

1	3	4	9
7	2	-5	8
-4	-1	6	-3
-7	5	0	-2

is the matrix

1	4	9
7	-5	8
-4	6	-3

```cpp
#include <iostream.h>
#include <assert.h>


//***********************************************************
//  CLASS NAME:      Matrix
//  PURPOSE:         To implement rectangular arrays (matrix)
//  STATE:           No special behavior in class objects
//***********************************************************
template  <class T>
class Matrix
{
    int  _RowDim, _ColDim; // total rows and total columns
    T**  _Data; // content of each cell
    public:  // class interfaces

        // constructor to create matrix without initialization
        Matrix(int = 1, int = 1);   // default parameters

        // parameterized constructor to create matrix from a simple array
        Matrix(int RowDim, int ColDim, T*   InitVal);

        Matrix(const Matrix<T>&); // copy constructor
        ~Matrix(); //destructor

        int row() const;   // Returns the row dimension.
        int col() const;   // Returns the column dimension.

        // overloaded plus sign operator
        friend Matrix<T>& operator+( const Matrix<T>&, const Matrix<T>& );

        // overloaded extraction (<<) operator
        friend ostream& operator<< (ostream& output, const Matrix<T>&);
}; // ENDCLASS
```

```
//*****************************************************
//    definitions of the class interfaces           *
//*****************************************************
// creates a matrix with empty cells
template<class T>
Matrix<T>::Matrix(int RowDim, int ColDim)
{
   _RowDim = RowDim;
   _ColDim = ColDim;

   _Data = new T*[_RowDim];
   for(int index = 0; index < _RowDim; ++index)
   _Data[_RowDim] = new T[_RowDim];
}


//***********************************************************

// class constructor: constructs a matrix from a simple array
template <class T>
Matrix<T>::Matrix(  int RowDim,  int ColDim, T* InitVal)
{
   _RowDim = RowDim;
   _ColDim = ColDim;

   _Data = new T*[_RowDim];
   for (int index = 0; index < _RowDim; ++ index)
   _Data[index] = new T[_RowDim];

   // initializing process
   for ( int i = 0; i < _RowDim; ++i)
     for ( int j = 0; j < _ColDim; ++j)
        _Data[i][j] = *(InitVal + (_ColDim * i + j)); // assigns
a value to each box
}


//***********************************************************
// copy constructor
template <class T>
Matrix<T>::Matrix(const Matrix<T>& matrix)
{
   _RowDim = matrix._RowDim;
   _ColDim = matrix._ColDim;

   _Data = new T*[_RowDim];
   for (int index = 0; index < _RowDim; ++ index)
       _Data[index] = new T[_RowDim];

   // now initializing
   for ( int i = 0; i < _RowDim; ++i)
     for ( int j = 0; j < _ColDim; ++j)
       _Data[i][j] = matrix._Data[i][j];
}
```

```cpp
//**************************************************************
// class destructor
template <class T>
Matrix<T>::~Matrix()
{
    for ( int index = 0; index < _RowDim; ++index)
        delete [] _Data[index];

        delete [] _Data;
}

//**************************************************************
// overloading + operator
template <class T>
Matrix<T>& operator+(const Matrix<T>& m1, const Matrix<T>& m2)
{
    assert (m1._RowDim == m2._RowDim && m1._ColDim == m2._ColDim);

    Matrix<T>   *result = new Matrix<T>(m1._RowDim, m1._ColDim);
    //   static Matrix<T>  result;     another alternative
    for ( int i = 0; i < m1._RowDim; ++i)
      for (int j = 0; j < m1._ColDim; ++j)
        result->_Data[i][j] = m1._Data[i][j] + m2._Data[i][j];
    result._Data[i][j] = m1._Data[i][j] + m2._Data[i][j];
    Matrix<T>&  m = *result;  // gets a reference to static data
    return m;
}

//**************************************************************
// overloading << operator
template <class T>
ostream&  operator << (ostream& output, const Matrix<T>&  m)
{
    for (int i = 0; i < m._RowDim; ++i)
      for (int j = 0; j <m._ColDim; ++j)
        output << "Data(" << i << " ," << j << " ) = "
                << m._Data[i][j]  << endl;
    return output;
}

//*********************************************************
//  a simple client code to test the class              *
//*********************************************************

void main()
{
    static int    table[] = {1,2,3,4};
    static double sales[] = { 2.3, 2.4, 3.1, 3.6, 4.1, 3.4,7.4,8.1,2.3};

    // makes a matrix from the table elements
```

```
   Matrix<int>        first(2,2, table);
   cout << first << endl;

   // makes a table from sales data
   Matrix<double>   second(3,3, sales);
   cout << second  << endl<< endl;

   // makes a matrix
   Matrix<int>  third;
   third = first + first;
   cout << third << endl;

   // a matrix of 1 x 1
   int single[] = {35};
   Matrix<int>  test(1, 1, single);
  cout << test;
}
```

Appendix A: Solutions to Self-Check Questions

CHAPTER 1 SELF-CHECK ANSWERS

Self-Check Questions 1

1. A typical C++ program normally starts with a unique C feature known as a *preprocessor statement*. A typical preprocessor statement is *#include <iostream.h>*. It is an instruction to the compiler to retrieve the code from the predefined *iostream.h* file and insert it into the source code on the line requested. Following the *include* statement is the *main()* function:

```
void main ()
{
        .
        .
        .
}
```

The *main* function is where the program starts. The body of the function follows the *main* function header. It is enclosed in { and } symbol pairs called *braces*. In C++ braces are used to encapsulate statements.

2. Comments are used to clarify the program for the reader. Therefore, a comment line must be brief but meaningful.

3. A variable is a location in the memory and the value of the variable is its stored contents. The value may vary during the execution of the program.

4. A semicolon (:) is a punctuation character used to terminate an individual statement.

5. Home address program:

```
//This program prints out my home address.
#include <iostream.h>  // Add the necessary I/O code.
void main()  // main function
{
   cout << "\n907 Prospect Avenue"  // prints each line
        << "\nNorth Vancouver, BC"  // on a new line
        << "\nCanada,  V7R 2M2";
}
```

6. The program for sum of the values:

```
//This program computes the sum of three four-digit values.
#include <iostream.h>  // Add the necessary I/O code.
void main()  // main function
{
        // declaration of variables
   int  first,  second,  third;  // variable names
   int  sum = 0; // Initialize the accumulator sum to zero.
        // Display the message
   cout << "\nType three four-digit numbers"
        << " each separated by at least a space"
        << " and press enter: ";

        // Input
   cin >> first
       >> second
       >> third;

        // Process
   sum = sum + first + second + third;

        // output
   cout << "\The sum of" << first  << " and "
                         << second << " and "
                         << third  << " is: "
                         << sum;

}
```

Self-Check Questions 2

1. A function is a self-contained element of the program that carries out a designated task. A function can be accessed from anywhere in a program.
2. In order to perform a task, a C++ function may or may not need information being passed to it from its calling function. The information passed to a function is called *function formal argument(s)* or *parameter(s)*.
3. A function to compute the number of seconds since midnight looks like this:

```
//  This function computes the number of seconds since
//  midnight.  It receives the time of the day in a four-
//  digit format, i.e., 0825  stands for 8:25 a.m.
```

```
#include <iostream.h>   // Add the necessary I/O code.

void main()
{
        // program constants
   const hundred = 100,
         sixty   = 60;

        // declaration of variables
   int    TimeOfDay;  // for a four-digit time
   long int   seconds;    //  for total seconds

cout   << "\nPlease enter the time in four-digit"
       << " format."
       << " For example, 0825 or 1235. Then press"
       << " enter: ";
          // process
seconds = TimeOfDay / hundred * sixty * sixty +
              TimeOfDay % hundred * sixty;

          // output
cout   << "\nThe number of seconds since midnight is: "
       << seconds;
}
```

Self-Check Questions 3

1. The illegal identifiers are

   Sales-Table

   Dot.Two

   4DigitNumber

2. Number 1234 is an integer suitable for arithmetic operations, whereas "1234" is considered to be a string of characters. Your name is also a string of characters.

Self-Check Questions 4

1. The value of the result on each line is

      1125

      1126

      1386

         1

         1

   −3524

2. The first statement is incorrect because in expression *first % second, second* is negative. The second statement is also incorrect because the variable *fourth* in expression *fourth % first* is of type *float*. It must be of type *integer* with a positive value.

Self-Check Questions 5

1. The code segment sets the value of variable *num* to 0 through *exclusive* OR operations. In *exclusive* OR, identical bits evaluate to 0.

2. The code segment may be rewritten as follows:

```
const int zero = 0;
int num = 65;
num = num & zero; // bitwise AND operation
cout << num;
```

Self-Check Questions 6

1. The code subtracts the value of variable *m* from the value of the variable *n* through two's complement operation, as shown. We used a 16-bit format to represent the integers.

```
int n = 10; //  with a binary value of 0000 0000 0000 1010
int m = 6;  //  with a binary value of 0000 0000 0000 0110
m = ~m;     //  reverses the bits of m 1111 1111 1111 1001
m++;        //  increments  m by 1      1111 1111 1111 1010
n +=m;      //  n = n + m; n == 4       0000 0000 0000 0100
```

The result of the operation is 4, which in binary format is 0000 0000 0000 0100.

2. The data will appear on the screen as shown:

> 6
>
> 24
>
> 0

3. Notice what happened as a consequence of the above code. The value of variable *n* was first changed from 26 to 6 as a result of a shift right (two times) operation. In other words, an integer division by 4 happened. Now if you do shift left on the variable *n* (two times), the result will be 24 or an integer multiplication of 4.

Self-Check Questions 7

1. The types and values of the expressions on lines 5 to 8:

   Line 5:   1234591 - long int

   Line 6:   1234594 (offset is demoted from 3.5 to 3) - long int

   Line 7:   'N' (14th letter) - char

   Line 8:   1234609 - long int

Self-Check Questions 8

1. A simple *if* statement:

```
int  maximum;  // an auxiliary variable
if (first > second)
   maximum = first;
else
```

```
        maximum = second;

    if (maximum < third)
        maximum = third;
```

2. A *while* statement to determine the sum of digits in a positive integer:

```
const int ten = 10;
int sum = 0; // an accumulator
while ( number != 0 )
{
    sum      = sum + number % ten;
    number   = number / ten;
}
```

Self-Check Questions 9

1. The declaration of a variable creates a memory location with an undefined value in it. Once you create the location associated with a name, you cannot change it, although you can change the value stored in it. The declaration also binds the data type to the variable.
2. The scope of a variable means the region of the program within which that variable has meaning.
3. A block variable is one that has meaning within a code block, or a sequence of statements enclosed in braces.
4. Unless *cast* is used, the type of the result of expressions is determined by default promotions and demotions.

Self-Check Questions 10

1. *Standard I/O* refers to two logical devices named *standard input* and *standard output*. The devices are assigned to screen and keyboard respectively.
2. The *cin* statement extracts (reads in) values entered by the user and places them into their variables.
3. The *cout* statement displays output to standard output.
4. Escape sequence characters are a group of unprintable characters used for special functions such as *newline, tab, backspace, carriage return*. All escape sequence characters are typed with the backslash character (\) called *the escape character*. They are used with *cout* statements.
5. The format flags are I/O facilities that allow the program to perform formatted input and formatted output.

Self-Check Questions 11

1. The purpose of each of the following I/O streams are:

   cin.get() is an input facility to read in a character from standard input.

   cin.getline() extracts a specified number of characters and places them in the addressed array.

cin.read() extracts a block of data specified by size into the addressed array.

cin.peek() returns the next character of the stream (or eof), but it does not extract it.

2. The *cin.gcount()* function returns the actual number of characters read in.

CHAPTER 2   SELF-CHECK ANSWERS

Self-Check Questions 1

1. The term *conditional execution* means that a statement, simple or compound, is executed only if a given logical condition has a specified value (either *true* or *false*).

2. The rules associated with the *if* statement are described in the following statement:

```
if (logical expression)  // Parentheses are required.
      statement;  // simple or compound statement
else statement;    //an optional part
```

Notice that semicolons should be used in every individual statement of the *if* statements.

3. A nested *if* statement is composed of several layers of conditional statements. It has this form:

```
if (logical expression1)  // if this is true
      if (logical expression2) // if this is true too
      if (logical expression3) // if this is true too
         statement3;
      else
         statement2;
      else
         statement1;
```

Statement3 will be executed if and only if the three logical expressions are true. *Statement2* will be executed if the first two logical expressions are true and the third one is false. *Statement1* will be executed if the first logical expression is true and the second one is false.

To avoid possible ambiguity, carry out *nested if* statements carefully. In addition, your programming style should show clearly the association between each logical expression (*if* part) and its related *else* part.

4. A compound statement consists of a sequence of two or more consecutive statements enclosed within two curly brackets ({ }).

5.
```
if (first > second)
if (second > third)
   result = first;
else
   result = second;
else                 // This else is unnecessary.
   result = third;
```

6a.
```
if(temperature > 30 )
      cout << "Hot\n";
```

```
        else if (temperature > 24 )
           cout << "Warm\n";
              else if (temperature > 19 )
                  cout << "Good\n";
                 else if (temperature > 14)
                      cout << "Chilly\n";
                       else cout << "Cold\n";
```
6b.
```
     if ( temperature > 14 )
         if ( temperature > 19 )
            if ( temperature > 24 )
               if ( temperature > 29 )
                  cout << "Hot\n";
               else  cout << "Warm\n";
            else  cout << "Good\n";
         else  cout << "Chilly\n";
     else cout << "Cold\n";
```
6c.
```
     // convert temperature to a code value
     int  code = temperature / 5;  //
         switch ( code )
         {
             case 2: cout << "Cold\n";  break;
             case 3: cout << "Chilly\n"; break;
             case 4: cout << "Good\n";  break"
             case 5: cout << "Warm\n";  break;
             case 6: cout << "Hot\n";   break;
             default: ;
         }
```
 7. Yes. It does the job. It does not need a break statement for this purpose.

Self-Check Questions 2

 1. *Repetition* refers to processing the same sequence of statements repeatedly until certain condition(s) have been met.
 2. The repetition statements of C++ are

```
while (logical expression) // as long as the expression is true
       statement;  // simple or compound

 do
 {
       statement;
 } while(logical expression);

 for ( initial; condition; action)
       statement;
```

 3. When the loop is executed, *initial* is executed first. *Condition* is evaluated next. If it evaluates to *true* (or a nonzero value), the *loop* statements are executed; otherwise, the *for loop* exits. If it does not exit after the loop body is executed, *action* is evaluated and the cycle repeats.

4. The minimum number of times the *while statement* executes is zero. It happens when the conditional expression of the loop evaluates to *false* (or zero). However, the *do-while* statement executes at least once, regardless of the result of the evaluation of its conditional expression.

5. The *do-while* statement looks like this:

```
int   digit;
do
   {
       cout << "\nEnter a valid digit <0..9>: ";
       cin  >> digit;
   }
while( digit > 9 || digit < 0 );
```

Self-Check Questions 3

1. The statement means that an array is a collection of elements that share a common name.

2. An array subscript indicates the position of an element of the array with respect to the other elements.

3. An array element refers to each component of the array, which is differentiated from other elements by its position.

4. An array element is a piece of data that represents the contents of a component and a subscript is an offset value from the start of the array showing the position of the element within the array.

5. The elements of the arrays in C++ are subscripted from 0, not 1.

6. We can only use character strings in single I/O statements. Other arrays should be read in or written out element-by-element using a loop statement.

7.
```
float   sales[12];
char    alphanum[36];
char    name[32];
```

8.
```
for (int index = 0; index < 12; ++index)
{
      cout << "\nEnter the sales amount <ddddd.dd>: ";
      cin   >> sales[index];
}

int  large       = sales[0],  // initialization
     second_large = 0;

for ( int index = 1; index < 12;  ++index)

  if ( sales[index] > second_large )
    if ( sales[index] < large )
        second_large = sales[index];
    else
      {
          second_large =  large;
          large = sales[index];
```

```
        }
  cout << large << '\t' << second_large;
```

Self-Check Questions 4

1. The statement reads in the elements of the matrix from the keyboard. The row index has been used before the column index because C++ is a row-major ordering language. That is, the language stores the matrix elements in the main memory row after row in a linear fashion.

Self-Check Questions 5

1. The three attributes associated with e memory location are *address*, *name*, and *content*.
2. Although pointers are used extensively for writing more compact and efficient code, their main use in C++ is the management of memory locations and objects allocated during the program execution.
3.
```
  int      number = 125;  // Declares a variable with initialization.
  int      *FirstPointer, *NextPtr, *ThirdPtr; // pointers to integer
  FirstPtr = &number; // Assigns the address of number to FirstPtr.
  cout << *FirstPtr;  // Displays what is pointed to by FirstPtr.
```
4. Incorrect statements are:

```
  FirstPtr = number;   // incompatible types
  ThirdPtr =&value;    // value is not a variable
  cout << *ThirdPtr;   // invalid redirection
```

Self-Check Questions 6

1. A two-dimensional array can be viewed as an array of arrays. It is stored in the main memory in a linear fashion. Therefore, the comment that an array of two dimensions can be thought of as a single-dimensional array is correct.
2.
```
  float    wage[MaxSize];   // Declares a float array.
  float    *left, *right;   // Declares two pointer variables.
  left = (float*)&wage;     // Left gets the address of the array.
  right = left + sizeof(wage) / sizeof(float); //Right points to
             // the address passed the last item of the array.
  while(left < right)
        cin >> *left++;  // Reads in the data into the array.
```
3.
```
  const  int rows    = 4,
             columns = 5;

  int  Two_D[rows][columns];
  int  RowIndex, ColIndex;
  for (RowIndex = 0; RowIndex < rows;  ++ RowIndex)
  for (ColIndex = 0; ColIndex < columns; ++ ColIndex)
       cin >> Two_D[RowIndex][ColIndex];

  int  *left  = &Two_D[0][0];  // Get the array's address.
  int  *right =  left + sizeof(Two_D) / sizeof(int);
```

```
while (left < right)
      cin >> *left++;

for (int i = 0; i < rows; ++i)   //row index
      for (int j = 0; j <columns; ++j)   // column index
         cin  >> *(*(Two_D + i) + j);
```

Self-Check Questions 7

1. When used with the name of a pointer to an object including a simple data type, array, structure, or class instance, the *new* operator allocates memory space for the object and assigns its address to the pointer.
2. The *delete* operator returns the memory, allocated by the *new* operator, to the free store.
3. The code fragment creates a single-dimensional integer array using the pointer variable *Time* along with the constant size of 3 representing the number of array elements. Each element of the array has been initialized to a time component of hours, minutes, and seconds.
4. The program must use the *delete* operator in order to return the allocated memory to the free store. Otherwise, a phenomenon called a dangling pointer will occur. Dangling pointers sometimes cause serious run-time problems.

CHAPTER 3 SELF-CHECK ANSWERS

Self-Check Questions 1

1. The grammatical structure of a C++ function is as follows:

```
type of returned value    function name ([list of formal parameters])
{
        statements;
        [return statement;]
}
```

The square brackets represent the optional parts of the function. In addition, in C++ the *declaration* or *definition* of the function must precede the actual call of the function. If it does not happen this way, the function declaration, also known as a *prototype,* must precede the function call. A prototype is similar to the function heading; it specifies the correct number, order, and type of parameters that match those of the actual parameters or arguments. If the function definition precedes the call to that function, it does not need a prototype.

2.
```
int  SignOf( int number)
{
     return (number < 0)? -1 : 1;
}
```

3. When calling a function, a number of arguments may be passed to the function. They must correspond one for one with the parameters in the function. As a conse-

quence, a linkage of actual arguments and formal parameters happens, which is also called *interface*.

4. The term *pass-by-value* means that at the time of the function call, the actual argument, provided by the calling function, is copied into a variable corresponding to its related formal parameter. This variable, along with other local variables of the function (if any), is used during the execution, and it is destroyed along with the other local variables upon termination of the function. The pass-by-value process does not cause any side effects and is normally used with simple variables.

5. The term *pass-by-reference* means that at the time of the function call, the actual argument and the formal parameter become synonyms referencing effectively the same memory location. This method is normally used when the formal parameter is used as an input-output parameter and when the formal parameter is an object of type structure or class to prevent overhead.

6. The term *pass-by-pointer* means that at the time of the function call, the memory address of the actual argument is passed the formal parameter of the function. As a consequence, the formal parameter must be declared as a pointer variable of correct type. All the references to this pointer variable, within the function, effectively reference the same memory location of the actual argument of the calling function. In many situations, the same results can be achieved by using either pass-by-pointer or pass-by-references. The former, however, is useful when the function is to interface with the operating systems or the run-time routines of the language for memory allocation and de-allocation.

7.
```
void  ProcessTime( int minutes,  int& hours, int& fraction)
{
    const  int  factor = 60; // minutes per hour
    hours    = minutes / factor;
    fraction = minutes % factor;
}
```

8.
```
void  ProcessTime( int minutes,  int* hours, int* fraction)
{
    const  int  factor = 60; // minutes per hour
    *hours    = minutes / factor;
    *fraction = minutes % factor;
}
```

9.
```
void ProcessTime( int, int&, int& );
void ProcessTime( int, int*, int* );
```

10. The arguments are of type pointer, array names, passed by value. The function prototype can also be rewritten using asterisks (*) in front of the array names instead of square brackets.

Self-Check Questions 2

1.
```
int     SumOfSquares(int  n)
{
        long int sum = 0L; // Long int is necessary.
```

```
            for (int index = 1; index <= n; ++index)
                        sum += square(index);
            return sum;
    }
```
2. `int SumOfSquares(int);`
3. `int Sum = SumOfSquares(n);`
4.
```
int     SumOfCubes(int   n)
{
        long int sum = 0;

        for (int index = 1; index <=n; ++index)
            sum = sum + SumOfSquare(index) * index;
        return sum;
}
```
5.
```
void (*DoIt)(float, float);
DoIt = swap;
```

Self-Check Questions 3

1. The *storage class* determines how storage is allocated to the variable and how long the storage exits. For example, a local variable comes into existence when the function that owns it is entered and goes out of scope when the function is terminated. A *static* variable comes into existence when the function is entered and continues to exist until the entire program terminates.

2. The term *scope of a variable* refers to the region of the program within which it is declared and can hence be used. Such a declaration may be external, within a function, or within a program block.

3. A *global* variable is visible and can be utilized anywhere inside of or external to the program functions. The scope of a *static* variable, on the other hand, is only limited inside the boundaries of the function within which it has been declared.

4. A block variable is declared within the delimiters of the block ({ }). It cannot be utilized anywhere external to the block. For example,

```
{
        int count = 0;   // a block variable
        while (*text != '.')
            count++;
        . . .
}
cout << count;   // illegal statement: undefined count
```

5. A dangling pointer is an existing pointer to a variable whose referenced data inside the memory has been destroyed. For example,

```
int process()
{
        int *p;
        int  number = 15;
        p = &number;   // address of a local variable
        return p;      //  The local variable number dies here.
}
```

CHAPTER 4   SELF-CHECK ANSWERS

Self-Check Questions 1

1. *Enumerated* data types enhance the vocabulary of description in the language and make it possible to describe every desired value. As a result, the program can be tailored to the terminology of the environment for which it has been written. In addition, there are a lot of values, expressions, and states that are suitable to be declared under a common umbrella name. Examples of these things are logical values of *true* and *false,* names of the months, names of the days, different colors, states of an electrical switch, and so on.

2. The syntax or the grammar of type declaration of an enumerated data type is as shown:

```
enum <type name> {enumeration constants};
```

For example,

```
enum ColorType { while, black, magenta, red };
```

3. Enumerated-type data are ordinal; that is, each element, except the first one, has a predecessor and, except the last one, has a successor. Therefore, the following operators can be used with enumerated-type data:

Assignment operator (=).

Relational operators (<, <=, ==, !=, >, >=).

Increment and decrement operators (++, --).

4. Yes. Enumerated-type data, similar to other ordinal data types such as integers and characters, can be used as a control variable of the loop statements or as a selector in a switch statement.

Self-Check Questions 2

1.
```
void Measures( cardinal   length, cardinal   width,
               cardinal&   area,   cardinal&  perimeter)
        {
            area      = length * width;
            perimeter = (length + width)  * 2;
        }
```

2. The short program using the given *typedef* names:

```
void main()
{
   string   ptr;
   DaysOfWeek days []= {"Mon", "Tue", "Wed", "Thu",
                        "Fri", "Sat", "Sun" };
   ptr = days[6];
   cout << ptr;  // Displays sun for Sunday.
}
```

Self-Check Questions 3

1. Templates are used to define generic types or functions with provisions for type checking. A generic function that accepts various data types, eliminates duplicate code and makes the function's algorithm independent of data.
2. Examples of suitable algorithms to be used with templates are sorting, searching, finding the mode of data, and finding the median of data.

Self-Check Questions 4

1. When a function is small and simple, it is better to declare it as *inline*. The amount of time spent executing the function is small compared to the time needed for the call and return processes of the function. An *inline* function improves the performance of the program especially when it will be called many times.
2. When two or more functions share the same name but differ in their parameter declarations, they are called *overloaded* functions.
3. An alternative to function overloading is using the C++ template. Templates are useful if your compiler supports them.
4. To write a default parameter function:

   You may specify the default parameters either in the declaration (which is preferred) or in the definition.

   When you assign default values to the parameters, you may or you may not use a parameter name. For example, both of the following declarations are correct.

   ```
   void ProcessArea ( int radius = 10 );
   void ProcessArea ( int = 10 );
   ```

   If the function will have a combination of default and nondefault parameters, the nondefault parameters come first.

   To call a default parameter function:

   Omit the default parameters' corresponding arguments.

   To override an argument through a function call, repeat the actual argument(s) before it. For example, if the function's prototype is:

   ```
   void process( int = 2, float = 3.14, char ch = '*' );
   ```

   Override the second parameter using the following function call:

   ```
   process( 2, 3.1415 );// repeats the first parameter
   ```

   The above function call will modify the second argument and will leave the first and the third arguments intact.

5. ```
   include <ctype.h>
   #include <stdarg.h>  //  macros to handle the function
   int  AreaOf(char  ch,...)
         {
             int area;
             va_list     data;     // open the list and call it data
             va_start(data, ch);   // Get the flag.
   ```
   ```

```
                ch = toupper(ch);      // Convert it to upper-case.
                switch(ch)
{
                    case 'S':  int side = va_arg(data, int);
                               area = side * side; break;

                    case 'R':  int length = va_arg(data, int);
                               int width  = va_arg (data, int);
                               area = length * width;  break;

                    case 'T':  int side1 = va_arg(data, int);
                               int side2 = va_arg(data, int);
                               int height= va_arg(data, int);
                               area = (side1 + side2) * height /2;
                        break;
                }
                va_end (data);
                return area;
}
```

Self-Check Questions 5

1. A preprocessor directive is not a statement to be terminated with a semicolon. It is an instruction to the compiler to invoke the preprocessor to perform certain tasks.
2. The macro is first defined by using the *# define directive* of the preprocessor. You then use it by placing its name in a subsequent place in the program. For example,

```
#define    average(x,y)    (((x) + (y)) / 2)
```

When the macro is called, the preprocessor expands it into *inline* code, replacing its name with a string of characters. For example, if the following macro call appears in the program,

```
int  first = 10,  second = 12;
 int  mean;

mean = average ( first, second);
```

it would be compiled as

```
mean = (first + second) /2;
```

3. The grammatical structure of a macro, as shown in the previous example, consists of three parts: the define directive, macro name, and statement(s).
4. The C++ alternatives to using macros and constant definitions are inline functions. An inline function provides type checking and is more suitable for program design and development.
5.
```
#include <stdlib.h>
#include <iostream.h>
void main(int  argc,  char* argv[])
{
      if (argc != 2)
      {
           cout << "\nWrong entry!";
```

```
              exit(1);
        }

    const int factor = 1.68;   //1 mile = 1.68 kilometers
    float kilometer;

    kilometer = atoi( argv[1] ) * factor;

     cout.width(6);
     cout.precision(2);
     cout.fill('*');
     cout << "\n"   << argv[1] << " miles"
          << " is " << kilometer << "kilometers";
    }
```

6. Conditional compilation allows you to skip certain code segments of the program and execute the rest. It is a very useful feature of the language that allows

    code portability across different platforms.

    implicit data declaration.

    debugging of certain regions of the program.

CHAPTER 5 SELF-CHECK ANSWERS

Self-Check Questions 1

1. The elements of an array are always of the same type, while the type of the structure elements are not necessarily the same. Moreover, the array name, unlike the structure name, is a fixed pointer to the start of the array.

2. A structure is composed of related components called *fields*. Each field in turn may be another structure or other built-in or enumerated-type data. A structure is declared as:

```
[typedef] struct StructType  // optional typedef keyword
{
              type      field1;
              type      field2;
                 . . .
              type      fieldn;
        };
```

3. You use a structure type in a way similar to other built-in data types. For example,

```
StructType record1, record2;
StructType *ptr = &record1;
```

4. An individual element of a structure is accessed using the *dot* notation (.) or in the case of pointer variables, the *arrow* notation. For example,

```
record1.fied1 or ptr ->field1 // similar to (*ptr).record1
```

5. Yes. As long as the two structures are of the same type, they can be assigned to each other. For example,

```
record1 = record2;
```

6. No. The elements of the structure must be read in individually.
7. No. The structure name is not a pointer.
8. The structure may be passed to a function using pass-by-value, pass-by-pointer, and pass-by-reference. Pass-by-value, however, is least desirable due to the overhead involved.
9.
```
enum  direction {south, north, east, west};
typedef struct WeatherType
{
   int temp;
   int pressure;
   direction wind;
};
```

Self-Check Questions 2

1. Union type and structure type
2.
```
typedef enum StockType {television, video};
typedef struct DateType
{
   int day;
   int month;
   int year;
};

typedef struct TvType
{
   short   power;
   int     watts;
};

typedef union TvSterio
{
   int      power;
   TvType   tv;
};

typedef struct ElectroType
{
   char         name[32];
   int          stock_no;
   int          quantity;
   DateType     date_purchased;
   StockType    type;
   TvSterio     set;
};
```
3. Yes. The C++ class may be used whenever there is a design requirement for structure declaration. The C++ class not only does the same job as a structure, it is also supported by several built-in features to represent and implement data abstraction concepts. The ability to use structures in C++, however, facilitates compatibility with the C language.

Self-Check Questions 3

1. Possibly the best examples of sequential files are program output destined for a printer and program I/O with a computer terminal. Other formal applications are inventory payroll files and customer billing systems. Although in the past these types of files were stored on tapes, today almost all of them are stored on direct access media or a disk system.

2. Since random-access files allow us to access any component directly, we use them with applications that require fast access operation at random order. Examples of this type of files are point-of-sale and interactive banking files.

3.
```
fstream    InOutFile;
InOutFile.open ("d:\\cs\\programs\\fileapp1.cpp",
                    ios::in|ios::append|ios::nocreate);
```

4.
```
char*     comment = "\\  "End of the program"
InOutFile << comment << endl;  //comment and end of line
```

Self-Check Questions 4

1. A file is normally passed to a function using the pass-by-reference concept.

2. A binary file is prepared by opening the file in binary mode *(ios::binary)* the first time you create it. For example:

```
OutFile.open ("d:\\cs\\programs\\myfile.dat", ios::out|
                    ios::binary|ios::trunc);
```

Files of structures, however, are automatically created in binary format.

A binary file is not directly printable. To display a binary file, you need to write the necessary code.

3. The program creates a text file composed of many lines of different sizes, each of which is started at a new line.

4. `OutFile.open ("a:\\myfile.dat", ios::append|ios::nocreate);`

5.
```
const int BuffSize = 128;  // line length
int LineNo = 0;
ifstream InFile;

InFile.open ("a:\\myfile.dat",
               ios::in|ios::nocreate);
InFile.seekg(0L, ios::beg);

while( !InFile.getline(buffer, BuffSize).eof() )
{
    cout << "LINE #"  << LineNo++  <<": "
         << buffer    << endl;
}
```

CHAPTER 6   SELF-CHECK ANSWERS

Self-Check Questions 1

1. The purpose of data abstraction is to isolate each data structure (or object) and its associated actions.

2. Domain defines the set of all possible values for an ADT.

   Primitives define the set of operations for an ADT.

   Rules describe the conditions and semantics of (the meaning) of the operations.

3. ADT: time

Domain:	hour, minutes, and seconds
Primitive Operations:	Initialization, subtraction, increment, decrement, conversion, formatting, etc.
Rules:	hour <= 24, minutes <= 60, and seconds <= 60

Self-Check Questions 2

1. A structure is simply an aggregate of related information. It is a passive data type; that is, once you create a variable of the given structure, it lies passively as you work with it. A class, on the other hand, is an active data type that has *state* and *behavior.* The state of the class is implemented through its data members and its behaviour is implemented via its member functions. Moreover, a class supports data abstraction through its conceptual features including data hiding, encapsulation, inheritance. Note that a struct can also have function members.

2. Access specifiers tell the compiler explicitly which class members are accessible only within the class domain and which are not. They are needed to implement the principle of data hiding.

3. Below is a brief explanation of each term:

   Specification defines the operations for the ADT, including those that alter its state and those that query its state.

   Representation shows the mapping of the ADT using built-in data types of the language or other ADTs.

   Implementation involves the operations according to the specifications and constraints by the representation.

4. Below is a possible class for ADT *Book:*

```
class Book
{
   Private:    // Makes the data members private.
     char     _title[128];
     char     _author[64];
     char     _isbn [11]; // International Standard Book Number
     char     _publisher[64];
     float    _price;

   public:      //// Makes the member functions public.
     Book( char*, char*, char*, char*, char*, float);
     void ShowTitle();
     void ShowPublisher();
     float GetPrice();
     char* GetISBN();
     ~Book();
};    // end of class Book
```

Self-Check Questions 3

1. A destructor:

   is named after the class.

   is *void* by default.

   cannot be overloaded.

   has no arguments.

   cannot be inherited.

   cannot be a *union* member.

2. When an instance of a class goes out of scope, the destructor is automatically called in order to free the memory allocated.

Self-Check Questions 4

1. A constructor is a function that automatically executes when an object (an instance of a class) is created to allow you to initialize the data members of the object.
2. A constructor is a public function or method that is always named after the class to which it belongs. Moreover, it is never called directly by the user and it never returns a value.
3. A constructor that takes no arguments is called a *default constructor*. A default constructor is also referred to the constructor that is provided by the compiler when an explicit destructor has not been provided by the program.
4. The implementation of class *Student:*

```
student::student() {_StudentNo = 0;}
student::student(long int IdNum)
{
     _StudentNo = IdNum;
}

student::ShowStudent()
{
     cout << "\nThe student Number is: "
          << GetStNo();
}

void main()
{
     student     first(97108612);
     student     next (first); // Uses copy constructor.
     first.ShowStudent();
}
```

5. The user-defined copy constructor for class *Student:*

```
student(conststudent& s)
{
   _StudentNo = s._StudentNo;
}
```

The constructor will be used as shown:

```
student     first(96309124);
student     next(97108628); // one possible application
```

Self-Check Questions 5

1. Inheritance provides code reusability and clarity. It allows us to describe common data and their related functions only once.
2. An access specifier, regardless of its place, defines the scope of accessibility of the data and functions that appear after it. An access specifier of a derived class, however, defines both the extent of accessibility of the inherited members and its own accessibility.
3. The compiler executes the constructor function of the base class followed by the constructor of the derived class.

Self-Check Questions 6

1. Using *virtual* function in class *message* ensures that the pointer variable *ptr* correctly calls the base and derived class functions. As a consequence, it will display the correct message. The output of the program:

```
This is a test.
End of test.
```

2. If the keyword *virtual* is removed, the pointer will call function *announce* in the same place twice and will display the following output:

```
This is a test.
This is a test.
```

Self-Check Questions 7

1. A class normally has several instances of objects, all of which share the same member functions of their class. The *this* pointer, a self-referential pointer, points to the instance of the class, including its data members and function members, that is active at a given instance. That is, it points to the object that is actually in process in the program.
2. In this particular exercise, the *this* pointer in constructor function and function *Inc* can be removed without any undesired effects.

Self-Check Questions 8

1. A *static* data member is shared by all instances of the class. That is, the compiler creates only one copy of the *static* data member to be shared among all class objects.
2. A *static* data member:

   is preceded by the keyword *static*.

   needs a global definition outside the class.

   is initialized, by default, to zero.

3. The following small functions are good candidates for declaration as *inline* functions by starting each function with the keyword *inline*.

```
inline UserFee::UserFee()
{
    const float increment = 25.50;
    _fee = _fee + increment;


}

inline void UserFee::DisplayFee()
{
    cout << "\nThe user fee amounts to: "
        << _fee;
}

float UserFee::_fee = 0.0;
```

4. The driver program to test the *static* data member looks like this:

```
void main()
{
    UserFee      user1, user2, user3;
    user1.DisplayFee();   // displays 76.60 ( 3 * 25.50 )
}
```

Self-Check Questions 9

1. *Friend* functions allow the sharing of private class information with nonmember functions. These functions, which are not defined in the class itself, share the same class information as member functions while remaining external to the class definition.
2. A *friend* class creates a bridge between two independent classes. When class *B* identifies class *A* as a *friend*, it specifies that all the resources of class *A* can be accessed by class *B*.

Self-Check Questions 10

1. Not necessarily. Although overloading operators violates some of the principles of true object-oriented programming, it simplifies coding. You can accomplish the same results by using named member functions with descriptive names, such as *add()*, *subtract()*, *multiply()*, and *divide()*.
2. No. The following operators cannot be overloaded:

```
.    .*    ::    ?:    sizeof
```

3. The implementation of class *Date:*

```
#include <iostream.h>

// default constructor
date::date() { _day = _month = _year = 0; }

// parameterized constructor
date::date(int d, int m, int y)
{
    _day = d;
```

```
    _month = m;
    _year = y;
}

//overloaded operator plus
date operator+(date& first, date& next)
{
  date  temp;
  temp._day   = first._day + next._day;
  temp._month = first._month + next._month;
  temp._year  = first._year + next._year;

  while ( temp._day > 30 )
          temp._day -=30, temp._month++;

  while( temp._month > 12)
          temp._month -=12, temp._year++;

  return temp;
}

// function print
void date::print()
{
  cout << _month << '/' << _day
       << '/'    << _year;
}


// driver program to test
void main()
{
  date    today(12,7,1998);

  // add 100 days to today's date
  date    next(100,0,0);

  date newdate = today + next;
  newdate.print(); // displays 10/22/1998
}
```

Self-Check Questions 11

1. The language allows us to overload the I/O operators to make them more universal and hence useful for input and output of user-defined objects.
2. The implementation of class *String* looks like this:

```
string::string(char*  str)  // class constructor
{
        strcpy(_text, str);  // Uses string.h for copy.
        length = strlen(text];
}
```

```
char*   string::operator+(char* another)
{
        strcat(_text, another); // Uses string.h.
        length = length + strlen(another);
};
```

A driver program to test the class *String* looks like this:

```
void main()
{
   string  comment = "Note: If you declare a string
                         as an automatic array,";
        comment + "there is no need to use the new operator.";
        comment.display();
}
```

3. Yes. You can replace an overloaded function with a regular named function to achieve the same results. Other object-oriented languages such as *Smalltalk* do not have overloading capability. They use regular functions.

Self-Check Questions 12

1. Class templates, similar to function templates, create generic classes and hence eliminate duplicate classes.
2. The implementation of class *Something* looks like this:

```
                // constructor with initializer
something::something(T value)
{
   _data = value;
}


                // copy constructor
something::something(const something <T>& another)
{
        _data = another._data;
}
friend ostream& operator<<(ostream&  output,
     const something<T>& object)
{
        return output << object._data;
}
```

Now, for a driver program to test the class *Something*

```
void main()
{
        something <int>    A_number(100);
        cout  <<  A_number;

        something <float>     Next_number(23.55);
        cout  << Next_number;
}
```

Appendix B: Basic Input/Output Operations in Standard C

Standard C does not define any I/O routines as part of the language itself. Rather, a standard library contains several functions that implement I/O traffic. This approach has made it possible to make the language machine-independent.

THE *STDIO.H* HEADER FILE

The basic routines for I/O operations are defined in the standard C library *stdio.h*. To use this library, include it in your program by using the C directive *#include<stdio.h>*. Note that the name is enclosed in angle brackets.

CHARACTER I/O

To output a single character, C provides the function *putchar(ch)* where *ch* is an integer value expression representing the code of the character to output. To input a single character, C has a parameterless function *getchr()*.

The following program reads two characters and displays them in reverse order, separated by a tab and terminated by the end-of-line character.

```
#include      <stdio.h>
main()
{
     char      alpha,  beta;   // two characters

     alpha = getchar();
     beta = getchar();
     putchar( beta );
     putchar('\t');
```

```
        putchar( alpha );
        putchar('\n');
}
```

> **Note:** Character I/O in some compilers (e.g., Turbo C) is carried out using *getch* (read with no echo), *getche* (read with a screen echo), *putchar,* and *putc*. Compilers with these facilities also support the standard I/O routines. The following is an example of character I/O:

```
#include <stdio.h>          /* standard I/O file */
#include <conio.h>          /* console I/O file */

main()
{
    char  ch;
    printf("Enter a character:");
    ch = getche();      /*input with echo*/
    printf("\nYou typed");
    putchar(ch);
    printf("\nEnter another character:");
    ch = getch();       /*input with no echo*/
    printf("\nYou typed");
    putchar(d);
}
```

FORMATTED I/O

C provides two special routines for formatted I/O. They are *printf* and *scanf* (print and read formatted, respectively).

To input an integer value, use *scanf ("%d", &n);* where *n* is a defined integer variable. Note that numeric variables are preceded by an ampersand *(&)*. It tells *scanf* where to store the value it reads because it returns the address of the memory object specified as its argument.

To output an integer value, use *printf ("%d", n);* where *n* may be an expression or a simple variable. Note that no ampersand is required here because the argument is not modified.

The following program reads an employee's number of hours and pay rate and displays the corresponding wage:

```
#include <stdio.h>
main()
{
    float  pay_rate;
    int    hours;

    printf("Enter hours worked and pay rate");
    scanf("%d%f", &hours, &pay_rate);
    printf("\nYour wage is: %6.2f\n",hours*pay_rate);
}
```

The specification *%6.2f* specifies a field width of six characters, with two digits after the decimal point.

THE SYNTAX OF FORMATTED INPUT

There are three input functions in the C language. To read from standard input:

```
int    scanf(format control string, arg 1, arg 2,... arg n);
```

To read from file *f*:

```
int    fscanf(f, format control string, arg 1, arg 2,... arg n);
```

To read from string *s*:

```
int    sscanf(s, format control string, arg 1, arg 2,... arg n);
```

Each function returns the number of successful assignments of input instances to arguments. This number may be less than the number of given arguments in two cases:

1. End-of-file for standard and file I/O and end-of-string for string I/O; in this case the value of end-of-file or end-of-string is returned.
2. Input data do not match specifications of the control string; in this case the number of successful assignments is returned.

THE FORMAT CONTROL STRING

The format control string determines the interpretation of input sequences as they are read in. It may contain:

- conversion specifications starting with the % symbol
- whitespace characters
- ordinary characters

CONVERSION SPECIFICATIONS

Conversion specifications determine how the input data is converted. The converted data is then placed in the location pointed to by the corresponding argument. The conversion specification is of the following form:

```
%*width size conversion-character
```

where the *, width, and size are optional.

The optional asterisk is an assignment-suppress character; that is, the input data is read but discarded rather than assigned to the argument. It is normally used with string I/O for reading a selected portion of a string. For example, assume that the input value to the following code is 123ABC5. The call scanf("%*d %4s %d", str, &n) skips the integer value of the input stream, assigns string ABC to the string variable *str,* and assigns number 5 to the variable number.

```
#include <stdio.h>
void main()
{
  char   str[4];  // a string of an arbitrary size
  int    number ; // an integer value

  printf("Enter a string:");  // e.g., 123ABC4
```

```
    scanf("%*d %3s %d", str, &number);   // Skips the integer part.

    printf("%d", number);  // Displays 4.
    printf("\n"); // new line
    printf("%s", str); // Displays ABC.
}
```

The field width, which is an unsigned positive decimal constant, specifies the maximum possible field width. For example, in the following statement up to and including fifteen characters from the input stream will be read in:

```
scanf("%15s", full name)
```

Note that in reading strings, the *scanf* function stops at the first whitespace character unless a field width has been specified.

There are two possible size flags; the letter *h* and the letter *l* (both lower case). The size flag *h* causes the argument involved to be treated as *short*. It can be used with decimal, octal, and hexadecimal values. The size flag *l* causes the involved argument to be treated as *long* when used with whole values to represent a *long* data type and as double when used with floating-point numbers. A list of conversion specifications follows:

- *d*   a signed decimal integer
- *u*   an unsigned decimal integer
- *o*   an unsigned octal integer
- *x, y*   an unsigned hexadecimal integer (with or without a leading 0)
- *c*   a single character
- *s*   a character string
- *f, e, E, g, G* a floating-point number
- []   a specified category of characters such as alphabetical or numerical

Let us write a program using the conversion specifiers with the following input stream:

```
#include <stdio.h>
void main()
{
  char          character;
  unsigned int  first;
  int           second;
  float         third;
  char          text1[5];
  char          text2[5];
  printf("\nPlease enter input line:"); // Enter 12   34   1.2abcd789m.

  scanf("%c %u %o %f %4s %4[0-9]", character, &first, &second, &third,
        text1, text2);
  printf(text2); //displays 789
  printf("\n");
  printf("%d",first);   //displays 2
}
```

The call

```
scanf("%c %u %d %f %4s %4[0-9]", character, &first, &second, &third,
      text1, text2);
```

assigns

the character 1 to character

the unsigned integer value 2 to first

the octal value 34 to second (two digits only)

the value 1.2 to third

the string abcd to text1   (four character plus the null character)

the value 789 to text2   (m in the input stream is not a digit; therefore, it will not be read in)

THE SYNTAX OF FORMATTED OUTPUT

The syntax of formatted output is similar to that of formatted input. It uses printf instead of scanf. In formatted output, however, the printed information can be displayed (formatted) as desired and it can also be mixed with special control characters or escape characters, including \f (form feed), \n (new line), \r (carriage return), \t (horizontal tab), \a (alert or beep), \b (backspace), \\ (backslash), \" (double quote), and \' (single quote). There are also three output functions in the C language:

To write to *standard* output, use the following format:

```
printf(format control string, arg 1, arg 2,... arg n);
```

To write to file *f*, use this format:

```
fprintf(f, format control string, arg 1, arg 2,... arg n);
```

To write string *s*, use this format:

```
sprintf( s, format control string, arg1, arg2, … argn);
```

This list of examples shows how formatting works.

Statement	Output	Description
printf("%#5X", 23);	0×17 (hexadecimal)	causes leading 0 or 0x to be displayed for octal or hexadecimal values (default right justified)
printf("%#5X", 23);	0×17 (hexadecimal)	causes leading 0 or 0x to be displayed for octal or hexadecimal values (left justified)
printf("%+d", 10);	+10	for signed numeric values only
printf("hello!");	Hello!	default left justified
printf("%7s!", "Hello");	Hello!	right justified using space for seven characters
printf("%-5s!", "Hello");	Hello!	left justified using space for five characters

Notes

- In %f, the default precision is 6.
- Use this declaration in the following table.

```
Int       first = 1345,
          second = -1;
float     third = 1234.567;
```

Statement	Output	Description
printf("%-5d", first);	1345	left justified format in a field width of five characters
printf("%7.2f", first);	1234.57	a field width of seven from which two paces are used for the rounded fraction part and one space is used for the decimal point
printf("%4e", third);	1.234567E+03	scientific notation meaning $1.234567 * 10^{03}$
printf("%4o", first);	2501	the octal value (base 8) of the number 1345
printf("%4x", first);	541	the hex value (base 16) of the number 1345
printf("%u", second);	65535	special calculation based on the values of the bits of the variable; it is different from the absolute value, which is the same number without a sign.

STRING I/O

String I/O in C is performed by two functions, *gets* and *puts,* that read and write strings to the standard output, respectively. Following is an example of simple string I/O.

```c
#include <stdio.h>
main()
{
  const int NameLen = 32; //length of names

  char name [NameLen];
  int index;
  printf("enter your name:");
  gets(names);
  puts(name);   /* printf("%20s",name);*/
}
```

IN-MEMORY FORMAT CONVERSION FUNCTIONS

The functions *sprintf* and *sscanf* may be used for data validation and data conversion in memory. The following examples show how these functions work.

Example 1:

```c
#include <stdio.h>

#define IntLen  6  /*  maximum size of an integer
void main()
{
    char  string[IntLen];
    int   number, index;

    printf("\nPlease enter an integer, e.g., 1234:");
    gets(string);

    /* convert string to numeric format */
    sscanf(string, "%d", &number);

    /* display the number  */
     printf("%d", number);
}
```

Example 2:

```c
#include <stdio.h>

#define  MonthLen  10  /* maximum size for a month name */
void main()
{
    char  month[MonthLen];
    int   day;

    /* initialize month and day variables */
    sscanf("April 30", "%s %d", month, &day);
    printf("%2d %s %d", day, month, 1998);
/* displays 30 April 1998 */
}
```

Example 3:

```c
#include <stdio.h>

#define length  10  /*  an arbitrary size for a string */
void main()
{
    char  string[length];
    int   first = 735, second = 130;
    int index;

    sprintf(string, "%d" , first + second); // Makes 865.

    index = 0;
    /*  displays the numbers in separate digits (formatting). */
    while( string[index] != '\0' )
    {
```

```
        printf("%5c", string[index]);   /* displays 8      6      5
        index++;
    }
}
```

THE UNGETC FUNCTION

C language has a very useful I/O feature that works with almost all types of input files. It returns a character that was just read into the input stream. The syntax for this function is:

```
ungetc(character, file);
```

Example:

The following piece of code scans an input stream (e.g., *abc1234df2*) until a valid numeric value is found; then it reads in that value.

```
char ch;
int number;
do
   ch = getchar();
while( ch < '0'|| ch>'9');   /*  skip non-digit characters */
ungetc(ch,stdin)             /*  put the last one back */
scanf("%d",&number);         /*  now, read the whole number */
printf("%d", number);        /*  print 1234 */
```

Bibliography

Barakati, N. (1991). *Object-oriented programming in C++*. Sams Publishing.

Cantu, M., & Tendon, S. (1992). *Borland C++ 3.1 object-oriented programming. New York, NY:* Bantam Computer Books.

Cargill, T. (1991). *An introduction to object-oriented programming.* Reading, MA: Addison-Wesley Publishing Co.

Eckle, B. (1993). *C++ inside & out.* Berkeley, CA: Osborne/McGraw-Hill.

Ellis, M. A., & Strousrup, B. (1990). *The annotated C++ reference manual.* Reading, MA: Addison-Wesley Publishing Co.

Gorlen, K. E.; Orlow, S. M.; & Plexico, P. S. (1990). *Data abstraction and object-oriented programming in C++.* New York, NY: John Wiley & Sons, Inc.

Graham, N. (1991). *Learning C++.* New York, NY: McGraw-Hill.

Gray, N. A. B. (1994). *Programming with class.* Baffins Lane, Chichester, England: John Wiley & Sons, Inc.

Hansen, T. L. (1990). *The C++ answer book.* Reading, MA: Addison-Wesley Publishing Co.

Kernighan, B., & Ritchie, D. (1978). *The C programming language.* Upper Saddle River, NJ: Prentice-Hall.

Lippman, S. B. (1991). *C++ primer.* (2nd ed.). Reading, MA: Addison-Wesley Publishing Co.

Murray, R. (September 1991). "The C++ puzzle." *The C++ Report.*

Saks, D. (December 1992). "Standard C++: A status report." Supplement to *Dobb's Journal.*

Sessions, R. (1992). *Class construction in C and C++.* Upper Saddle River, NJ: Prentice-Hall.

Shildt, H. (1994). *C++ from the ground up.* Berkeley, CA: Osborne/McGraw-Hill.

Stevens, A. (1990). *Teach yourself C++.* Portland, OR: MIS Press.

Strousrup, B. (1991). *The C++ programming language.* Reading, MA: Addison-Wesley Publishing Co.

Wirfs-Brock, R., & Wilkerson, B. (1989). *Object-oriented design: A responsibility-driven approach.* OOPSLA'89 conference proceedings. *24(10):* 71–75.

Wirfs-Brock, R.; Wilkerson, B.; & Wiener, L. (1990). *Designing object-oriented software.* Upper Saddle River, NJ: Prentice-Hall.

Index